INTRODUCTION TO REFERENCE WORK

VOLUME II *Reference Services
and Reference Processes*

INTRODUCTION TO REFERENCE WORK

Volume II **Reference Services and Reference Processes**

Eighth Edition

William A. Katz
State University of New York at Albany

Boston   Burr Ridge, IL   Dubuque, IA   Madison, WI   New York
San Francisco   St. Louis   Bangkok   Bogotá   Caracas   Kuala Lumpur
Lisbon   London   Madrid   Mexico City   Milan   Montreal   New Delhi
Santiago   Seoul   Singapore   Sydney   Taipei   Toronto

McGraw-Hill Higher Education

A Division of The McGraw-Hill Companies

INTRODUCTION TO REFERENCE WORK, VOLUME II
Published by McGraw-Hill, an imprint of The McGraw-Hill Companies, Inc. 1221 Avenue of the Americas, New York, NY, 10020. Copyright © 2002, 1997, 1992, 1987, 1982, 1978, 1974, 1969 by The McGraw-Hill Companies, Inc. All rights reserved. No part of this publication may be reproduced or distributed in any form or by any means, or stored in a data base or retrieval system, without the prior written consent of The McGraw-Hill Companies, Inc., including, but not limited to, in any network or other electronic storage or transmission, or broadcast for distance learning.

Some ancillaries, including electronic and print components, may not be available to customers outside the United States.

This book is printed on acid-free paper.

domestic   1 2 3 4 5 6 7 8 9 0 DOC/DOC 0 9 0 9 8 7 6 5 4 3 2 1
international   1 2 3 4 5 6 7 8 9 0 DOC/DOC 0 9 0 9 8 7 6 5 4 3 2 1

ISBN 0-07-244143-7

Editorial director: *Phillip A. Butcher*
Sponsoring editor: *Valerie Raymond*
Project manager: *Diane M. Folliard*
Production supervisor: *Heather Burbridge*
Designer: *Gino Cieslik*
Producer, Media technology: *Lance Gerhart*
Compositor: *Electronic Publishing Services Inc., NYC*
Typeface: *10/12 Baskerville*
Printer: *R. R. Donnelley & Sons Company, Crawfordsville*

Library of Congress Cataloging-in-Publication Data

Katz, William A., 1924–
    Introduction to reference work / William A. Katz.—8th ed.
        p. cm.
    Includes bibliographical references and index.
    Contents: v. 1. Basic information services—v. 2. Reference services and reference processes.
    ISBN 0-07-244107-0 (v. 1) — ISBN 0-07-244143-7 (v. 2)
    1. Reference services (Libraries) 2. Reference books—Bibliography. I. Title.

Z711.K32 2002
025.5'52—dc21

                                                                00-069536

INTERNATIONAL EDITION ISBN 0-07-112073-4
Copyright © 2002. Exclusive rights by The McGraw-Hill Companies, Inc. for manufacture and export.
This book cannot be re-exported from the country to which it is sold by McGraw-Hill. The International Edition is not available in North America.

www.mhhe.com

ABOUT THE AUTHOR

WILLIAM A. KATZ is a professor at the School of Information Science and Policy, State University of New York at Albany. He was a librarian at the King County (Washington) Library for four years and worked in the editiorial department of the American Library Association. He received his Ph.D. from the University of Chicago and has been the editor of *RQ*, the journal of the Reference and Adult Services Division of the American Library Association, and the *Journal of Education for Librarianship*. Professor Katz is now editor of *The Reference Librarian*, a quarterly devoted to issues in modern reference and information services, and *The Acquisitions Librarian*, concerned with collection development. He is the editor of *Magazines for Libraries* and has compiled a second edition of *The Columbia Granger's Guide to Poetry Anthologies*. He is editor of a series on the history of the book for Scarecrow Press including his *A History of Book Illustration* and *Dahl's History of the Book*. Presently, he is writing a cultural history of reference books.

CONTENTS

PREFACE

The goal of *Introduction to Reference Work Volume II, Reference Services and Reference Processes,* is to give the reader a thorough overview and a broader understanding of the possibilities of reference services than could be encompassed in *Volume I, Basic Information Services.* This second volume introduces the reader to the sophisticated, imaginative, and, some think, more interesting aspects of the complete reference process. Another purpose is to indicate the ongoing and important changes and developments in information technologies and particularly the role of the Internet in the reference process.

NEW TO THIS EDITION

Almost everything in this edition is new, not simply revised from the seventh edition. The decision was necessary because of new technologies and the evolution in the practice and theory of reference services. In the seventh edition, for example, there was a single chapter on the Internet. In this edition there are four chapters in a section given over to the subject, as well as related chapters on the Internet and on document delivery.

A primary problem in any text of this type is the rapid change in information delivery. It is pointless, for example, to explain in detail how to reach point "c" and "d" on the Internet. Tomorrow the points of reference, the methods, will have changed with new networks, new hardware, and new software. Conversely, it is important to recognize the far-reaching implications of networking, if not the specifics of how to find this or that bit of datum. And it is to that purpose the second section was written, as well as most of the remainder of this second volume.

The second volume is a pragmatic, practical approach to information sources and theory. Basic developments are covered and explained. The footnotes and "Suggested Reading" sections guide those who wish to explore further. Leaders and followers in research and information science are responsible for much of what is revolutionary in reference services today. There are other courses, other places where information science can be considered in depth; all that can be done here is to hint at the joy of the intellectual fields open to the information scientist and researcher.

PLAN OF THE BOOK

The text opens with a discussion of traditional and new reference services in the community. Here the word community embraces almost every situation from the typical middle-class public library to the library serving the special needs of equally special groups of users. Problems and possible solutions are considered, especially in terms of limitations of budget and the new technologies. Enough is offered to suggest, if only in the broadest way, the people a librarian serves and hopes to serve.

The second chapter, "Information and the Community" explains how information is collected and made available for libraries and individuals. This is followed by related matters from reference telephone services and copyright to information and referral programs.

The second part, "The Internet and Reference Services," begins with a consideration of the Internet in the broadest sense with statistics and comments about what it means to the United States and to the world as well as a section on evaluation Web sites. The next chapter is concerned with the role of commercial and non-profit reference librarians on the present and future role of traditional reference services. In Chapter Five there is a discussion of networks from commercial to regional. The unit concludes with details about availability of full text.

The third large section is devoted to chapters on the reference interview and various methods of searching. Here the primary focus is on the role of the librarian as mediator, as the person who filters out the useful information for the hapless or even well informed client. Given this role, the searching process changes. Chapter Seven addresses the problems of the ubiquitous reference interview. Whether the librarian is working with digital databases or retrospective print indexes, the interview itself is much the same. It deals with the human process of communication rather than with the content and form of information sources. Chapter Eight is concerned with the search. The first of from the general search process to sophisticated searches. Attention is given primarily to the search for content rather than technology. It is the author's contention that whether the required data are on a CD-ROM, online, or in print, the important factor is what it contains or does not contain. The technologies, which carry the message, are important and today's reference librarian must be as familiar with computers and software as the databases themselves.

The fourth and final section, "Instruction and Policies," contains two chapters. Beginning with the pros and cons of bibliographical and computer instruction. The Tenth Chapter concludes with a discussion of related distance learning. The final chapter moves on to a consideration of reference service policies and methods of evaluation.

Students and teachers alike should be aware that much of the material covered in this book is updated, argued, and dutifully considered in information science related journals. Knowledge of the rapid changes in the field is not easily acquired. One must keep up to survive; a painless method of doing just that is to read current issues of journals as well as consult online listservs, chat rooms, etc. which are involved with reference services. (Many of these are listed throughout this text.)

ONLINE VERSION OF THE TEXT AND UPDATES

This text, and its companion volume, can be purchased in electronic format. Contact either your McGraw-Hill sales representative or visit www.mhhe.com/primis/online for more information.

Updates to the text will be available on an accompanying website: www.mhhe.com/katz.

ACKNOWLEDGMENTS

Thanks are due to the reviewers who critiqued this book: Lesley Farmer, California State University, Long Beach; Judith V. Lechner, Auburn University; Ketty Rodriguez, University of Southern Mississippi; Gail M. Staines, University of Buffalo; Ibrahim M. Stwodah, Longwood College.

Thanks are also due to the editors for this volume, Valerie Raymond and Amy Shaffer, as well as thanks also to the indexer, Kelly Lutz.

William A. Katz

INTRODUCTION TO REFERENCE WORK

VOLUME II   *Reference Services*
and Reference Processes

PART I
INTRODUCTION

PART
INTRODUCTION

CHAPTER ONE
REFERENCE SERVICE
AND THE COMMUNITY

Reference librarians identify their public with the people who walk in the front door and take the time to ask questions. Add home computers and the walk may be electronic; yet the queries are much the same. Day to day the view from the reference section rarely changes. For a broader look at the great library visitor, let's begin by considering the chain bookstores.

Chain bookstores from Barnes & Noble to Borders have an appeal not often found in libraries. Why? According to an informal survey of college students, the answer is the store is more comfortable, has a more current selection of books, is well organized (if only in broad subject areas), and is open often till midnight and beyond. Many now choose the bookstore over the library as a study center. " Students who are practiced users of libraries avoid the library whenever possible."[1]

Librarians are learning. At least several public and academic libraries now have more comfortable surroundings, longer hours and even 24-hour cafe service. For example, the public libraries in Portland, Oregon and Stamford Connecticut have commercial coffeehouses besides the stacks. (Firms such as Starbucks pay a fee each year to use the space.) Superficial? You bet. Does it draw in more readers? It does. The bookstore-library comparison has a major lesson. The librarian seeking to attract a large part

---

[1]"For Research Students Now Head to Barnes & Noble," *The New York Times,* November 3, 1999, p. B11. Copying bookstore attitudes and practices may not be the answer, though. At the height of prosperity, sales were down for bookstores in 1999. "As Booksellers Shuffle, Readers Depart," *The New York Times,* May 3, 1999, p. C13.

of the community has to go beyond the old goal of simply being a warehouse outlet. Parenthetically, some librarians may argue that the library is not a main street attraction and has more important tasks.

Nationally, libraries continue to hold their own as major cultural and information sources. In Cleveland, for example, "a surprising 81 percent responded that they believe libraries are more important" than ever before.[2] A major reason includes ready access to both print and electronic sources. No one mentioned coffee.

The bookstore is an arena of wide taste, which appeals to a mass public, as well as the esoteric needs of individuals. Reference librarians, in particular, should study what goes on in these large stores. For example, what type of health books do people buy? Is this trend useful for a reference librarian to know? It is. Without belaboring the obvious, the chain bookstore is a mirror, no matter how imperfect, of public taste and wants which may not always be evident in the library or at the reference desk.

In numerous areas the library differs from a typical bookstore.[3] But in particular it is a matter of emphasis. If a store stresses entertainment and best sellers (along with specialized interests), the library has a primary focus. The role of the library remains educational. Traditionally, this has been the attitude, if not always the realization, of library reference librarians. It is a view shared by the American public that believes an important role of a library is as an education center and research center. An average of 85 percent of Americans see the public library as: (1) an educational support for students of all ages (88 percent); (2) a learning center for adult independent learners (85 percent); (3) a discovery and learning center for preschool children (83 percent). The other role of the library as "a recreational reading center of popular materials and best-sellers" was down the list (under 45 percent).[4]

The library exists to serve the community. No one will argue with that platitude, although almost everyone has a somewhat different definition of *community*. People accept that the public library serves the pub-

---

[2]*Library Journal,* April 1, 1998, p. 14.

[3]Bookstores not only differ from libraries in extremely important ways, but so do other common comparisons from how banks are operated to department store efficiency. Any librarian can learn from the good and bad points of a business serving the public—from animal stores to undertaking parlors—but it is well to remember the unique status of the library. A good summary of comparisons with other types of organizations is: Steve Coffman, "Reference as Others Do It," *American Libraries,* May, 1999, pp. 54–56.

[4]*The Bowker Annual* (New York: R.R. Bowker, 1994) pp. 430–431. Subsequent studies and surveys, i.e., until 2000, find these attitudes remain constant.

lic, and the school and academic libraries students and teachers. Beyond these generalizations, it is necessary to look at America as a community in terms of income, education and interests.

Library Finance

How influential can a library be in a given community? The answer, of course, relies on numerous factors and variables. Something, again, can be learned by statistics.[5]

1. Statistically, there are some 9,050 public libraries in the United States with about 1500 urban and country libraries reporting an additional 7,000 or so branches. Close to one-half the public libraries (about 45 percent) have budgets of under $50,000 a year. Nearly 37 percent spend between $50,000 and $399,000. Only about 20 percent, or about 1,800 libraries, have funding over $400,000. Close to 70 percent of the population is served by only about 950 libraries, primarily in urban and closely aligned suburban communities.

2. Americans spend from $4 per capita to $100 per capita for public library support in various communities. The national average is $16 to $18 per capita.

3. There are some 3,280 academic libraries, with 488 of the institutions offering doctoral degrees. The 488 take close to 60 percent of all funding, although the 488 represent only about 15 percent of the total number. The same 488 institutions have about 60 percent of all books held in academic libraries. They account for 50 percent of all professional libraries employed. Again, most of the 488 are located in wealthy to relative wealthy areas and are privately endowed. At the same time, some 50 percent of academic libraries have only enough to sustain minimum services, minimum staff and certainly a minimum stake in new technologies.

4. Statistics for school libraries (or media centers) are not as precise. Still, if one considers the public library and academic library comparisons fairly standard, it is safe to state that only about 15 to 20 percent of school libraries are adequately financed.

5. What did American government spend its money for, from 1940 to 2000? Almost $19 trillion was spent on defense. Federal spending on nuclear weapons has exceeded spending on welfare payments, state medical insurance, health and education. Comparatively some $1.5 trillion was spent for the same period on education, training, and employment/social

---

[5]*Ibid.* Statistics are from various issues of the *Annual.*

services, which includes libraries. On the whole library support in the United States remains comparatively low.

WHO USES THE LIBRARY?

Studies of the American way of life agree on two points: (1) Society is becoming more stratified, more polarized, with the rich and the poor, the educated and uneducated wider apart than in any time in our history. (2) Limited cognitive skills are associated with lack of proper education, lack of information, and a myriad of social problems.

Less obvious, particularly to younger people, is that the country is growing older and older. People over 50 have half the nation's disposable income and those over 65 enjoy twice the discretionary income of people 25 to 34. The younger are a vanishing breed. The future lies with the old. The largest circulation magazine in America is neither the *Reader's Digest* nor *TV Guide*, but *Modern Maturity* with a total circulation of 20.5 million.[6]

Another truism is constant. The more income, education, and stability, the more likely an individual will turn to a library for information, education and recreation. As the income-education-stability level rises in a community, so does library use. Conversely, in many urban areas where income, education and stability are low, the library is usually underfinanced and underused.

The paradox is obvious: The more people need a library, if only to gain information about better jobs and education, the less it is fiscally prepared or relevant to the community. The division between the information rich and information poor seems to be increasing.

Ideally, libraries should reach out for the poor, for those most in need of information. So called "operations outreach" have been popular, and remain so in some communities, but on the whole have faded with fading library budgets and increased demands of expensive technological aids. The problem is national, and, in the opinion of this author and others, the only way the library will reach the nonreaders, the income-education deprived, is via massive federal aid. Is that likely to happen soon? And what form should it take? The questions are open for discussion, although by 2000 were hardly even considered to be on the table.

Profile of Readers

Where are the majority of staunch library supporters who vote funds for libraries and schools? The political parties will tell you. The middle classes

[6]"A Madison Avenue Fantasy," *The New York Times,* July 2, 2000, p. BU11.

are in the suburbs. Here politicians seek votes and bring up issues (such as library support) which have wide acceptance. "Fifty years ago fewer than a quarter of Americans lived in the suburbs; now roughly half do. Every 10 years, another 10 members of Congress represent predominantly suburban districts."

And these middle-class Americans vote, e.g., "In 1996, when President Clinton was re-elected, the suburbs cast 40 percent of the state's vote, Chicago only 20 percent." And the crucial demographic group for library support is parents who have children under 18 living at home in the suburbs.[7]

Enclaves, sometimes large, in urban centers which are made up of middle class citizens add to library support. Suburb or city, those who use libraries are pretty well defined, as are those who are readers and take advantage from time to time of reference services.

A market research group for eight years methodically collected information of the daily activities of 3,000 different people each year—chosen to reflect the national population spanning the ages of 18 to 90. The research through the 1990s found:

1. Only 45 percent say they read at least 30 minutes each day, but most of that comes from newspaper reading. (This fell from 51 percent in 1992.) Actually the proportion of American who had *not* completed a book in the past year doubled to 16 percent in 1990 from 8 percent in 1978.

2. Reading is falling off for younger people under 55, but about the same for those over 65. About 22 percent of men between 18 and 34 read 30 minutes a day (1999) as compared to 36 percent in 1992.

3. No one is sure why the pattern of reading shifts. One idea is that young people before the 1980's tended to read more because they were better educated than older readers. Now the attention of younger readers is wandering.

In rough terms, based on the aforementioned study and scores of others since the 1920s (well documented in the index, *Library Literature*) only about one-third of the population are considered readers who more or less regularly use a library.

Education and the Library

America is well educated, at least in terms of the number of people who now graduate from high school. Comparatively, the United States remains on top of other Western countries in the percentage of students who

[7]"Two Parties Seek to Exploit a Relentless Suburban Boom," *The New York Times*, May 4, 1999, p. 1, A22.

enter college, but the country had one of the highest dropout rates in the industrialized world—37 percent. Also, whereas twenty years ago some 80 percent of students graduated from high school, by 2000 that figure decreased to 72 percent. At the same time by 2000 some 87 percent of Americans were saying a college education is as important as a high school diploma used to be. Apparently many try for the degree but too few (about 25%) graduate.

The demographics of illiteracy are frightening. Despite levels of education, more than 47 percent of adults or about 90 million people lack basic reading skills. Another 50 million are only marginally literate, i.e., they can read, but have difficulty with complex sentences or ideas. Most live in large urban centers, although another big group is scattered in the poorer agricultural sections of the country. This set of statistics, reported by the National Adult Literacy Survey, has obvious results for libraries.[8] It explains, in no small way, why only a minority are regular library users, i.e., regular readers. It points out, too, the necessity of reaching out to poor readers.

Middle Class Libraries

Essentially the library is a middle class institution. Readers are from that class, as are the majority of financial supporters. And while the United States has the most unequal distribution of wealth of any major industrial nation few are concerned about all of this. Why not? Because most Americans believe they are middle class.

Middle class is defined in many ways, but income and education are major factors in the definition. Although about one-half of the population makes less than $35,000 a year, most consider themselves middle class or bordering on this distinction. Actually the Commerce Department considers middle class as those in the median family—household income of about $47,000, meaning that half the nation's households earn more and half less. This represents, usually, both husband and wife working. The same Department classifies people as "affluent" who make $75,000 a year and up.

There is a growing income disparity in America, e.g., in mid-2000 one-fifth had income (after taxes) of $8,800 a year; one fifth $20,000; middle two-fifths, i.e., the "middle classes" $31,400 to $45,100; highest one-fifth $45,000 to $102,000—and within that group about one percent have incomes after taxes of over $515,000. The top one-fifth of American households with the highest income earn half of all the income in the United States. The top one percent accounts for 7.3 percent of all income. The

[8]Reported in *Reference User & Services Quarterly*, Winter, 1997, p. 155.

gap between rich and poor is so wide that (in 2000) the richest 2.7 million Americans, the top 1 percent has as many after dollars to spend as the bottom 100 million. That ratio has more than doubled since 1977.

A constant barrage of studies and reports about middle America—as dear to politicians as to advertising agencies—is an accepted and acceptable statistical cliché. Some are relatively amusing and, yes, instructive. For example, one of the more unusual, was "the narcissus survey," a fearless inquiry which appeared in *The New Yorker*. The poll group was in sectors; "main street" (i.e., the majority); "easy street" (college graduates between 30 and 60 with personal incomes—not family—of over $100,000 a year). Not unexpectedly, the majority of the population on main street had the narrowest point of view about sex tolerance and drug use. "Easy street," that is those who are better educated and with higher incomes, are considerably more tolerant of drug use and liberal sexual attitudes.[9]

Reference Services Profile

When polled people responded favorably to library service and reference support. This may change, if only gradually. Short budgets and more focus on electronic aids seem to have cut into the positive response. Comparing, for example, replies from a 1989 and a 1995 poll of academic libraries in England, 67 percent indicated the library met their needs fairly well. This compares to a 77 percent level in 1989. Problems: (1) The library's failure to meet journal needs, brought on by cancellations and not subscribing to new titles. (2) Deteriorating book collections—not enough new titles. While these figures were for England, similar studies indicate much the same response in America and for much the same reasons.[10]

In an informal check of what people need in a small college library several points were made which are valid for almost all types of libraries for reference services in all types of libraries.[11]

1. No more than one in ten users ever goes to a reference librarian with a question. They either do not think of that type of assistance or are confident they do not need assistance.

2. In helping themselves, most laypeople choose the wrong sources, e.g., ones familiar to them that normally are not the best for their particular type of query.

[9]Hendrik Hertzberg, "The Narcissus Survey," *The New Yorker,* January 5, 1998, pp. 27–29. The survey was conducted by an opinion consulting firm.

[10]Bob Erens, "How Recent Developments in University Libraries Affect Research," *Library Management,* Vol. 17, pp. 6–16, 1996.

[11]Eileen Kramer, "Why Roving Reference," *Reference Services Review,* Fall, 1996, pp. 67–80. One of numerous studies that confirms this finding. See, too, references for earlier studies.

3. Few people have any idea how to carry out a basic, more or less refined reference search.

4. Frustration is the key descriptor of people seriously trying to find information in a library without the help of a trained reference librarian.

What do most students want from the reference librarian? Experience indicates it is what many librarians think—help with online searching. They would like this both in the library and at home on a 24-hour basis.[12]

SPECIAL GROUPS SERVED

There is a major problem with any discussion of library service to special groups. As long as "special" is read to mean the middle and upper classes, all is well. As soon as the label is used as a disguise for the underclass, there can be disagreement. The argument goes that the underfinanced library has no business trying to solve gigantic social problems such as illiteracy and outreach programs for the poor. It is a logical value judgment about the mission of the library and librarian. Others, including this author, grant that these are terrible problems, but they believe the role of the library is to serve all, not just the few. In this text, the library is seen as a social as well as an information service. The two, particularly at the public library level, are inseparable. Even the reader who rejects this assumption should at least know there are millions of nonlibrary users out there, as well as clients who need special attention. And that is what this section is about, argument or no.

Multiculture Groups

There are various ways to designate groups that are composed of other than white, middle-class, "average" users of the library. The descriptions of these groups vary—such as disadvantaged or underprivileged. It is impossible, and unwise, to lump all members of the groups under a single name. Whatever they are called, the majority of their members unfortunately represent nonusers of library services today.

Primarily, there are two large groups in the category of the disadvantaged. The first is composed of those lacking necessary education. The second, which may be a part of the first, is the poor and includes many ethnic minorities: African-Americans, Hispanics, Native Americans, and so forth.

[12]Maribeth Ward, "A Disconnect Between Academic Librarians and Students," *College & Research Libraries*, vol. 16, no. 10, 1996, pp. 22–23.

While not all members of minority groups are underprivileged, enough are to identify them as part of the larger, deprived group. In any case, and whatever the descriptor, the disadvantaged include both adults and youngsters, both city and country dwellers.

In providing reference services for ethnic minorities, several factors must be considered: (1) Foreign language materials, particularly the basic reference works, for example, encyclopedias, dictionaries, geographical sources, and so on, should be part of acquisitions whenever possible. (2) Members of the reference staff should be familiar with the language(s) of the ethnic groups. (3) Community information files should be tailored for the needs of these groups. (4) Maximum effort should be made to reach these groups through information and referral centers, publicity, and so forth. The use of television, radio, and door-to-door canvassing are effective tools here. (5) Including local members of prominent minorities and ethnic groups on the staff is an obvious benefit.

It is necessary to pay close attention to cultural differences simply as matters of sensitivity, courtesy, or diplomacy. Give it any name, but the name of the game is success at answering questions, and any barrier, cultural or otherwise, that stands in the way of that goal are to be routed out and overcome.

Each year there are a growing number of reference works dedicated to various cultural groups. See, for example: The *Booklist* (January 1, 2000, pp. 956-957) which lists and briefly annotates "Native American Reference Sources." See, too, the same journal's longer annotations for basic books covering both Africa and African-American interests (February 15, 2000, pp. 1130+). The librarian should follow the standard reviews for new additions suitable for the reference library.

Foreign Born

America's foreign born leapt from 10 million in 1970 to more than 20 million in 1998-1999. Immigrants historically favor public libraries over bookstores, and turn to the library for everything from romance novels to assistance with reference type questions. How important an audience is the immigrant? In comparing the "busiest libraries" in the nation, the American Library Association found that the Queens Borough Public Library in New York (with 62 branches and 15.5 million circulation in 1997) was by far the "busiest." Why? In Queens more than one-third of the population is foreign born. Immigrants, who use the library, place a heavy emphasis on education and book learning as a means of securing the family's future. "The numbers also reflect an extraordinary effort by library officials to reach out to their multinational neighborhoods. Queens residents speak more than 100 languages, and the library system circulates material in more than 40 of them, including Spanish, Chinese, Icelandic, Zulu, and Gaelic."[13]

While one in ten Americans today was born abroad, not all, by any means, are either poor or not that well educated. A new breed, the immigrants of this time are better educated, economically more secure and routinely hop a plane to visit the old country. These expatriates use the library, but more likely to find information on international trade and stock markets rather than helping to build railways and working mines and production lines as earlier immigrants.

The librarian looking at the immigrant population soon realizes it is not a neat group, which can be categorized in terms of reference services use. The same message is apparent when evaluating needs of any large group of people.

Disabled

Nothing illustrates better the problem with lumping groups of people under a descriptive heading, than the "disabled." This can mean anyone from a bed-ridden patient to, more likely, an individual bound to a wheelchair or crutches. They all have different needs independent of their ill fortune with health, and at the same time the library must provide reference facilities so they can tap the resources of the library either in person or at home.

One example of a specific problem: learning disabilities. "In a service area of 100,000...around 15,000 people have LD," claims a specialist in this field of library work. "Factor in parents, teachers, spouses, and bosses next; count at least one additional person for every one with LD. That brings the total to at least 30,000, probably a lot more."[14] Note that this type of speculative mathematics may be used for almost any disabled group.

Generally the most prevalent type of query is how to find information about the disability. Depending on the attention given the disability by librarians and others, there may be a little or a great deal of data available. The reference librarian should know how to find just the right type of work for the person(s) putting the questions.

The Other Side of the Desk

Not all readers follow standard "behavioral guidelines" and these individuals have come to be known as "problem patrons," an unfortunate

---

[13]*The New York Times*, May 31, 1998, p. 30. The other "busy" libraries are all in urban areas. They are, in order of circulation: New York Public Library (11.5 million); Brooklyn Public Library (10.1); Los Angeles Public Library (9.6); Chicago Public Library (7.9); and Houston Public Library (5.9).

[14]For a brief explanation of what is involved in serving the disabled, in this case the learning disabled, see Audrey Gorman, "Better Reference for 40% of Your Community," *American Libraries*, May, 1999, p. 73.

phrase for an individual searching for information, and/or trouble. In a banal, unintentionally amusing approach, one authority explains that these odd fellows and odd women may be divided into three classes. At the bottom is the "nuisance group, annoying but harmless." They are identified easily by such things as knuckle cracking, sleeping, chattering, and, yes, laughing. More serious are the Class II types that include those who bring pets to the library and the "highly emotional" as well as more commonplace drunks and exhibitionists. Downright dangerous, and classed as "very serious" are readers who come to the library armed, "openly hostile," "combative," and "emotionally disturbed." While at least some categories may be less than ordinary, and sometimes pose administrative difficulties, the primary loss of such lists is the public's view of the good sense of the librarian, e.g., the aforementioned listing was carried in *Harper's Magazine* under the title "Trouble at the Reference Desk."[15]

The catch with the so-called "problem" patrons is one of categorization. Who is simply eccentric or truly a problem in that he or she may be a danger to others? This is summarized by a chart from a book on how librarians are supposed to identify unusual patron behavior. It was reprinted, without comment, but with a decided sense of irony and a dash of humor in a national magazine. First there is the "nuisance class, annoying but harmless." Under this category one finds a dozen labels from "knuckle cracking and coughing" to "amorous" (consensual and malodorous (i.e., someone who does not use deodorant). Next comes the "unclear (potentially serious)" and here we have the standard exhibitionist, drunk and homeless along with staring and "bringing pets." Finally is "Class I (dangerous)" these are identifying characteristics such as predatory, openly hostile, threatening, combative or verbally abusive.[16] The problem is that these might apply to almost any relationship of two people over a given period of time.

Despite such banal lists, meant, to be sure, to be useful, there is no real way of deciding on appearance or even action who is truly a "problem."

SUGGESTED READING

American Libraries, August, 1999, pp. 44+. There are a half dozen articles in this issue given over to the serving of special groups from "information needs of displaced people" to serving "organized workers." Written by librarians, the articles reflect real activities, not theory.

Aronson, Marc, "Teenagers and Reading," *Journal of Youth Services in Libraries,* no. 2, 1999, pp. 29–30. Why don't teenagers read more and at the same

[15]*Harper's Magazine,* November, 1997, p. 32.

[16]*Ibid,* p. 32. The quotes/lists are from an American Library Association book: *A Handbook of Positive Approaches to Negative Situations,* Chicago: 1997.

time use the reference section of the library more? The author discovers numerous reasons, but a primary one is the lack of understanding by adults (librarians) about the needs and reading habits of teenagers. Aronson found, too, that teenagers really do love to read, if only to escape the problems of the teen years.

Bowman, Karlyn, "The Family Dinner, Alive and Well," *The New York Times,* August 25, 1999, p. A23. In an "op ed" piece an American Enterprise Institute resident fellow points out that most people, no matter how busy, take time off for the traditional family dinner. More important to librarians, the majority now has more free time than ever before—despite stories to the contrary—to do everything from watching television to, yes, going to the library. Studies show "that there may be less to the fabled time crunch than meets the eye."

Lee, Earl, *Libraries in the Age of Mediocrity.* Jefferson, NC: McFarland, 1998. A practical look at the role of the library in modern society by a working librarian, this calls for a traditional view of the mission of the library. Along the way, the author discusses censorship, automation, women's studies and "the ongoing corruption of the arts." A wide ranging view, this is highly recommended for both veterans and beginners.

Li, Suzanne D., "Library Services to Students With Diverse Language and Cultural Backgrounds," *Journal of Academic Librarianship,* March, 1998, pp. 139–143. The author stresses the needs of undergraduates who have problems with coursework, and the library, because of language problems. Most are born outside of the United States. There is a good literature review and notes on library instruction.

Marcella, Rita and Graeme Baxter, "The impact of social class and status on citizenship information needs." *Journal of Information Science,* vol. 26, no. 4, 2000. While this article reports the results of a British survey, the conclusions are applicable to America and other Western countries. The study finds: *(a)* social class and status shape information needs and demands; *(b)* lower income and education classes rarely use the libraries for information needs; c) certain groups are not using the new library technologies. The conclusion: the poor in terms of income and schooling are "in a real danger of exclusion" from library information services.

Massey-Burzio, Virginia, "From the Other Side of the Reference Desk: A Focus Group Study," *The Journal of Academic Librarianship,* May, 1998, pp. 208–215. How do people look for information? What problems do they have, and how can the library counter with suggestions and services? These are answered by the author who is head of the resource service department of Johns Hopkins University Library. The main conclusion is that there often is a wide difference between what librarians think is needed and the actual wants of the users.

McCook, Kathleen, ed. "Ending the Isolation of Poor People," *American Libraries,* May 2000, pp. 45+. The editor introduces four articles "on how libraries change impoverished people's lives." Worth reading as so few articles in library literature carry information on the important role of reference services for the poor. See, particularly: Patrick Grace, "No Place to Go (Except the Public Library)."

O'Connor, Daniel and Robert Fortenbaugh, "Socioeconomic Indicators and Library Use," *Public Libraries,* May/June, 1999, pp. 156–164. In this chapter much is made of economic and social aspects of library service. The two authors of the article, based on research, stress the need to understand such material in order "to promote library development." While primarily of value to those contemplating library evaluation, the article stresses the "two stage mode...to link community characteristics to library funding and then link funding to use."

Poor People and Library Services. Jefferson, NC: McFarland, 1998. A collection of statistics and papers from both librarians and nonlibrarians outlines the position of the American poor and library services. Useful for both raw data to help improve a budget to how to pry questions out of some reluctant people who desperately need assistance. A guide for all public and school libraries.

Sarkodie-Mensah, Kwasi (ed). "Reference Services for the Adult Learner." *The Reference Librarian,* nos. 69/70, 2000. Moving from the information explosion to "understanding the characteristics, needs and expectations of adult learners," to serving diverse populations, this is the single place to find anything about reference services and the community. In over 400 pages (both as a journal and as a separate book), the editor has brought together the latest in thinking about the broad dimensions of reference services. All the contributors are experts in their fields. Must reading.

Schuyler, Michael, "Adapting for Impaired Patrons," *Computers in Libraries,* June, 1999, pp. 24–29. The author explains how the new technology can help the disabled to use the library. He draws his information and suggestions from experience and careful consideration of all of the possibilities in terms of cost and ease of use. A basic article for anyone interested in the subject.

Steckman, Betty et al., "Library Services to a Linguistically Diverse Community, *Reference Services Review,* Summer, 1998, pp. 57–66. The results of a workshop which considers the various aspects of serving a community where different languages are spoken. Practical advice is given on how to reach this audience. A highly recommended approach for all libraries.

Westbrook, Lynn, "Analyzing Community Information Needs," *Library Administration and Management,* January, 2000, pp. 26–30. The author shows how the library staff and community members may band together to carry on a community library need survey. The end result may be a change in library services as well as a method of continual community analysis. A practical article for small- to medium-sized libraries in particular.

Willis, Mark, *Dealing With Difficult People in the Library.* Chicago: American Library Association, 1999. In the publicity blurb for this excellent guide it is noted that "Libraries need patrons, but unfortunately one cannot predict the behavior of every person who walks through the door." Perhaps it should be "fortunately," but no matter. Here the author gives practical advice on how to handle difficult (impossible) people from the slightly mad and talkative to the really dangerous. Highly recommended.

CHAPTER TWO
INFORMATION AND
THE COMMUNITY

The major technological transformation in America, and a good part of the world, concerns information. The digital age has made this not only apparent but has changed the whole pattern of the way the economy operates and how it is analyzed. The new economy has pushed traditional industrial patterns aside in favor of information technology. Once again the skills of the workers (from managers and computer specialists to researchers and, yes, librarians) is of major importance. "Or to put it differently, in an age where information is so widely available, it is not the information that is valuable but what is done with it.[1] Studies are valuable in understanding how information is matched with the needs of the individual. Several generalities have emerged. Some are outlined here.

The average client study is based on demographics, that is, an evaluation of education, age, occupation, economic status, and so forth. Often the study is balanced with such variables as the size of library collection, the education of the staff, the distance of the user from the library, and so on.

Another type of patron study considers communication patterns and such things as how and why the reference section is used, and why one person may prefer periodicals to books or databases. Several conclusions have emerged:

1. People have different patterns of behavior when they are seeking information, at least information other than the ready-reference variety. Although libraries may separate information into the classical

---

[1]"How New is the New Economy?" *The New York Review of Books,* September 23, 1999, p. 50.

divisions, such as the humanities and science, and their subdivisions, people rarely seek information within those specific, logical areas. The wide use of the Net has torpedoed traditional library categorization of information for laypeople. At the same time experienced searchers realize the value of forms and categories which speed up information retrieval.

2. Few people seek information as an end in itself; rather, it is used to help trigger decision-making or to enhance understanding of the immediate environment or the world. Most clients want the information. They are not interested in how it is obtained. Again this attitude is reinforced by wide use of the Net.

3. The average patron does not contact the reference librarian. Signs indicating where to get the right type of help, and an understanding among staff about directing an individual to a reference librarian, are helpful in improving information communication. The fact that most young people prefer to go to a computer, not the librarian, indicates the need to stress availability of expert help. It is vital for users to understand that such assistance is freely available.

4. Despite the mass of material on communication and information, the general public still knows too little about these specialized fields. The average person copes with a glut of information from radio, television, newspapers, and magazines very simply. Most often, the public does not hear, view, or read—it ignores. When information is "received," the receiver may:

a. Accept it, that is, use it as a means of reinforcing existing opinion or reject it because it challenges existing opinion. A characteristic verbal response is often "I know that," or else, "I didn't know that."

b. Add it to memory without allowing it to make any real impression. Verbally, the response would be "Yes," or "Oh, I see," or, simply, "O.K., I understand."

c. Use it to answer a latent question, that is, "the information may be pictured as connecting two previously isolated elements of knowledge." Here the person would say, "Oh, that explains things."

d. In some cases, the person accepts the new information and uses it to transform an opinion or an idea. Verbally it would be expressed: "That does change matters" or "That alters my position."

5. Information may be graded in terms of potential value to users. For example, a finding in an otherwise undistinguished article may trip the thought processes of one researcher, who is then led into a completely new approach to a problem. There are many relationships among information sources, and there is no valid way to determine what is or is not valuable for all people at all times and in all places.

6. The successful decision-makers are those who are able to acquire and process information quickly, no matter what type of situation they happen to be in. The ability to acquire and process information is very difficult to achieve. Reference librarians should see their primary function as one of assisting in this important processing operation. Inability to separate knowledge, facts, and understanding from the masses of data often results in what one author has come to call *information anxiety.* Anxiety can reach the nervous breakdown stage when the average layperson (or student) is confronted with technical material from almost any field. The inexperienced solve the problem by turning to the Net and only the Net. They may not be able to search well, but at least they find something they understand—something which may or may not be adequate, but at least it is information of sorts.

7. It is harder and harder for experts to understand even what other experts are saying. Using a scale from plus 50 to minus 50, the vocabulary of the more technical fields ranks close to 50. Popular magazines and newspapers would be between 0 and 10. A boy chatting with a cow would be about *minus* 50. Some laypeople feel more at home with the cow. Reference librarians must be comfortable with cows and with vocabularies in the plus 50 bracket. More important they must be able to interpret to laypeople what the experts are about.

GATHERING INFORMATION

How information is used, and particularly by different individuals from different educational, economic, and cultural backgrounds, is too rarely addressed. In the larger context of reference services it becomes imperative to understand who uses information and how it is gathered. The importance of this is underlined with each new digital database, with each new full-text service, with each new network. There are simply too many data. Someone has to be able to mediate between it and the user. This cannot be done until one appreciates not only the information sources, but also the individual seeker of data. The librarian is concerned with the ability to access what is needed for X or Y query. Access in turn implies an understanding of the information process.

Packaging Information

The steps in the creation and packaging of information may be traced in various ways. While not everyone will agree with this or that analysis, a general overview of the different communication packages is possible. And what follows is as applicable to digital data as to print and other media.

The information, or message, goes through three phases before its eventual publication in some traditional reference form, such as a book or periodical article. These phases are: (1) the origin of the message, (2) the informal communication of the message, and (3) the formal communication of the message.

Even with the Internet, e-mail, Listserv, and other forms of digital communication, the basic pattern of information packaging remains the same. What differs is the amount of control by a second or third party. Whereas print publishing usually requires not only an author, but a publisher, distributor, bookstore, etc., the Net allows a "one to one" passage of information. The author goes online and offers free access to what he or she has to say or report. No middle persons. Democracy applauds. Economists shudder. Librarians simply ask: "Yes, but how reliable is this data?"

Phase 1—Origin of the Message

The message originates when the individual author begins to think about his or her next novel and puts the thoughts on paper. Or it can originate when the inventor developing a better mousetrap is working on the project with six other mousetrap experts. Each is thinking, exploring, and experimenting, but none has yet arrived at the final version—the polished fiction or the decisive way to catch a mouse.

The same process goes on when one undertakes the common task of writing a paper for a class. First there has to be an idea for the paper, even if it is only a suggestion from a teacher, a friend, reading, television, and so forth. The idea generation may be the most difficult phase, although the consequent efficient solving of the problem posed by the idea offers another major challenge—deciding how the idea is to be implemented by research and eventually modified for the purpose of the paper. Still, those who have struggled with the innovative process itself recognize the difficulty of phase 1 of the communication process.

The formality, even some say the thought behind the origin of the message may disappear with the computer and e-mail. On the other hand, even the most informal chatter does require some consideration. The difference here is that e-mail and its many cousins may or may not be a formal way of communication. It is important to distinguish, say, the quick response to a message of love to a plea from a student or researcher for a detailed analysis of drinking water.

Phase 2—Informal Communication of the Message

Once the message is conceived, how is it passed on? Librarians are familiar with the formal method of communication, the translation into the printed word. They are equally familiar with informal channels, but, as will be shown, rarely use them in reference situations.

The information in phase two of the communications chain may be labeled in many ways but, essentially, it is the familiar inside information, or "inside dope." Knowledge of this information may give the receiver a certain status from knowing something few others know, or it may help the receiver in an instrumental way by supplying evidence for a decision—a decision regarding whether to go ahead on this or that experiment, business deal, or research project, or whether to modify the experiment or project. The content of the informal message varies, but the transmission process is somewhat the same in all disciplines:

1. Informal channels of transmission. These days this translates into use of the Internet one–to–one, or group–to–group. Beyond that:

2. Face-to-face discussion with colleagues and those interested in the project.

3. Discussion through the computer, telephone or private correspondence.

4. Drafts of manuscripts to be circulated among friends and colleagues—by mail, computer, and so on.

5. Discussion at meetings and seminars.

6. Semiformal channels of transmission:

In addition to formally published works, there are:

a. Works in progress. A communicator may report the current status of the project. In the case of the author of the novel, this communication may be totally informal and may be picked up from a variety of sources, from *Publishers Weekly* to *The New York Review of Books;* that is, a note may appear to the effect that Y author's next novel is finished. In the case of the mousetrap consortium, there may be a formal outlet for the communication such as a series in a journal that reports works under way by X and Y scientists.

b. Semipublished studies. If one accepts "semipublished" in the sense that the work has not been offered for general circulation but is in a printed form, this would include computer downloads. There are several online services, such as FINDEX, which focuses on abstract research reports, studies, and surveys otherwise not published. In fact, many scientific and social science reports, studies, and talks can be found online for many months, if not years, before they are formally published.

What is peculiar about both the informal and semiformal channels of transmission indicated here is that generally the information packages are not available to libraries. "Generally" is used advisedly because online services make many of these previous relatively inaccessible forms part of the reference process. Also, the alert reference librarian may tap into the semiformal levels of transmission when those are committed in some form to print—works in progress are often parts of journals and books; reports that are unclassified and not private are indexed and abstracted, and many are available to librarians; dissertations are generally available by means of well-organized indexing.

However, this merely skims the surface, tapping only the obvious aspects of the semiformal channels of communication. Much more is needed in terms of bibliographical control of traditional print and nonprint materials.

Phase 3—Formal Communication of the Message

Time passes, and the communication chain is completed. In terms of our model, this means that the communicator's message has been codified, having been transmitted formally in a format that may range from an online journal article to a book. The time from gestation of an idea until the publication of a report or journal article varies with individuals and disciplines. However, in most disciplines this is usually two to three or more years.

It is generally only when the chain is complete that the reference library comes into play by (1) acquiring and organizing the message in whatever form it may take; (2) acquiring the necessary indexes, abstracts, bibliographies, and cataloging to gain ready access to the message; and (3) organizing the reference system in such a way that the message may be retrieved with a minimum of effort and a maximum of relevancy for the user.

The communication packages in phase three include the standard resources found in any reference situation. They are listed here in the general order of most current, next most current, and so forth.

1. Databases, particularly those updated hourly or daily.

2. Reports (printed and other, including computer e-mail, tapes, and televised news shows and news events)

3. Periodicals, the timeliness of which increases when they are digitally published online.

4. Indexing and abstracting services—databases are usually, though not always, available faster than printed versions.

5. Annual reviews and state-of-the-art reports.

6. Bibliographical reviews.

7. Books.

8. Encyclopedia summaries.

9. Almost any other resource in print or in nonprint form, that is, textbooks, conference proceedings, the library catalog, audiovisual materials, and so on.

Library Access to Communications Forms

The guides to this morass of information become increasingly scarce as one moves from published to semipublished sources. The Internet, for example, is a jungle when it comes to discovering a particular piece of unpublished information, especially if the data retrieval is not within the experience of the searcher. In fact, some information is extremely hard to come by because it is private (office memoranda, for example) or has never been indexed, abstracted, or otherwise made available. Totally unpublished material has little chance of circulation except at a computer terminal, in conversations, conferences, meetings, and the like, where one might learn about, and sometimes even view, the materials.

What is needed is effective access and retrieval systems that will make it easier to acquire, control, and access records. The records available should include not just those in libraries, but others as well—as long, of course, as they are available to the public, as limited as the public may be. A method of discrimination and evaluation must be built into these devices to eliminate the records that need not be maintained. To date we are closer to a system of acquisitions and control than we are to devising a means of evaluation. It is likely that for generations to come the essential task of the librarian will be the establishment and implementation of standards in information storage.

Another major consideration is the highly international nature of information. It is increasingly the case that the well informed draw upon data from all over the world, not simply the country of origin. True, most of the time the information has to be in English, but everyone from U.S. industrialists and scientists to European technicians and businesspeople understand a language that is a key to modern markets and products. This is not to argue against knowing a foreign language, but only to admit a basic weakness of most Americans from all professions. The development of the European Community, with a population of over 350 million and a gross national product exceeding that of the United States, gives the librarian more opportunity for information channels.

DESKTOP PUBLISHING

Although reading printed matter (such as a magazine or book) online has proved less than popular, the use of the computer to publish print books and magazines has taken hold. The same steps are employed as in electronic publishing, except the end product is a printed work.

The mimeograph machine, followed by photocopying, revolutionized what has come to be known as "desktop publishing." For the first time an individual was able to "print" a pamphlet, magazine, or book at home. Distribution remained (and remains) a problem, but the author-editor no longer had to depend on expensive typesetting and printing equipment. Today desktop publishing is linked to computer, word processing, and software programs.

Thanks to scores of software programs, anyone can now generate and combine text and graphics at a computer keyboard. Pages may be arranged in almost any form. They are then printed on a laser printer, bound, and mailed. A more sophisticated, as well as expensive, process is to use the laser printed pages as camera-ready copy. This is then the basis for lithography or printing on a large system. To a reader the desktop publication appears no different than one done by standard production methods. An editor has the ability to publish a magazine or book that, in appearance, may be even better than one pulled from a million-dollar printing press.

Everything from creative layouts and incorporation of various typefaces and artwork into a page is possible. More important, money and time are saved. Expensive, individually typeset pages are no longer required. The result is evident in many places, but particularly in the rapid growth of small presses. There is now 6,000 or more of these across the United States publishing, usually at a desktop, everything from one-page political tracts to how-to-do-it books, poetry, and fiction.

Other Publishing Possibilities

What one technology gives, another takes away. Consider, for example, the limited possibilities of CD-ROMs for the small press publisher. The high cost of preparing and producing CD-ROMs makes it an unlikely place for small publishers or self-publishing. It is estimated that $800,000 to $1.5 million are required to have a successful CD-ROM product, often with nearly half of that going to marketing and promotion. The result is that CD-ROM publishing, like book publishing, is controlled by a dozen or so publishers. The decline of the small and independent publisher is likely to be more marked in CD-ROM publishing than in print.

At the same time, many more avenues for small publishers are opened up by networks, and particularly the Internet. Here there is almost total freedom to publish what one wishes and has the time and patience to prepare. Overhead is small, and there are few technological barriers to publishing, say, a poem or a book of poems online. The drawback is lack of control and, for many, lack of profit. This is not to say a whole new method of publishing is not open to the same people who brought the small press to the world, but it is going to take time before it becomes as popular, as well known.

A computer, linked to a network, can produce a completely digital journal, newsletter, or magazine. There is no true estimate as to how many such titles are available, say on the Internet, but they cover the globe. Some are free and pay their way by generating other work for the people who produce them.[2]

INFORMATION SUPERGLUT

What is the single biggest problem concerning information today? There is too much of it. It is that simple, and it is the topic of countless articles, discussions, books, and even television programs. Some call it information overload, others label it information anxiety, and still others consider it an abundance of garbage.

The problem is twofold: (1) Does the public, general or specialized, really want or need all the new or rehashed data? (2) Does the public really need still another technology to speed along the mass of material to the person at breakfast time who can hardly get through the front page of a newspaper much less another conference speech or a journal article? A serious error in today's reflections about information science is the sometimes unconscious and unconscionable assumption that the more information available, the better off the society. Total undifferentiated access to information can well enslave the poor user.

Reference Librarian as Information Mediator

One major, significant answer to the problem is for the reference librarian to serve as an information mediator, to determine what is useful, what is needed, and what can be rejected. As an information mediator, the reference librarian of today is ensured a major role in the information

---

[2]Space does not allow a lengthy discussion of online publishing possibilities for individuals or small groups, but there are over 1,500 books on the subject. The odds are that in the next decade small press publications (known by many as "zines") will dominate online, not in print or in other digital forms. Online opens the world to all publishers, small or large. The small presses stand to gain more via the Net.

society of tomorrow. Where once the librarian was a useful individual, tomorrow, as mediator, he or she will be absolutely necessary.

Librarians might consider the mass of information a blessing for, if nothing else, it (1) increases the chances of finding the best, current, precise answer(s) and (2) it encourages the layperson to think of the librarian as an individual trained to cope with the overload.

In the past the reference librarian has had the opposite concern. Never quite certain that the user was receiving enough information about a given question, the tendency was to give as much as was available and let the user select and choose. Thanks to information overload this formula today is one that can lead only to disaster and a frustration for most users. Specialists, of course, may still want "all" that is available, but they are rare.

Common sense dictates the professional reference librarian command and control information. The ability to determine what is good, bad, or indifferent for a given individual with a given question is at the heart of the matter. In its broadest context it is one exercised almost every day by the librarian. For example, how does one select just the right periodical, or the best article from among over 120,000 to 140,000 journals now being published? Which of the 40,000 to 50,000 books issued each year in America can be of help to a particular reader? Should the baffled high school senior turn to the online *Readers' Guide,* or rely on a more specialized service to find current data on hunger in America?

Turning to the Internet, as most students and many laypeople do today, what page out of the one billion plus possibilities on the Net is relevant for the student's assignment? Which website will have necessary links to bring numerous dimensions to a question about minority groups in America? What is the fastest search engine to determine an address, or find a reliable source of business information?

The reference librarian *selects what is relevant* and thereby helps tame the information giant.

Beyond exclusion and inclusion of information, the librarian must deal with what is at hand and, furthermore, what can be had at the computer terminal. So, while it is important to wage war on too much information by careful selection, the second weapon in the battle is an understanding, and appreciation of individual information needs. This assumes the librarian has certain capabilities when fielding questions:

1. An understanding of what the individual client requires. In most cases the librarian must have an appreciation of the research process. How does one move from an unqualified mass of data to a particular fact or group of facts which, in turn, may be employed to solve a larger problem?

2. An understanding that most people with questions not only have a query about the information itself, but also are often working blindly toward a thesis that they may or may not fully understand. This hit-and-miss aspect of research is evident in such problems as attempting to *(a)* pinpoint the solution to juvenile crime; *(b)* appreciate the contribution of Henry James to the class novel; or *(c)* solve the meaning of the expanding universe.

The individual moves from the general to the particular and hopes for assistance from the librarian. Examples include a frustrated carpenter who needs all the information available for construction of a garage roof and does not want everything on the subject of carpentry and certainly not a history of garages; or a high school student searching for material on "democracy versus socialism," where the librarian must narrow the query and select a minimum amount of material to meet the time limits and educational background of the student.

Copyright[3]

Laypersons understand vaguely that a copyright or patent protects the originator of a work. It assures an author of exclusive rights to a novel or scientific treatise. Under most (but not all) circumstances the author must be paid each time the novel is purchased or the article is faxed or photocopied. However, because of exceptions and gray areas, understanding copyright law has developed into one of the great mysteries of modern times. It truly takes an expert to fathom its various aspects. When the new Library of France opened in Paris, some 300,000 documents were available both in print and in electronic format. All had to be used in the building because of publishers' concerns over copyright.

Who owns the rights to reproduce articles online or on a CD-ROM, or another electronic form? The person or corporation who owns the copyright of the article is the usual answer. Problems arise when a freelance writer, who has been paid X dollars for an article, demands royalties when the piece is used on a CD-ROM, online, and so on. The publisher claims the X dollars gave the publisher full rights to the article. The writer's claim, "Yes, but only when printed in the magazine." Outside the magazine format, the writer should receive royalties. Although some publishers fight this, the common approach today is to give the writer an extra one-time amount for future electronic use of work. (Magazines, for example, whose articles appear on America Online give freelance writers $100 for each article, above and beyond what they received for publication in a magazine.)

---

[3]*The Copyright Website* (www.benedict.com) is a site of a copyright and trade mark attorney. It offers current information on what is going on with the ever changing copyright law. Particularly useful for the latest on information, libraries and digital databases. See, too, the American Library Association's *Copyright and Database Protection* (www.ala.org/work/copyright).

In the midst of the confusion the librarian continues to offer public access to data from the author's novel or article. Perhaps this is acceptable, but when is there a limit to how many photocopies one can make of an article, a book, a chapter, or whatever? When and how is the author paid or recognized for such use? While the U.S. Copyright Revision Act of 1976 is clear about authors' rights, Section 107 concerning "fair use" is vague. Fair use is a method of defining what someone may do with a copy of an article, or a page out of a book, or a video recording, and so on, without violating the rights of the copyright holder or author. In general, one is free to photocopy an article as long as the copy is not put to commercial use, but is used for research, scholarship, teaching, and so forth.

There is no strict legal definition of "fair use." The term is employed in copyright to indicate how much one may quote from a work (book, article, report, etc.) without having to seek permission from the copyright holder. Thanks to the vagueness of the present copyright law there are cases where some authors and publishers have refused permission to quote anything from a given book. With that, though, there are rough guidelines, which prevail in 99 percent of the time and are generally recognized. In prose, an extract should not exceed 400 words and the total words taken from the complete work should not be over 800 words. Rules vary for different types of composition, i.e., for poetry the quote should be no longer than one quarter of the whole poem. (The question of unpublished work, such as letters, becomes truly complicated and may call for legal advice.)

Section 108 of the copyright law concerns photocopying in libraries and interlibrary loan. Essentially, it says that copying is legal as long as it is done without a profit motive. Beyond that there are problems: (1) It is legal for the library to make up to 10 copies of an article for students to read in the reserve section of the library. (2) It is *not* legal to store an article in the library electronic data file in anticipation of future use. This assumes systematic commercial copying, and requires that the copyright owner be paid. The key is the verb "to transfer." Information transferred from a printed or electronic source to the single user's file is legal. But to transmit the article to a library server for future use is not legal. (3) Books may be borrowed, but only if the book cannot be purchased at a reasonable price. That is, almost any book in a current edition of *Books in Print* should not be sent on interlibrary loan. While this protects the publishers and the authors, it does raise sticky problems. Some librarians conveniently overlook the rules, others pay for the periodical articles, and still others may claim that an interlibrary loan from a library within a system does not infringe on the copyright law.

Studies show the copyright law has not had much effect on libraries. The average library is not likely to request an article, book, or report more than once. The chance of a periodical article or of a single periodical being requested on interlibrary loan more than once is largely accidental. One may also interpret broadly the section on books, particularly since it is stipulated that the book must be sold at a "fair price." This is not to say the copyright law is not an important consideration and one of much interest to librarians but it has not had real (as opposed to theoretical) influence on the activities of the majority of libraries.

Copyright Fees

Copyright is a major issue with moving from only a citation to the full text online. Librarians and the public are opposed to paying an author/publisher each time they read or download an article. At the same time, the author/publisher justifiably feel they should receive some revenue, or equivalent to what the same library/reader would have to pay for the magazine or book. A parallel dilemma: if payment is due should the library bear the cost or pass it on to the reader. Most librarians opt for the former, but this could have serious budget consequences.

Copyright fees may be paid in a number of ways:

1. Through the Copyright Clearance Center where a certain sum is set for each article that is copied. This is paid to the copyright owner. Numerous periodical and book publishers are registered at the nonprofit center, but almost as many are not. Be that as it may, it has proven to be one way to simplifying the problem of who owes what to whom.

2. Ordering articles from document delivery services that build in royalties to authors and publishers in their fee for the copyright work. These services have arranged licensing fees from the individual publishers.

3. Licensing of CD-ROMs or online databases by the publisher or vendor. The license then sets the rights as to what may be copied, if anything, and how. Most licenses, for example, forbid the user to use the data to create a new database, printed work, and so forth.

4. The library can exercise its "fair use" option to pay no fee, and pass on the little or no cost per copy to the user. Under law the commercial service is obligated to collect and pay the copyright holder some royalty fee.

Copyright in the Electronic Age

Networks provide major questions for copyright experts. How can multimedia—using both new and older works—meet the rights of copyright owners of only a small part of, say, a multimedia CD-ROM? Is the present copyright law a feasible way to govern computer networks? Most important: Can copyright be enforced online? On the Internet it is possible for anyone to use a service called "anonymous remailer," and send copyrighted material to thousands of places online without being identified. Why would one want to pay for copyrighted books, magazines, reports, and so forth? Today, quite literally, those with access to a computer network can avoid copyright protection. The ease of infringement is made even more so by the lack of any method of enforcement. (The FBI and other enforcement agencies do monitor bulletin boards and regularly arrest notorious copyright infringers. While this discourages organized groups, it is no protection against the single teenager.)

The answer to all of this is threefold. First, the copyright laws will be rewritten and constantly updated. Second, major copyright violation in the past, present, and future is done for profit by professional criminals, not by librarians. Third, the photocopying machine, the fax, and the computer laser printer open the way for individuals to avoid copyright, but they are hardly important players in the game.

In 1998–1999 Congress approved the Digital Millennium Copyright Act designed to protect electronic information copyright holders. A provision which differs from earlier laws: The library can now make three rather than one copy of a copyrighted work for the purpose of preservation. Without all of that, how long can present copyright survive? No one knows, but the vast use of the Net indicates something will have to give and it is most likely to be copyright. What will replace it to satisfy authors and publishers? No one knows, but in the next decade the answer will be there.

PATHS TO INFORMATION

How do most people collect the information they need to make a decision or simply to answer some persistent query? Most often the researcher finds the answer in the so-called invisible college, and by the layperson at the "back fence." Although more analysis has been made of the phenomenon of the "invisible college" than of the "back fence," there seem to be similarities in both approaches.

Several studies indicate that the procedures in information gathering are common to us all.

1. The first and possibly the single best source of information for both laypeople and subject experts is conversation with a friend who knows the subject matter. Lacking someone next door or in the next room, the curious individual may turn to the Internet, pick up the telephone or even write a letter to the expert.

Most research on the "invisible college" has been limited to the scientific community, but the few profiles available of other information seekers confirm the general pattern followed by scientists. When scientists, social scientists, and those involved with the humanities are asked to list their information sources, all note that informal personal contact is valuable. When asked the method most often employed for locating a reference, all include personal recommendation, although in different orders of importance. Social contact at conferences and meetings is also cited as valuable for information gathering.

2. Thanks in good part to the Internet, and low-cost communication by e-mail, today's "invisible college" is most likely to be through a network channel. Where heretofore one might chat on a phone, now one talks person to person over the Internet, or uses a Listserv or the ubiquitous Usenet discussion group. Meetings are arranged without benefit of conferences; and papers and findings are exchanged without print publication. In effect, the computer network may have made the "invisible college" all too visible in that privacy can be short-circuited and, where at one time it was a one-to-one conversation, now it can turn with intent or not into a one to a thousand discussion.

3. The third source of informal information may be the personal library of books, periodicals, newspaper clippings, or like material. These days an individual is likely to have numerous reference sources on CD-ROMs or downloaded on personal discs, as well as Net bookmarks.

4. Should the personal library fail, the user is then forced to turn to the formal library and perhaps even ask a reference librarian for assistance. The librarian is likely, through networks, to have access to data that may or may not be in either the personal or institutional library.

The common denominator of these various approaches is convenience and ease. Most people turn first to what they can find with the least amount of effort, with or without a computer. Many are willing to sacrifice an in-depth article available in a library for a quick, possibly shallow, answer from a friend, or an online or a digital database.

Parallel studies show that user expectations are highest for the formal library—although this may be the last place one goes—and lowest for the personal library, including the Net.

Selective Dissemination of Information (SDI)

Selected dissemination of information, or SDI, is a term commonly employed in the computer-assisted search, and is a way of saying that once a day, once a week, or once a month, the librarian searches the available new literature and prepares a bibliography of materials likely to be of interest to a particular person. For example, if X client is involved with hospital administration, the librarian would search databases likely to give the latest information on the topic. The computer printout is then sent to the client or it may be sent electronically to the user's computer or to an organizational computer to which the user has access. In this way the material is "selected" from the latest periodical indexes, that is, databases, and the "information" is "disseminated" to the user.

SDI is by now almost an automatic system in many libraries. Why? Because of electronic servants. Several examples:

UnCover Reveal (http://uncweb.carl.org/reveal) has a two-pronged attack on current awareness: (1) The user lists tables of contents of journals he/she wishes to view as they become available. (2) In addition, the reader submits subject interests. These are matched with new articles added to the database weekly. (Note: This is in addition to the requested table of contents.) Results are sent to the individual at his or her e-mail address. Be careful. Too many content pages, too many subject interests will flood the mails.

When an article of interest appears the reader may either go to the library for the piece, or order it directly from *UnCover.* Each article is priced: "service charge," usually from $8 to $15; and "copyright fee," around $3 to $12. The order is sent through e-mail and the article is faxed to the user, usually within 24 hours.

ArticleFirst/ContentsFirst are available through OCLC, (http://new firstsearch.oclc.org) and discussed in the first volume. Here one finds an article (either by subject, author, title, etc.) or by searching tables of contents, and then there is an opportunity to have it delivered through fax within 24 hours at a price range of $10 to $30; by rush mail, for example, overnight delivery at $19 to $35; by regular mail, $8 to $21; or by interlibrary loan, usually free to library users. The actual request takes no more than typing in the number, or method, or supplier. And, to be sure, details are available.

EBSCO Alert: (http://eadmin.epnet.com/ealert/home.asp). Individual profiles are established to search the table of contents of over 14,000 journals. Also, includes reports and papers from conference proceedings. System allows the user to tap into a maximum of 25 journals. Each week the service sends e-mail updates to the individual. Copies of all articles are available through the EBSCOdoc.

Information and Referral Services (I&R)

A term frequently seen in connection with reference service at the public library level is *information and referral,* or simply *I&R.* The term comes from the fact that the librarian begins by giving information, but if this is not enough, will refer the person to the proper agency or individual. The referral process may go as far as having the librarian make an appointment with an agency for the individual. There are other terms used to describe this service, such as *community information center.* Essentially, the purpose of this special reference service is to offer the users access to resources that will help them with health, rent, consumer, legal, and similar problems. Libraries can provide free information on such subjects.

In even the most traditional library, it is now common to (1) call individual experts, including anyone from a local professor to a leader in a local special-interest group, for assistance; (2) provide files, pamphlets, booklists, and so on, which give users information on topics ranging from occupations to local housing regulations; and (3) provide a place which active groups in the community may identify as an information clearinghouse for their needs.

The "reachout" aspect of I&R is its most important characteristic, and this has been implemented in a number of ways. The most common is the storefront reference center where someone may wander in from a shopping center or a main street in a downtown area to find a helpful reference librarian. I&R is an effort to overcome an inequality attendant on people who do not know that certain information exists and are therefore unaware of their rights. These rights can range from free school lunches to the minimum wage, and many people forego what is legally theirs out of pure ignorance.

Another basic problem which I&R tries to solve relates to an individual's inability to understand information in the form that it is presented. This not only includes the illiterate, but many others who are borderline literate, or who simply have a difficult time deciphering legal or social jargon. I&R tries to offer information in various formats that can be understood by the user who has a reading problem.

I&R services are as varied in scope and purpose as the imagination of librarians and the needs of users. A major stumbling block is budget. No matter how willing the librarian or how great the need, without funding, the program is likely to go nowhere. Another requirement is staff involvement: Librarians must be convinced that the course of action is worthwhile and practical.

TELEPHONE SERVICE

The telephone can be the bane of a reference librarian's existence. Deciding how to handle the constant ringing while responding to patrons in line at the desk can be complicated. Libraries have routinely turned to the business world to find solutions to customer service problems and this may be another case.[4]

Unequal reference service is often given when someone telephones with a query and the librarian drops everything to respond. Understandably, the people waiting at the desk may be less than pleased. There are three ways of overcoming this problem:

1. Install a telephone answering service, which can be done at minimum cost, to be used when the librarian is busy. The message: "What

[4]"Reference Call Centers?" *Library Currents,* June, 1999, p. 1 (Quoting from Steve Coffman, "Reference as Others Do It," *American Libraries,* no. 5, 1999, p. 54).

is your question(s)?" and "I will get back to you as soon as possible." In this way, the person on the phone feels satisfied and the individual in front of the desk is not overlooked.

2. If the library is large enough, there is a specialized telephone reference service that allows librarians to screen calls. Here the usual process is to identify the question, which usually is no more than a ready-reference problem ("What is the address of X or Y"; "Where can I find information on colleges"; "What is the height of the tallest building in the world?"). If specialized assistance is needed or if the answer requires materials beyond those in ready reference, the call is transferred to the regular reference librarian.

3. A third approach is to make a reference e-mail address available to the public for reference questions. This works well, but only, of course, if the answers are prompt. Then, too, one to one "immediate" calls may be made via the computer to the library. Still, the problems remain much the same whether traditional telephone or computer.

Most libraries provide telephone reference service and use many types of reference works, including print and digital telephone books. Larger libraries have separate sections for phone reference, usually out of view of the public. The smaller- and medium-size libraries perform the service from the main desk.

The telephone aspects of reference follow specific procedures. For example, libraries differ in such matters as answering requests by patrons concerning whether the library has a needed book or periodical. Some will look to see if the library owns the item; others will ask the user to come in and check. Should one answer legal or medical questions over the phone? Should the librarian give out city directory information over the phone? These and countless other policy issues must be established if effective service is to be given.

In many libraries a special group of reference works is set aside for telephone service. These vary from place to place, yet inevitably include local directories and telephone books, as well as national works such as *Facts on File* and *Books in Print*. Normally, too, a great deal of emphasis is placed on how-to-do-it types of manuals and handbooks from music and sports to first aid and gardening. The reference sources that are used most often tend to be dictionaries, various almanacs, and local guidebooks.

While the telephone service requires the same basic steps needed when dealing face to face with people at a reference desk, some particular skills are necessary. One must be able to ascertain the nature of the question quickly and be sure it is clearly understood. Interviewing procedures tend to be somewhat less personal than at the desk and yet are even more necessary to master. One must know when to terminate a query, when to call back, and when the question should be referred to another section. As more than one reference librarian has observed, telephone reference service can be a unique type of work that requires specific skills—and certainly much experience.

A model of its kind, the New York Public Library's telephone reference service draws upon 1,500 reference works to answer some 1,000 calls a day. Staffers can answer most questions without leaving the desk, but when an answer is not readily available they transfer the call to various subject areas within the library. The limitations to the service are those followed by many other libraries: Questions one must be able to answer involve contests, crossword puzzles, or school homework.

E-mail

Augmenting, some say possibly replacing telephone services, e-mail has become increasingly important in larger libraries. Here the user is encouraged to put questions to the librarian through the computer. Often this service is part of the library home page or an intregal section in the services of the so-called "virtual" library discussed in another chapter. At any rate, it has proven successful for students particularly. It is less of a charmer with older people and adults who either do not have a computer, or prefer the speed and the personal touch of the telephone.

What will be the future of e-mail, or some such derivative in libraries? No one knows, of course. Actually, where it is in place it has tended to increase the use of the telephone. Users who learn about and use one service are inclined to use similar services.

One possibility is 24-hour digital reference services which will draw upon libraries from the world around, e.g., if it is 3 a.m. in America a librarian on day duty in Australia will be able to field the early morning query. And there are numerous other technological solutions to 24-hour service such as "instant" e-mail. Internet based video is another possibility.

Beyond that, consider the telephone which still is almost ideal for serving remote users, at any time of day or night.

INFORMATION BROKER[5]

The information broker is a private individual or organization that sells the type of reference information that is free from libraries. There are two basic types of private information services.

1. The information broker, or search service, tends to deal with specific questions and problems. The paid response includes citations and documents that will aid the user in the solution of the problem. The documents are screened, and only those thought to be of benefit are presented.

---

[5]The best current guide on the subject: Sue Rugge and Alfred Glossbrenner, *The Information Broker's Handbook.* 3rd ed. New York: McGraw-Hill, 1997.

2. The consultant, who may have one or more information brokers in his or her employ, goes a step further and not only validates, but also evaluates, the information. Recommendations for action are made based upon the documents.

The specialists do many things, but essentially they act as consultants, advising the paying client about the course to take based on the best sources of information. This usually means that the broker takes the question and does extensive research that provides a list of citations or the actual information required. The search will be manual or online, or a combination of both. For example, a client may want to know the advisability of opening or expanding a business that sells X products. The information broker will identify information sources that will help identify trends in the area of X products, show strategic planning for development, and even provide market forecasts. This may be done by providing citations, that is, a bibliography, but more likely it will be a written report.

Today there are information brokers across almost all the United States and the Canadian provinces. The actual number of for-profit information organizations is somewhere between 1,500 and 2,000, of which the majority are one- or two-person operations. Only a few, probably no more than two dozen, employ more than three or four professional people. Each maintains its own unique fee structure, although billing tends to be based upon (1) the time spent on the question or project by the organization, (2) direct costs from photocopying to online searches, and (3) miscellaneous costs, from typing and phone calls to travel. The broker may itemize the bill, or simply charge a flat fee normally set before the project begins.

The information broker came into existence for many reasons, but the primary one was the failure of the library to meet the information needs of some parts of the public. Perhaps "failure" is not the right word, because librarians consciously do not provide certain types of services either because of lack of funds and personnel, or simply because of tradition. It tends to be more the former than the latter.

Of particular interest to librarians is the opportunity to turn to an alternative career as an information broker. This can be done, and is done most often by starting up one's own operation, or, for experience, joining a larger firm.

One response to the competition or threat of the information industry impinging on traditional reference services is for the library to develop its own private fee-based information model. Here the librarians perform many of the duties of the information broker, but with an essential break with the past—there is a charge. This does not simply mean charging for an online search, but sometimes using the fee structure for detailed studies and reports.

One may argue that this competes with what should be a private type of operation, and discriminates against the user who cannot pay for such in-depth services. Conversely, if the library does not offer such services there is a good chance that support from the business community will dwindle. There are now some 250 to 300 libraries in the United States and Canada that offer fee-based services. This includes everything from rapid document delivery to translation services and, of course, individual research and reference assistance. University and college libraries make up the greatest number of such services.

What's This?

Digging out accurate data is the primary role of the information broker. Working out of an office, often in the home, the broker finds most of what is needed through print and online databases as well as websites.

There are other approaches. Take the example of James J. Rapp and Touchtone Information of Denver. The company sells "information that ended up in the hands of everyone from the tabloid press to a reputed member of the Israeli Mafia."[6] The material was gathered "through a subterfuge known in their business as a pretext: calling banks, phone companies and other businesses and claiming to be the customer whose records were sought."[7] The legal question is whether practices which on their face are deceptive also are illegal.

"Mr. Rapp...maintained that there was nothing inherently wrong with using deception to get confidential information.[8] The law does not agree. Mr. Rapp was indicted by a grand jury in the case that is the first known criminal prosecution against the growing business of peddling confidential information.

No matter how the case works out, *The New York Times* labeled Mr. Rapp and his company as "information brokers."[9] The process of gathering information is one which information brokers might go out of their way to avoid. Besides, a good deal of what Mr. Rapp found through calls, might be had almost as easily via the Internet.

SUGGESTED READING

Harmon, Amy, "Copyright and Copying Wrong's: A Web Rebalancing Act," *The New York Times*, September 10, 2000, p. WK4. A discussion of MP3.com's online music service and the copyright laws. The author points out the "current system is seen as an obstacle by Internet music entrepreneurs." The

---

[6]"Law Confronts Seller of Private Data," *The New York Times*, July 1, 1999, p. 1.
[7]*Ibid.*
[8]*Ibid,* p. 15.
[9]*Ibid.*

conclusion is that something will have to give on the Internet, and it eventually will be current copyright laws.

Leibovich, Lori, "Choosing Quick Hits Over the Card Catalog," *The New York Times,* August 10, 2000, pp. G1, G6, G7. Teenage students and even younger ones now find that using the Web is much easier than using a library. They may take much longer to find what is needed—if they find it at all—but prefer the at-home atmosphere to the library. The result is a generation of students with little sympathy with standard research methods and even less appreciation of equally standard reference works. Note: much of this section of *The Times* is devoted to student use of the computer for looking up answers, e.g., see a useful guide to "smart searching" for students who can't bother with Boolean logic.

Rowley, Jennifer, "Current Awareness in an Electronic Age," *Online & CD-ROM Review,* August, 1998, pp. 277–279. How has current technology, including the Internet, changed the role and nature of current awareness services? The author answers this question with two examples of what she terms "state-of-the-art" of current awareness services.

Talab, R. S. *Commonsense Copyright.* 2nd ed. Jefferson, NC: McFarland, 1999. One of the best books available for an easy-to-understand, up-to-date review of copyright and how it influences library circulation. See, too: Sinofsky, Esther, "Copyright," *Booklist,* June 1 & 15, 1999, pp. 1880–1881. An annotated list of copyright references available free of cost on the Web. The compiler, an expert on the subject, offers alternatives to expensive reference works. Here evaluative-descriptive annotations suggest precisely how and when the sites should be employed. An excellent source for reference librarians.

Taylor, Arlene, *The Organization of Information.* Englewood, CO: Libraries Unlimited, 1999. Here is a clear introduction to how to organize and, yes, create information in the library. The author offers a sound historical background for basic sources, as well as current data on catalogs, indexes, etc. A considerable amount is found on the finer points of classification.

Tennant, Roy, "Copyright and Intellectual Property Rights," *Library Journal,* August, 1999, pp. 34–35. A brief, informative overview of the problems of copyright and electronic databases. The legal situation is summarized as are various problems faced by libraries. See, too, the valuable "link list" which guides the user to a dozen websites which deal with the topic.

Tour, Debra, "Quest Line (Telephone Reference)," *Public Libraries,* July/August, 1998, pp. 256–258. A discussion of how a Florida Library System provides reference services on the telephone without slighting people who come into the library. QuestLine "operates with a relatively sophisticated database that tracks questions, tallies statistics, and is used for quality control."

PART II
THE INTERNET AND
REFERENCE SERVICES

CHAPTER THREE
THE INTERNET

Internet information channels are fundamental to a library. Yet, this is only one aspect of an international revolution. The new globalization, the "economic interdependence facilitated by electronic technology and financed by the electronic herd of investors and traders has replaced older systems of international relationships grounded in the constraints and ideologies of the cold war. Economic technology...has trumped military technology."[1] Beyond that, the combination of the personal computer and the Internet has democratized not only technology but also finance and investment.

Connecting the traditional military-industrial-academic complex, the Internet developed and grew in the 1990s because it was based on the convergence of technology (computers and phone lines) and social need (i.e., you pass on or answer my message and I will pass on or answer your message). What began as Pentagon technology developed into connectors for government administration, then turned to linking business and industry for conferencing, and to networking production-line schedules. Along the way the academic community joined to pass on and download research data as well as open each other's catalogs and archives. Not far behind, the information business joined the link with everything from reference works and newspapers to indexes. Paralleling this were millions

---

[1]Benjamin M. Friedman, "The Power of the Electronic Herd," *The New York Review of Books,* July 15, 1999, p. 41. Friedman is reviewing Thomas L. Friedman's *The Lexus and the Olive Tree* (New York: Farrar, Straus and Giroux, 1999). The controversial book offers a wide view of the practical results of technology and the Internet on the world, not just on the United States and the consumer.

of individuals and interest groups that widened the Net into an every person's communication system.

Behind the backs of officials and planners, and with only accidental aid from the government and corporations, the Internet has become the universal and common information highway spanning the world. True, it lacks a board of directors, it seems to lack any planning or programmers, but on the wild frontier the diligent searcher may find almost any bit of information needed.

Because of its accidental growth, the Internet was the only large-scale communication system that sold itself rather than selling an audience. The Internet has become so popular that people flock to it without being urged.

The daughter of the Internet is the Worldwide Web, or simply Web. Initially it was for scientific research and was put together by the European Particle Physics Laboratory. Unlike the Net, it provided images, icons, drawings, etc. rather than simply words. The addition of "hypertext" with lateral links for browsing, turned it into an international telephone-television line available to everyone with the hardware and software. Today it serves the needs of everyone. The Web long ago left the home of the physics lab.

The electronic revolution has and will continue to change the face of the globe. Beyond the library, although information is a major reason for the Net's success, are further implications: (1) Limitations on natural resources no longer need constrain a country's prosperity. The new technologies make it possible to move resources and labor from one point to another in a matter of seconds. Given the right technology and prosperity is now a matter of choice rather than of what is in the ground or manufactured. (2) The growing number of people on the Net, or as some say, "the electronic herd" will be the energy source of the century.

Optimistic? Probably. There will be setbacks,[2] some major, but in the decades ahead the world will have changed considerably, and probably for the better, because of improved methods of communication and new forms of technology.

NET STATISTICS

No one knows just how many people are using the Internet or how much information is available.

That is a given which is not likely to change.

[2]The United Nations' Human Development Report for 1999 studies the advantages and disadvantages of globalization. Among the latter it reports the Internet has helped to build the organized world crime syndicates to a point where their gross $1,500 billion a year, more than England's 1,200 billion total budget. Advances in telecommunications and the opening up of borders via the Net "creates new and exciting opportunities, and among the most enterprising and imaginative opportunities are the world's criminals." *Guardian Weekly,* July 8–14, 1999, p. 2.

On the other hand, not a week goes by that some commercial or nonprofit organization does not do a scientific sampling to at least indicate the approximate amount of information and the amount of Net use. As of mid-2000 there is at least a rough consensus about what's out there. One rough rule of thumb: double the numbers each one to five years.

1. There are about one billion plus Web pages. Some reports set the number at one-half to three-quarters that number, but most agree Web pages double about every six months to one year. By 2004, estimates are that there will be over 13 billion pages, of which only a small fraction (about 16 to 20%) are likely to be available via a search engine.[3]

   There are some 10 million worldwide registered domains. (Of these over one half are commercial. Only about six thousand are educational).[4] There are approximately 4 to 5 million Web sites, both public and private. Thanks to lack of use, of these close to 800,000 are unreachable.

2. Just as in a million plus volume library only a small percentage of books are used or read, websites show the same pattern. Some 6,000 websites receive 75 percent of all Web traffic. The top five percent of adult sites receive 42 percent of total visitors. When limited to educational sites, only five percent receive 60 percent of visitors. Once a site catches on, its popularity tends to increase rapidly. Others fall further and further behind.[5]

3. Who is on the Net, and where do they live? First, "among the hype for everything online it is easy to forget that 80% of the population of the world has never even used a telephone, let alone sent an e-mail message."[6] North America and Europe have almost a monopoly on Net use.[7]

4. If a decade ago there were only about 100,000 computers connected to the Net, more than 300 million people are expected to be using the Net by 2001—and almost exclusively in developed nations. Approximately 50 percent of the American population are familiar with Net service, although not all are

[3]Greg Notess, "The Never Ending Quest: Search Engine Relevance," *Online,* May/June 2000, p. 38. See, too: "Searching for the Essence of the World Wide Web," *The New York Times,* April 11, 1999, p. wk1.

[4]*Wired,* October 1999, p. 108.

[5]Findings based on statistical analysis on Internet traffic by both Xerox and IBM. *The New York Times,* June 21, 1999, p. C4.

[6]"Cyber Utopia?" *Guardian Weekly,* July 15–22, 1999, p. 14.

[7]Net users per 1,000 people are highest in Iceland and Finland with the U.S. coming in fifth. *Yahoo!,* September, 1999, p. 119.

connected. Net users constitute about one-quarter of the American population. Net use in educational, business and government institutions is almost 90 percent, if not higher.

5. It is hardly a surprise, but minorities are under represented on the Net. The disparity is apparent in college where 73 percent of white students have access to a home computer, compared with only 32 percent of black students.[8]

6. The primary online activities underline the commercial present and future of the Web. Some 65 percent of the users are after "business/work information," while another 87 percent "get information about a hobby or personal interest." Reading news occupies 74 percent.

The statistics support the general opinion that the growth of the Internet may worsen the nation's existing social and economic gaps. While it is no surprise that Americans with lower incomes are less likely to own a computer, studies highlight what are the racial disparities in who has access to digital technology.

Beyond Information

So much for the information aspects. The majority of users are involved in other matters: 92 percent browse the Web, much as couch potatoes skim television; 88 percent send e-mail; 81 percent shop; 63 percent get travel data; 60 percent download pictures; 58 percent look up events from movies to concerts, and the same percentage check out the weather.[9]

With a limited number of hours in the day something has to give when 50 million people are avid Net users. "The activity taking the biggest hit is television and VCR watching...Nearly 65 percent of 500 Net users surveyed said they had sacrificed television time for Net time. Forty-eight percent said they spent less time reading, and 29 percent said they slept less."[10] One way of both watching television and cruising the Net is to have the tube used as a computer screen as well.

At home and at work the average American spends close to an hour each day on the Net. With a drive to gain more advertising, firms such

[8]"Big Racial Disparity Persists in Internet Use," *The New York Times,* July 9, 1999, p. A12.

[9]*Yahoo!,* September, 1998, p. 77. Subsequent figures (see *Yahoo!,* September, 1999, 2000) support the initial study.

[10]"Survey finds TV is a major casualty of Net surfing," *The New York Times,* July 16, 1998, p. G3. The results validate a trend reported in similar polls. The only thing, though, that is certain is that while it took 40 years for radio to gain 50 million domestic listeners it took only 4 years for the Worldwide Web to reach the same number. Granted the population is larger, but it is an impressive figure.

as America Online are developing new services to lure users to stay online as long as three hours a day. "Sad, lonely world discovered in Cyberspace," headlines a report on a lengthy Carnegie Mellon University study, the first of its kind. The result: "people who spend even a few hours a week online experience higher levels of depression and loneliness than if they used the computer network less frequently…These were normal adults and their families…The interactive media may be no more healthy than older mass media."[11]

One out of every nine Internet users in America qualify as "addicts," at least according to sporadic studies. The disturbance, which makes headlines on feature pages of newspapers and magazines every year or so, was discovered in 1994 by a psychology professor. He and others define the addiction as "staying online for 38 hours a week or more in leisure time. Symptoms include lying to family or colleagues about the amount of time spent on the Internet; restlessness, irritability and anxiety when not engaged in computer activities; a neglect of social obligations; and a consistent failure to quit."[12] Incidentally, more information will be found at the *Internet Addiction Service* (www.computeraddiction.com).

The United States dominates the information industry.[13] Figures make the case: (1) About 90 percent of the world's websites originate in America and from 80 to 90 percent are in English no matter where they originate. (2) Some 40 percent of the world's computer industry are American. (3) About 30 million new jobs have been created in America by information industries.

France is typical of Internet progress outside of the United States. A leader in the use of the low-tech Minitel system, a videotext entertainment-information source, it is much behind the United States on the Net. Only 16 percent of French families own computers. Some 3 percent of the French are on the Net. Comparatively, England, Germany and the Scandinavian countries have about 8 to 10 percent of the population on the Net.

This side of the economic factors such as the cost of computers and getting onto the Net, one French official put it plainly. The Net with over 80 percent of its text in English is another way of colonizing Europe. The U.S. has taken over fast food places and movies across Europe, and the Net is another example of American colonialism.

---

[11] *The New York Times*, August 30, 1998, pp. 1, 22.

[12] *The Times Union* (Albany, NY), March 16, 1998, p. 1. The newspaper is quoting an article of the previous month, which appeared in *Psychology Today*.

[13] This is not to discount contributions by other countries, if on a smaller scale. For example, in "little old Holland" there are card operated computers that deliver the Web and e-mail. The kiosks with the computer are found on street corners along with telephones. Some express extreme pessimism about the practicality of open air unsupervised keyboards. Meanwhile the Dutch are the first in Europe to have such a service. *Guardian Weekly*, May 3, 1998, p. 21.

Porno and Hate

The blunt truth is that many laypeople are primarily interested in the Net for sex and commerce. According to one survey, "six of the top 10 search words...typed into computers...are about matters lewd and lascivious."[14] The complete ten: (1) sex; (2) chat; (3) XXX; (4) Playboy; (5) Netscape software; (6) nude; (7) porno; (8) games; (9) weather; (10) Penthouse. A dozen of other sex based words clog up the top 200.

Fear of pornography, particularly for young people, results in massive concern, genuine and otherwise, to "protect" the young from some Net content. Close supervision or censorship—call it what you will—extends as well to violence and questionable political, religious, etc. materials. The catch, of course, is the meaning of "questionable" and the ability to "protect" in an electronic age.

One answer is parent supervision where those closest to the child may define and check, if they wish, every descriptor from "porno" to "questionable." Be that as it may, from Congress to talk show hosts there is an ongoing cry to take public action. This usually means to shift the responsibility from family and parent to the public sector, i.e the library.[15]

Foes of hate sites have another case—made apparent in the aftermath of various shooting rampages, arson, and beatings by racists and similar groups.

An argument can be made to protect children, e.g., "The scariest thing about many of these sites are the links. You can start with a traditional racist group and wind up at specialized sites for children who are 8 or 9 years old, very creative sites."[16]

The reference librarian must be aware of the hate sites and the natural questions about censorship they bring up.

The American Library Association, as related groups, takes a strong, well considered stand against any type of library censorship, on or off line. This includes the use of Internet filters in the library—a position not all librarians or (of equal importance) the public, school, or academic chiefs of library budgets agree about.

[14]*Guardian Weekly*, November 2, 1997, p. 8. This is a report on a survey found in the American Web magazine for the previous month.

[15]Once or more a month, a national newspaper or a library periodical has stories about censorship and the library—particularly calling for filters for the Internet. Laura Schlessinger, for example, is a radio talk show host far, far to the right. As a radical conservative she fights for online filters in libraries. She is representative of groups who do battle to keep the Net policed. The fascinating problem: are people like Ms. Schlessinger going to be the cops? See, "ALA Under Attack from Dr. Laura," *Library Journal,* June 1, 1999, pp. 20–21. For another point of view and ways of "keeping it out of your house" see: "What Sex Sites Can Teach Everyone Else," *The New York Times*, September 22, 1999, p. 46.

[16]"Net Monitor," *Yahoo! Internet Life*, August, 1999, p. 102.

The tug-of-war between intellectual freedom and downright censorship on the Net will go on for many years to come. Every librarian, every reader of this text has to take a stand on the issue or be killed in the crossfire. If not obvious, the position of this author is no institutional censorship of any kind. Period. Accept or reject, but there is no way of being neutral.

Beyond Reference: Commerce On The Net[17]

By definition and scope, this text is limited to reference services, digital and print. The Net is a major information element. Too often, though, the librarian may lack perspective on the much broader effect of the Internet. The long term effect on commerce, on companies yet has to be understood or realized.[18] At the same time there is a very real question: will the Net create and at the same time destroy the system built up from the mid-19th century to the present which is based on large corporations manufacturing goods? It is a question of concern to all, and has numerous dimensions. Here, though, consider only one, and the one that eventually will have more influence on American, on world attitudes than the glories of finding information rapidly and efficiently.

Shopping, for lack of a better descriptor, is the heart of the commercial-online revolution. Virtual stores may be the most significant element of the online age. Consumers in the United States are expected to spend more than $36 billion on Internet shopping in 1999, up from $15 billion in 1998. Expectations and the amount will more than double each year to an estimated $6 trillion in 2005.[19] Some forecasters see 20 percent or more sales of all kinds will be online in less than a decade. On the other hand, less optimistic types claim goods bought electronically will amount to only 5 percent of U.S. retail sales or 2.5 percent of total retail spending within five years. The real growth rate, at least eventually, will depend on profit which by mid 2000 did not seem to worry e-commerce investors.

[17]An estimated 17 to 20 percent of Internet users purchase products online.

[18]A downside of free newspapers online, along with ready access to their classified advertisements, real estate, and employment, is that it has driven numerous newspaper dealers out of business. People who once scanned out-of-town or foreign papers they had to purchase at a kiosk, now turn to the Web. The single example highlights what many economists see as a massive trend away from standard sources of supply—from newspapers to recordings and yachtes—to the Net. This in turn indicates major shifts in business and manufacturing. "…Vendor of Distant News, Closes Store," *The New York Times*, July 31, 1999, p. B3.

[19]"Study predicts huge growth in business to business web sector." *The New York Times*, June 27, 2000, p. C6. Actually the largest volume of "shopping" is not retail, but business to business. Suppliers of large companies increasingly use the Net to increase the efficiently of inventories, delivery speed, etc. Some suspect the consumer side of shopping, except in certain areas such as books, will diminish while the business to business size will grow tremendously.

As a mass medium to end all mass medium, the Internet Worldwide Web threatens to turn the United States and the world into a gigantic, multi-faceted commercial for every product from accordions to zinc oxide ointment. By 2000, for example: (1) eBay (www.ebay.com) was only one of dozens of sources where the user can purchase at auction everything from cigars to watches and gourmet foods.[20] (2) Day traders can now get in and out of the stock market in minutes or years, but they are free to trade on the Net without brokers, e.g., see *Trading Places* (www.trading-places.net). About seven million individuals or households trade on the Net and over 20 million tap into the Internet for investment advice (i.e., as of 2000). The numbers increase each year. (3) Romance is available at *Romance Classics* (www.romanceclassics.com) where one can find books, films, video clips, etc.

EVALUATING WEBSITES

Online: Gale Directory of Online, Portable and Internet Databases, Farmington Hills, MI: Gale Group, 1998 to date, semi-annual, www.gale.com. Also, DIALOG file 230. Rate varies.
*Print: Cyberhound's Guide to Internet Databases.*1995 to date, annual. $110.

There are several reliable guides to both old and new Internet sites. The best place to turn for a quick overview of what is available for a given subject or area of interest is the print *Cyberhound's Guide to Internet Databases.* For an ongoing appraisal of new or relatively new databases, nothing quite measures up to resources found on the Web itself.

The online version includes not only the print *Cyberhound's Guide* but two other related databases: *Gale Directory of Databases,* vols. 1 & 2. For many this is overkill (there are over 23,000 records online). It often is easier to use the better focused print work.

Reviews of about 6,000 sites are found in the print edition. The description generally is no more than a few sentences, if that, and the ratings (with stars, scale of one to four, etc.) tend to like almost everything equally, i.e., three to four stars.   There are several indexes, including an index to the whole book as well as a subject index. Information for each entry is more complete than found in any other guide, e.g., there is the usual rating (almost all get top grade, so this is of limited value); the address; a description of the database; search routines and full information on the sponsor. Despite faults this is the first place to turn for accurate, current and *full* data.

[20]George Pappas, "Going, Going...Gouged!," *Yahoo!,* June, 1999, p. 80. Reliable auction sites do monitor for fraud, but there are more than 1.8 million auctions a day across the Web. Fraud is a problem—as it can be with all shopping on the Web.

The Good Web Guide to.... London: GoodWebGuide, 2000, 160 pp. $15. (www.thegoodwebguide.co.uk) offers what the editor claims to be the best 100 Web sites for a given topic. As of mid-2000 the topics: "to gardening"; "to money"; "to food"; "to parents." While published in England, most of the sites are applicable for North America and, for that matter, other Western countries. Editors are experts in their fields, e.g., David Emery who edited the guide to money sites offers insights into strengths and weaknesses of each.

Note the *Cyberhound* and the other large systems not only include information on Web sites, but give evaluations of related information sources, e.g., gophers, newsgroups (usenet), listservs, libraries, etc.

Journal Reviews

The major library oriented journals and magazines feature good to excellent reviews of Web sites as well as individual online indexes, abstracting services and other reference works. (See previous chapters for comments about reviews in the major library journals from *Choice* to *Library Journal*). Almost all library-oriented journals have some reviews, e.g., *College and Research Libraries News, Online, Database*, etc. For a complete list see the latest edition of *Magazines for Libraries.*

Popular reviews are found in Web magazines, the best being in *Yahoo!*. There are articles in which reviews are embedded, as well as subject by subject analysis of sites. Most emphasis is on entertainment. The information reviews vary wildly in quality. Too often they are more concerned with the technology than with the content. Still, they are required reading for any reference librarian.

Another current guide is in the Thursday edition of *The New York Times*. Here a weekly section, "Circuits," examines the latest sites as well as information on developments in electronic databases from entertainment to sophisticated science. Note: This section, plus ongoing technology news is combined in a daily free Net feature. This is *CyberTimes* (http://nytsyn.com/syndicate/fs/features/cybertimes) an excellent source of current information.

Site reviews are found in various print guides. One example: Shirley Kennedy's *Best Bet Internet* (Chicago: American Library Association, 1998). A columnist for *Information Today*, she incorporates her experience of the field in her guide as she points out the best places to find information. Similar guides, although possibly not quite so good, appear almost every month.[21]

---

[21]See S. Gandhi's "Internet Directories: A Subject Guide to Monographs," *Choice*, April, 1999, pp. 1,409+ for a subject by subject listing of guides to the Net for everyone from an accountant to the sports fan.

Site Reviews on the Web

With the number of single Internet pages estimated to be over one billion, the need for even the broadest discrimination is evident. This is done in two or three ways. First, the guides listed here briefly describe the best, the most generally used site. Second, new sites are reviewed regularly in the standard review sources considered elsewhere in this text. Third, there are scores of online sites, which concentrate on new sites. Some of these are evaluative, although the majority simply list the sites by subject, e.g., in one study a total of "24,075 sites were categorized into the 20 subject areas. There are so many possibilities that one expert points out: "The use of popular Web-based *What's New* sites for locating appropriate new Internet resources for an academic library home page is problematic...Services can add 1,000 or more new sites each day."[22]

Evaluation of Net sites is by now a cottage industry threatening to become a major source of even more information about more information, about more information, etc. The problem is not to find evaluative sources, but to find the best ones in order to avoid spending more time reading about information than finding it on the Web.

Beyond the giant rating systems, are smaller, although for many purposes much better guides. They tend to focus almost entirely on the *best* information sites and, as such, should be consulted first. Also, they are frequently updated.

Maylaine Block (http://marylaine.com). A librarian and expert on Net sites, Ms. Block is a reliable guide to old and new websites as well as guides and related material. She regularly updates her "Neat new stuff I found this week and bookbytes." This is of particular value to reference librarians. An unusual site, this has the advantage of being put together by a person with a first-class mind and an understanding of library needs. Highly recommended for one and for all.[23]

The Scout Report (http://scout.cs.wisc.edu/report/sr/current) begun in 1994, this is a superior evaluation site sponsored by the University of Wisconsin with the help of the National Science Foundation. Sites are carefully screened for accuracy and use in education (K–12 and through graduate university work). Search is by Library of Congress subject headings or keywords. There are descriptive annotations for each recommended site. Information is under three broad headings: research and education, general interest, and network tools. About 20 sites are described each week.

---

[22]Laura Cohen, "What's New on the Internet..." *Reference Services Review,* Spring 1998, p. 12. This is a superior article in that the author points out the results of a study of new site sources as well as lists preferable Web-based sources of new Internet sites.

[23]For an interview with Ms. Block see: "Marylaine Block: A Librarian with All but Walls," *Searcher,* June 2000, pp. 65–69.

Librarians' Index to the Internet (www.lii.org) is the work of librarians at the University of California. The sites are under 45 to 50 subject headings with numerous subheadings and links. All are annotated and represent the work of not only the compilers, but librarians throughout the United States and Canada. Focus is on much used and/or new sites.

The *Argus Clearinghouse,* University of Michigan Library (www.clearninghouse.net). An uneven, although excellent guide to what is best on the Internet in terms of information. Various people, including students, compile the subject guides, which range from how to find information on education to current political problems and debates. There is a rating system for the sites, which is a bit uneven but at least indicates relative importance in the eyes of the compiler. There are between 450 to 600 guides available, all of which can be located by entering keywords. For example, "women's issues, law, public policy," will turn up "Internet Resources for Women's Legal and Public Policy Information." Also there are broad subject areas to search from arts and entertainment to science. In explaining the site the sponsor notes it is meant to identify and "describe and evaluate Internet-based information resources. Our mission is to facilitate intellectual access to...the Internet."

OCLC, which charges for the service, has what it calls "Net First" online (www.oclc.org/oclc/menu/home1). This is a descriptive, and sometimes evaluative view of close to 60,000 worldwide websites. (It includes, too: Usenet newsgroups and listservs). The database, according to OCLC, increases at about 2,000 records a month. The positive side of this is that the majority of sites have something to do, directly or indirectly, with education. There are a few "fun and games" listed.

A general site that covers everything from online stocks to "sex on the Web," puts the rhetorical query: "If technology is advancing at an amazing speed, why are you still learning about it the same old way?" *C/Net* (www.cnet.com) not only is a major source for investing, but includes reviews of sites as well as products. A quick look often will update current news about the Net's technology.

For ongoing information about new Net sites, see "What's New" on the State University of New York at Albany's Library homepage. Masterminded by Laura Cohen, this offers assessments of sites, which will be of assistance to working reference librarians and researchers. The address: (www.albany.edu/library).

There are numerous listings of various website sources, but one of the best, which includes related tips from file transfer protocol to wide area information servers, is: The Library of Congress, *Internet Search Tools* (http://lcweb.loc.gov/global/search).

SUGGESTED READING

Anghelescu, Hermina and Donald Davis, "Books and Libraries in the New Millennium: A Review Essay," *Choice*, September, 1999, pp. 87–97. Summarizing the conclusions of 57 authors from three basic collections, the compilers of this review essay conclude, "many traditional roles of the book seem secure." They agree there will be a place for print, libraries and librarians for a considerable number of years to come.

Berners-Lee, Tim, *Weaving the Web*. San Francisco: Harper, 1999. The 44-year-old English physicist who created the Worldwide Web explains how it came about and how it complements the Internet. Berners-Lee began the Web as a set of protocols for transferring, linking and addressing documents to send over the Net. This gave the Net the global reach it has today.

Cohen, Laura, "Librarians on the Internet," *Choice* (Annual. August Supplement 1998 to date). An excellent overview article, which leads off a special issue of *Choice* magazine on basic Net sites, this discusses search engines in the kind of detail needed by librarians. The author is an expert who writes clearly and touches all major points.

Cooke, Alison, *Neal-Schuman Authoritative Guide to Evaluating Information on the Internet*. New York: Neal-Schuman, 1999. Checklists for evaluating information on the Net are given as well as a text filled with practical ideas on how to judge what is or is not of value. There is a brief introduction to how to find information online. Note, too, the numerous lists of references at the close of each chapter or section.

Goldman, Alvin, *Knowledge in a Social World*. Oxford: Clarendon Press, 1999. One, of by now numerous works on the philosophy of information, this has the benefit of being relatively current and equally easy to understand. The author considers the Internet as well as the broader aspects of the information revolution in terms of how it works for and against the human condition.

Gordon-Murname, Laura, "Evaluating Net Evaluators," *Searcher*, February, 1999, pp. 57–59, 60. A short discussion about how websites are evaluated followed by a descriptive-critical evaluation of those evaluators from the Scout Report to Argus Clearinghouse.

Harris, Lesley, "Improving Information Services and Beyond," *Information Outlook*, March 2000, pp. 24–30. The author shows how to "go about incorporating e-commerce in your special library." Much of the article will be of equal interest to academic and public libraries who feature business reference services.

"Internet Books: New and Forthcoming," *Choice*. Supplement (August) 1999 to date. Highlights new and forthcoming books about the Internet in four categories: reference guides, technical guides, Internet & Society, and Internet and business. Basic bibliographic information, but not annotated. About 100 to 150 titles in each annual issue.

Kautzman, Amy, "Digital Impact: Reality, the Web and the Changed Business of Reference," *Searcher*, April, 1999, pp. 18+. The Harvard Lamont Library head of reference explains how the new technologies fit in (and don't fit in) to modern reference services. Much of the problem is the gap between technology aware students and older adults (particularly teachers). More important, the article shows the day to day activities of the new digital library.

"Librarian of Congress," *Yahoo! Internet Life,* September, 2000, pp. 74–80. This is a conversation-interview with James Billington about the Net and the future of the book. Of particular value because Billington points out why librarians are needed: "The fact that we call it the information age and not the knowledge age proves how much we need librarians...Information has to be turned into knowledge...And that's the role of the librarian."

Mayo, Diane and Sandra Nelson, *Wired for the Future: Developing Your Library Technology Plan.* Chicago: American Library Association, 1999. Yes, this starts with a planning committee and ends, one hopes, with a sensible plan for public librarians (and for other librarians, as well) on how to establish a working electronic library. More a management tool than a daily report from the reference front, the guide has good advice on how to keep everything going with the staff in accord.

"Net Commerce," *The Economist,* February 26, 2000, various pages. An overview of net commerce and what is or is not important in terms of profit. The future of online commerce is examined, but with a word of caution. It may or may not attract enough people to make it worthwhile.

Schuyler, Michael, "Porn Alley: Now at your local public library," *Computers in Libraries,* November/December, 1999, pp. 32–35. A Kitsap County librarian (Bremerton, Washington), explains why librarians "are out here in limbo trying to figure out the best approach, all the while being assaulted by well-meaning souls who would protect us from porn...."

Sheehan, Mark, "Faster Broadband Access to the Internet," *Online,* July/August, 1999, pp. 19+. While there are countless articles on how to speed up Net access this differs in that it addresses the practical—economic aspects of speed. See, too, on p. 20 a list of "promises" for speed and what has resulted in actual connections of sometimes highly expensive systems.

Stoker, David and Alison Cooke, "Evaluation of Networked Information Sources," *Omni* (http://omni.ac.uk/agec/essen.html). This is a free article on the Internet, which gives a detailed description about how to evaluate basic sources on the Web. Along with the bibliography it consists of a 14-page printout. Highly recommended for its thorough, point by point analysis and it's easy to understand approach to a difficult subject.

Tenopir, Carol and Jeff Barry, "Are Online Companies Dinosaurs?" *Library Journal,* May 15, 2000. This is the fourth annual marketplace survey and it will continue in *Library Journal* each year. It has charts and diagrams to show the development of various for online reference companies from Bell & Howell and EBSCO to OCLC and Wilson. A marvelous place for details on a fast moving market.

Well, Amy et al., *The Amazing Internet Challenge.* Chicago: American Library Association, 1999. A study of 12 libraries where Internet reference services is the primary consideration. The joint authors consider selection criteria, evaluation process, funding sources, and other basic elements, which are common to online libraries. Practical advice for the librarian creating Web pages and indexes for their individual libraries.

CHAPTER FOUR
INTERNET REFERENCE
LIBRARIES

One excellent solution to the Net disorder is the online reference library. The winners in the technology age are the knowledge workers, or, if you will, the reference librarians. Their task of ferreting out information, despite the most refined search engines, cannot be handled by technology. As more than one critic has put it: "artificial intelligence" is merely a myth of the computer age.

Online reference libraries serve as guides to numerous reference links. In describing themselves, one of these libraries (at the University of California, Riverside) explains the mission of *Infomine*, (http://infomine.ucr.edu) their version of the virtual reference library. The summary pretty well covers all such systems:

> INFOMINE is intended for the introduction and use of Internet/Web resources of relevance to faculty, students, and research staff at the university level. It is being offered as a comprehensive showcase, virtual library and reference tool containing highly useful Internet/Web resources including databases, electronic journals, electronic books, bulletin boards, listservs, online library card catalogs, articles and directories of researchers, among many other types of information...As with most Internet resources, INFOMINE will be undergoing continual change in the pursuit of better service provision.

The "virtual library" is the library without walls whose major resources may be examined on a computer. The online reference works range from the library's catalog to basic indexes.

Examples of the virtual library are everywhere, and most particularly at universities and colleges. Here there normally is a direct connection
between the teacher or student's computer and a campus network. That
network may include everything from free access to the Internet-World
Wide Web as well as major online/CD-ROM indexes and other digital reference works which the library pays for and makes available free to qualified users. One may weave back and forth between what is free on the
Net to traditional, sometimes expensive, reference sources and conclude
a search in a small amount of time, certainly less than if one had to rely
exclusively on the free Net sources.

Most of the online reference libraries, which are called by a variety of similar titles, i.e., "virtual library," "reference desk," etc. begin with
a page which briefly indicates what is available. Then appears, or one
calls up, a menu that lists the major divisions. These range from periodicals and newspapers, to broader subjects from arts and entertainment
to science. Major sections and subdivisions are reached through standard links. The number of links depends on the number of divisions and
single sites available.

LIBRARY WEBSITES

Almost all libraries of any size these days have websites. Most serve two
purposes. First they are a public service, a method of "advertising" what
the library can do for the individual reader. Second this service usually
embraces reference functions, and more particularly links to specific
information aids from the local online catalog to Net links with reference
sources from Washington, D.C. to London, England. In particular: "Dissemination of information can be reflected on the Web through the following: internal search engines, online reference service, stable links to
other Internet sites, access to the online catalog and other databases,
basic information about the library (hours, staff, collections, etc.), and
timely updates. Perhaps the most important of these is access to the
online catalog of the library's local collection(s).[1]

"So what's a Webmaster anyway?"[2] Asks one of the breed from a
library in a private corporation. The answer is that while duties vary wildly
from place to place, in general it is someone who has various tasks but
essentially maintains the library on the Web and who controls the technology and the knowledge of how to disseminate information to the
greatest number of people with the greatest ease.

[1]Mark Stover, "Library Web Sites," *Computers in Libraries*, November/December, 1997, p. 56.
[2]Jon Pardue, "So What's A Webmaster, Anyway," *Internet Reference Quarterly*, vol. 3, no. 1, 1998,
pp. 7–14.

Universal Net Research Libraries

There are several excellent all embracing library sites. The best "universal" online libraries include:

The Library of Congress (http://lcweb.loc.gov) contribution is impressive, and discussed in some detail in the chapter on Bibliography. In addition to access to its massive catalog, if only in part, there are numerous other links to federal sites. See their home page: (http://lcweb.loc.gov/homepage/lchp.html).

The Berkeley Digital Library Sunsite (http://sunsite.berkeley.edu) is sponsored by the University of California Library at Berkeley and Sun Microsystems (hence "sunsite"). It particularly is useful for: *(a)* Some 4,000 links to information which have been, and are under constant watch by professional librarians. These are arranged by subject with brief descriptive annotations. *(b)* Superior links to most local, national and international library home pages that, in turn, have valuable data and links to other sites. Note: This includes, too, some 3,000 links suitable for children.

The Internet Public Library (www.ipl.org/ref) is sponsored by the University of Michigan, and foundation grants. The system opened in early 1995. It has a full-time director and staff operating with a budget of $450,000. Its future will depend on continuing financial support.

While the IPL is a complete Net library, the focus here is on the Reference Center. In essence, the IPL Reference Center is a grand experiment. The purpose is to maintain and run a quality reference service, based on traditional library models, for the Internet community. Questions are answered on the Net, or by e-mail. Note: Lack of funding makes answers slow, and sometimes there is no response.

The "ready-reference collection" is an annotated collection, chosen to help answer specific questions quickly and efficiently. Sources are selected according to ease of use. The sources move from "reference" and "arts and humanities" to the social sciences. A "ready-reference collection expanded subject tree" breaks the primary sections down by forms and subsections. See, too, the close to 8,000 full-text works online, for example, links to some such as modern collections of fiction, nonfiction and poetry.

The searching is accurate and usually results in relevant hits. The problem, as the sponsors are more than aware, is the lack of standard basic reference works on the Net. The result is that success is more likely when one is either looking for out-of-the-way data or historical material. It is weak on lengthily background articles.

Michigan Electronic Library (http://mel.lib.mi.us). Offering close to 200 reference formats, and menus for subjects from agriculture to weights and measures, this is an ideal source of information for the public at large. The links are well chosen and searches, by keywords or Boolean operators, are easy to master. Examples are given for the various types of search word orders.

A joint operation by the University of Michigan, the State Library of Michigan and Merit Network this is tailored "to serve the state's libraries and its citizens." It may be used by all. Only a few sites are of pure Michigan interest. Some sites are access restricted...although a password is available. Sample searches indicate the sites are well chosen and relevant to most questions.

BUBL (Information Service) (http://bubl.ac.uk). An excellent browsing tool for any reference librarian or researcher looking for material on England as well as much of Europe. It is based in Great Britain at the University of Strathclyde. BUBL "provides subject based service to the academic and research community." The key is the 29 page WWW Subject Tree, a mass of links to libraries, reference works, experiments, research and even a "librarian's home pages' directory" that includes pages from around the world. See, too, the "e-mail-library related e-mail lists" that is a description of library oriented discussion lists worldwide.

Virtual Library (http://vlib.stanford.edu). Operating out of Stanford University and operated by "a loose confederation of volunteers," the *Virtual Library* is a model of its kind. It offers the best sites on the Web by subject, for example: Agriculture, Computer Science, Communications and Media, Education and 10 other areas, all with subdivisions. Volunteers, too, add material. The site manager asks, "Do you have a good list of sites for a particular area? Would you like to make your favorite area of the Web safe for unwary travelers? If so, consider joining the VL."

The Library in the Sky (www.nwrel.org/sky/teacher) is the work of the Northwest Regional Educational Laboratory and is a source of information for teachers, students and parents. The primary focus is on material likely to appear in the school curriculum from the early to late grades. Each audience section has a clear, easy to understand index to materials and there are numerous links to related subcategories.

Individual Library Web Pages

There are over 3,000 individual library Web pages.[3] What follows are a few examples of what this author considers the best, but they are only examples. The proper place for students to turn is the local library Web page.

[3]Among lists to find such home pages: *Libraries on the Web* (http://sunsite.berkeley.edu/libweb/usa-state.html) and *Braintrack* (www.braintrack.com) which concentrates only on major sites.

Infomine, Scholarly Internet Resource Collections (http://infomine. ucr.edu). Sponsored by the University of California at Riverside, this valuable resource began in 1994. It is updated and modified several times a month. While it serves as a home page for Universities of California campuses, the heart of the system is the links to "8,500+ academically valuable resources in: biological, agricultural and medical sciences; government information; instructional resources, K–12 and university; maps & GIS; physical sciences; regional and general interest; social sciences and humanities; and the performing arts."

The user calls up the particular area and then is asked to enter a key word subject, or title entry. The results are particular works that usually are of great value. Most can be used outside of the university.

Other major sections: news resources, e-journal guides and search/finding tools. The one of interest here, is "general reference." General reference embraces close to 20 typical ready reference forms from acronyms and directories to fact books and biography. Each lists links to good to sometimes less than good sources. Still, the most valuable subheading is the "reference desk collections." Here are 13 links to both public and private types of virtual reference libraries similar in purpose, if not scope, to *Infomine.* The majority is annotated in this guide.

Columbia University. ILTweb Virtual Reference Desk (www.ilt.columbia.edu/net/guides/ILTrefdesk). Primarily useful for four screens of "Internet reference sources" in alphabetical order. For example, on the first screen are links to *CIA World Factbook,* five dictionaries, *Directory of Electronic Journals and Newsletters,* Electronic Forums (listservs), etc. Major guides, such as "resources on the Internet" and "education resources" precede the list of reference titles.

The New York Public Library (www.nypl.org) has numerous links and data that are of more than parochial interest. As one of the world's leading research libraries it offers valuable access to media from books and photographs to manuscripts.

COMMERCIAL NET LIBRARIES

As a generic descriptor of almost any type of information or service, "library" is widely used on the Net. In a restrictive sense of serving the similar purpose of the non-profit virtual reference libraries, the best of these are immensely popular. "Ask Jeeves" moved from serving about 1.3 million people per month to over 5 million in early 2000. They receive some two million questions per day. Other services report equal gains. Comparatively the National Council for Education Statistics reports that in 1996 (the latest date covered) there were about 285 million reference questions in all United States public libraries. This compares with Jeeves' 485 million questions. Raw statistics may show popularity, yet fail to chart rate of satisfaction. Be that as it may, librarians have much to learn about service from Jeeves and its numerous competitors.

At the same time the online libraries suffer from numerous drawbacks, at least for those familiar with library services. First and foremost almost all charge in part or in whole for securing articles and other documents. One may find an article from a popular magazine only to learn it will cost X dollars to view online. In a library this is free. Second, the indexes and other services are considerably more shallow than in the library. For example, Contentville allows the user to search *Dissertation Abstracts,* but there are no essential abstracts—only author, title and the inevitable charge for securing the dissertation unbound or softbound from $30 to $58. Again all is free in the library. Another major factor is the library boasts a reference librarian to give personal assistance, to help in the search, etc. The commercial services expect the user either needs no help, or if he or she does is willing to do combat with another computer miles away. Some offer personal service, usually at a fee, but this is only for certain types of questions. And so it goes. Library wins every time.

Ask Jeeves (www.askjeeves.com). This online library "allows you to ask a question in plain English." Actually it is a search engine, but with a difference. Instead of simply replying with a list of sources, Jeeves puts questions to the user. The questions narrow or broaden the search...if only in a rather simple way. The commercial organization, based in Berkeley, California, gives an example: "If you ask: Who is the King of Siam? Ask Jeeves would respond with Who is the head of State of Thailand? When you click on that question, Ask Jeeves takes you to a particular page on a site that answers the question. Also, there are links to other search engines from AltaVista to Excite with the number of matches on each. Does this work? Yes, for rather unsophisticated ready-reference queries with a single answer. No, for anything more involved. In the latter case the questioner is back to the usual list of multiple sites.

Electric Library (www.elibrary.com). Concentration here is on magazine and newspaper articles and a few basic reference works. This Microsoft library, unlike the *Internet Public Library* or the *Michigan Electronic Library* charges a $9.95 monthly fee. There is a free trial period. Search is word by word and relatively easy to use. The company says the library has more "than 150 full text newspapers, 900 full text magazines, two...newswires, two thousand classic books (i.e., those not copyrighted), hundreds of maps, thousands of photographs..."

If one looks up John Kennedy there appears 3 primary and some 35 secondary entries with "scores" of relevance and reading level—in this case from grades 6 to 12. The lead, overall articles are from the encyclopedia. With that background one may then turn to magazines and newspapers. The "catch" and a major one is that the related pieces are about other members of the Kennedy clan and even President Johnson. Articles are from 1995+. The weak link is the relevancy scores. All, in this example, are 100. However, 100 seems to mean any time the ex-President's name is mentioned, e.g., "The Federal Reserve chairman as hero..." and other completely tangential pieces gives one pause as to actual relevancy.

There are several sites on the Net that are dedicated to homework projects. *Electric Library* has two different entrance paths, with features and signs, for the first time or amateur term paper writer. The first "Homework Helper" (www.homeworkhelper.com) is for the high school student and possibly the first-year college student. It has numerous features such as "tips about asking questions" that are fed into the system as well as more general advice on term papers. One enters a question and then picks a source, i.e., magazines, maps, books, newspapers, etc. At this point the regular *ElectricLibrary* kicks in with the citations under subheads such as "biography," "literature," etc. A typical citation: "Score 100. *Great Works of Literature;* Carlylye, Thomas; Size 36K; Reading level: 12." Unfortunately in almost all cases the "score" is always 100. Beyond that the links to reading matter are fine, but at the end of the line the text usually is extremely brief.

A similar system, but with the focus on college students, is found under the rubric "Researchpaper.com" (www.researchpaper.com).

Essentially, no matter how useful the added features, this is simply the *Electric Library* database. When a question is framed it is referred to the *Library* and the procedures are the same as for the person who goes first to the *Library* without stops at the *Researchpaper* or *Homework Helper* sites.[4]

Contentville (www.contentville.com). Opened in mid-2000, this site follows the general pattern of all others but differs in its base of support, i.e., those who are taking part in bringing the service online. Among the sponsors: Ingram Book Group, the wholesale jobber who puts up the section on the sale of new books, and thus offers competition to *Amazon.com* and company. Bell & Howell offers *Dissertation Abstracts,* but without the

---

[4]The less than satisfactory "homework" sites are scattered throughout the Web. Another example will suffice: *Yahooligans* (www.yahooligans.com). This follows much the same pattern as the *Electric Library*. There are a series of links to "homework answers," "cultures, politics, history" and "science and oddities," among others. It adds such touches as "comics," games and entertainment that is an effort to attract teenagers who might be less enthusiastic about a total homework site. Still, the educational aspects of the system are good to excellent.

abstracts. EBSCO provides the archive of articles and indexes—but this is far from complete and hardly rivals library offerings. The service itself is underwritten with advertising by CBS and NBC as well as individuals. Other services include a limited number of legal documents, speeches and even screenplays. Off to a rocky start as far as satisfaction in answering questions is concerned, it may grow and develop into a real powerhouse because of the philosophy of taking in information partners. While the indexing services are free, one has to pay about $2.80 per article—a standard type of charge with all of the commercial services listed here.

Webhelp (www.webhelp.com). Online since the end of 1999, this follows the pattern of other commercial reference services, i.e., the user puts a question, the service may modify it with other questions, and, if available, an answer is given. Unlike the other services, though, there is a real person, not a computer, available when help is needed. If, for example, the user can't find a satisfactory answer to what is manufactured in Ethiopia, he or she can turn to the individual for personal help. Here, to be sure, much depends on the resources available to the online reference persons (who may be located in numerous cities around the United States), but generally answers are forthcoming. While elementary questions are fielded free, those which are more complicated, or where the user wants an "immediate" answer, instead of waiting in line for days or longer for an e-mail reply, then he or she must pay a fee of $10 a month, or so much per search. Meanwhile, the free service is little more than a search engine, i.e., one enters a query and dozens of possible sites are given. The answer itself, except for the fee or wait-in-line queries, is not given.

AskMe.com (www.askme.com) uses another approach. Under broad categories, which can be narrowed to specific areas, one finds a series of experts who answer the questions. The experts are self selected, i.e., asked by the online company to "share your knowledge with the world." They receive no pay for answering queries, but have the satisfaction of "gaining recognition as the next Internet columnist." The user asks a question and is given a list of authorities, with the number of questions each has answered. One then picks the expert, or if in a hurry skips this person, and tunes into what essentially is a search engine. A report on audio speakers, for example, may refer the user to numerous links from an encyclopedia article to a magazine piece. But if more data is required, then the expert is called in. If a rapid answer is needed the user pays a fee, otherwise gets in line and waits with anyone else. The system works well enough, although reference librarians could find answers for all the questions, at least those given as examples, much faster and for nothing.

For a library-sponsored site of this same type see *Ask an Expert Page,* which is examined in this chapter.

Yahoo! Reference (www.yahoo.com/reference). All of the search engines offer links to reference works, but none is as well organized as Yahoo. On this page one finds both broad and specific titles. "Journals," "libraries," "searching the net," etc. lead to several step quests for information. Narrow links are to encyclopedias, acronyms and abbreviations, quotations and similar reference sources. While hardly as satisfactory as the direct link to specific titles, it certainly offers numerous possibilities not found in other reference libraries. Note, too, that after each category or subject Yahoo! gives a specific number of links. "Libraries" takes the lead with 1,119, while "directories" comes in with seven. As usual, though, there are numerous blind alleys.

ELECTRONIC TUTORS

Quick, relatively easy to answer fact questions often are answered by the librarian over the telephone. Now another avenue is open. This is putting the question—from the ready reference query to the research problem—to an expert (often a teacher or librarian) on the Web. The assumption here is that a student simply needs to find a single Net site, click the mouse a few times and all the material needed for a term paper is, presto, at hand. This may work for a two- or three-page paper. Generally, though, it is much faster to use a standard full text online index to find two or a dozen current articles on the subject at hand. Historical, or any material of more than a year or two old, can be mined equally fast in a print/CD-ROM/or online encyclopedia, or from other standard reference sources in the home or in the library.

There are two basic types of online tutorial systems. The first is sponsored by educational institutions and libraries. The second is commercial, where there may or may not be a fee. The first type tends to be more efficient and reliable, although both are good enough for relatively simple queries.

Electronic tutors can be helpful. They are not, by any stretch of the technological-educational imagination, a substitute for a one to one discussion with a trained reference librarian. This becomes evident to anyone comparing the two approaches. Still the reference librarian should know about these electronic tutors in order to appreciate what the layperson may be talking about, particularly in relation to his or her children.

Numerous academic and public libraries offer a modified "tutor" service via their home pages. One excellent example: *University of Albany*

Libraries Internet Tutorials (www.albany.edu/library). This is clear advice on how to use the Net for research along with links to basic guides and search engines. There is an explanation of how to evaluate Net information as well as "recommended sites and search techniques." Here the pattern is to ask the student to put a question and then wait for a reply. Only short fact queries are encouraged. Longer research problems usually will not be considered. Normally only the answer is given without an effort to explain what the user should do next.

How do the tutors work? There are numerous approaches, but in a general way the method is much the same for both library and commercial sites. First, the user is given a list of subject and subsections to narrow the question. Second, the student is asked to enter a question within the subject area that may be narrowed even further by such limits as dates, country, language, etc. Third, one of three things are suggested: *(a)* The student should turn to the "archive" or to "frequently asked questions" to see whether his or her query has been answered previously. *(b)* There often are links provided to other resources on the Web, which should meet the user's need. *(c)* Failing to find a suitable response, the student may then reach the ultimate point—query an expert.

The usual procedure is to fill in an online form or e-mail the question to the tutor site. A reply will come, via e-mail, in two to ten days. Some sites are faster, some are slower, but in no case is there an instant response.

Experts tend to be layperson volunteers in subject areas, or teachers and librarians. America Online's service, for example, has over 1500 laypersons who volunteer assistance and receive free online service for their trouble.

Some commercial sites limit their tutor services to a particular group, e.g., America Online only to its customers; or an academic or public library only to those served in the immediate area. On the other hand there are enough nation-wide general tutorial sites to meet the needs of the average user on the Net.

Just how good are these electronic tutorial sites? It depends. If it is a matter of asking and getting an answer to a quick ready-reference type question, they are good. Answers tend to be short and supported with citations. Conversely, if the query is involved, or calls for more than a 100 to 150 words in reply, the system tends to break down. Usually the answer comes in the form of suggested sources to search rather than the answer itself.

Still, if nothing else, the tutorial sites do suggest answers, further paths of pursuit. And some of them can be particularly helpful when the question is limited to their archive of frequently asked questions. The typical question is given and then a short answer is provided. The average user cruising through such a list may find what is needed. Here it is much like browsing through an encyclopedia, or fast fact book. It takes little time and the answers usually are reliable.

Tutorial Educational Sites

Among the best noncommercial electronic librarian-tutorial sites are:

Stevens Institute of Technology (http://k12science.ati.stevens-tech. edu/askanexpert.html). This is the best of the group for two reasons. First, it offers numerous links to experts and to reference sites. Second, it has a good list of links "to other ask-an-expert" pages. While specifically directed to students and teachers in elementary grades through high school, a good deal of the expert advice may be used by older adults. There are nine broad subject areas, each replete with experts: science and technology, medicine and health, computing and the Internet, economy and marketing, professionals, personal and college advisors, library reference, literature, and just out of curiosity. One finds the subject area of interest, which often is broken down further, and then enters a question (usually a short, factual type) to an expert via the usual form/e-mail. The results take several days, as a rule, but are quite good. Experts tend to be both volunteers and trained teachers and librarians.

Ask a Question at the IPL Reference Center. Internet Public Library (www.ipl.org/ref/que). Here the expert is a volunteer librarian who works at the Internet Public Library in Michigan. The process follows standard public and academic library procedures. "Use the reference form and fill out a form with information about your question." When the message is received, the user receives a "message as soon as possible, advising on the status of the question." Note: it may be accepted or rejected. Answers are sent back in a day or two, or "possibly a week if it's a harder question." The response, again, is typical: "You'll get a brief factual answer if you've asked a specific question, or, if you have a broader topic of interest, you'll get a short list of sources that you can use to explore your topic further. These sources will be primarily Internet-related, but may include traditional library resources."

At the same site (www.ipl.org/teen/aplus) see "A+ Research and Writing for High School and College Students," a guide to the Net and links that will help in preparing a paper.

A search of any academic, public or special library home page will indicate usually the institution offers a similar a service. Obviously, it is wise to pick a library in the immediate vicinity. One example:

World Lecture Hall (www.utexas.edu/world/lecture). Sponsored by the University of Texas this "contains links to pages created by faculty worldwide who are using the Web to deliver class materials...You will find course syllabi, assignments, lecture notes, exams, class calendars, multimedia textbooks, etc." There is a menu of close to 100 subjects (from

Accounting and Agriculture to Women's Studies). A click of the mouse and there are scores of possibilities, say under "History." The first entry here is typical; "American history: civil war to the present." Outlines and summaries of each lecture...Professor Stanley K. Schultz, University of Wisconsin-Madison." Another click and the Professor Schultz entry is given in full. The links are to university courses primarily in the United States with a few from England and other countries. The amount of useable material for an outsider varies from extensive notes to simple outlines. A site for both teachers and for students. The latter may use to obtain, at least in most cases, well considered outlines of both broad and narrow topics. Note: The Lecture Hall concludes with links to Web servers at universities and community colleges in the U.S. K–12 sites are located as well.

Tutorial Commercial Sites[5]

Expert advice is not confined to libraries. Recognizing the potential profit, companies now offer similar services. These usually are free...at least up to a point. Where documents may be required there may or may not be a charge. Advertising and hopes for future methods of reaping profit have made tutorial commercial sites a booming business.

There are problems. How reliable are commercial tutors? Libraries normally can be trusted. That's not always true when the person putting the question has no real idea about the qualifications of the site and/or the individual who gives an answer. The best commercial sites allow the user to check the qualifications of the individual who has given an answer. Others skip this. Another difficulty is how fast does one receive a reply. If a simple query it may be a matter of minutes, but if involved it can take some time. And, in fact, the student may never receive a response. In fairness, though, at least some of the time a commercial tutor will be faster than an overworked library site.

Librarians can learn much about setting up their own tutorial sites by studying the good and bad points of commercial operations. Three examples of sites follow:

Abuzz (www.abuzz.com) is a website of *The New York Times* and follows both standard and a few unique paths. Termed "a knowledge network," it is a group to group, individual to individual method of both answering questions and sharing "your knowledge with other Abuzz mem-

---

[5]"Getting Expert Advice" *Yahoo! Internet Life,* September 2000, pp. 83–85. A dozen tutorial sites are examined and evaluated. Useful as much for what not to expect as what to hope for by way of information from the site.

bers." The group method is to join a "circle" (living, news, fun, working, etc.) where the individual can ask questions which are answered by other members of the circle. Individuals pose questions via e-mail. Answers come back the same way. Who are the people involved? The sponsor reports "They aren't experts. They don't even get paid. They're educated, smart, opinionated people. They range from professors to parents to...bar hoppers." Given this assembly of people willing to share information for free it remains to be seen how valuable the answers are likely to be. First put online in mid 2000 it is much too early to evaluate, although it does offer if not a unique method of gaining information at least a new structured approach.

AskMe (www.askme.com). The reader is given broad subject headings and usually these are subdivided to meet the needs of the average student or layperson. Another approach is to use a keyword search to find both the subject area and the expert. (Note: this is one site where full information is given about the person who is going to answer the query. Most are qualified to well qualified.) If the question is difficult, the user may request subdivisions and, yes, other experts to pitch in to find the answer. Note, too, a shortcut is often to turn to the archives where a similar question may have been put and answered. On the whole the response time is relatively fast—hours to several days. When an expert fails to answer, the user is asked to notify the site.

Learn2 (www.learn2.com). This differs from other tutorial sites in that most of the focus is on answering "how-to-do-it" queries. These cover everything from repairing a car to building a shed, i.e., the typical ready-reference questions heard in libraries each and every day. The limits are dependent on what is available, and while the scope is wide not everything is found here. But where a reply is discovered it tends to be accurate, full and easy to understand. Note: This is an excellent site for the library with a limited supply of books, periodicals or online sources for this type of question.

Research Papers

Students who wish guidance in preparing a research paper (from what topics to select to how to find information) can be directed to several sites. The best has been mentioned, i.e., the *Internet Public Library* service. Others, in order of preference:

Research Paper (www.researchpaper.com). A commercial site, unlike the IPL above, this primarily does two things: *(a)* It features an "idea directory" with possible topics for various interests and grade levels. *(b)* It provides links to research materials. This helps to narrow down the field, but just. Primary value here is the "idea" section.

Info Zone (www.mbnet.mb.ca/~mstimson). An expert on preparation of research papers explains, as found in many printed guides, the basic steps to take to get started and complete the work. In addition, there are links to information sites.

Paradigm Online Writing Assistant (www.powa.org). Prepared for college students by teachers at Boise State University, this, as the Info Zone, above, takes the student through the steps.

There are numerous variations on this type of help. Say, for example, a ready-made speech is required. Try *Speechwriters* (www.speech-writers.com). A perfectly legitimate organization, this offers speeches for special occasions, customized for an individual at $150. Prewritten speeches not tailored for an individual go for about $25. Incidentally, these come from masters of the genre. The firm is located in Dublin.

Electronic Citations

How does one cite an article, book or whatever taken from the Internet? The Modern Language Association has the same rules it applies for standard citations.[6] Basically the electronic citation should include the author's name, the title of the book or article, the date of publication or time the information was created (not always easy to find on the Net), the online address and the date when the source was accessed by the person who used the material.

A typical citation for a magazine article:

Landsburg, Steven E. "Who Shall Inherit the Earth?" *Slate,* May 1, 1997, May 2, 1997 (www.slate.com/economics/97-05-01/economics.asp).

If the citation is from a book, magazine or journal online the wording should be the same as for a print format, but with the addition of the Net address and the date it was read. Newsgroups, mailing lists, and e-mail follow much the same procedure. The user gives the address online in all cases and the day the information was accessed.

Further details may be found in the print *MLA Handbook for Writers of Research Papers.* (New York: Modern Language Association, various dates) which virtually every library has in the reference collection. On the Web an abbreviated form of these rules will be found at *MLA-Style*

---

[6]Scientists and some social scientists prefer to use the American Psychological Association (APA) style sheet. The MLA approach is much the same except the APA provides the primary name of the citation, and date within the text of the article.

Citations of Electronic Sources (www.mla.org/style/sources). Also, by now, standard style manuals have a section on citation of electronic sources. Note: For additional information, see the chapter on dictionaries and the section on "style guides."

Term Paper Mills[7]

The dark side to the Internet-Worldwide Web has many aspects. Not the least of which is access to the prewritten term paper.

The term paper mill is known to many high school and college students as well as alert teachers. Advertisements for the prewritten papers appear in college magazines. Word of mouth has been the best advertisement, at least until recently when the Net took over.

The ready-to-hand-in prewritten term papers are available on the Net at scores of sites. Simply enter "term paper" in almost any search engine box and the possibilities are everywhere. Most companies charge a fee (from $6 to $10 a page). A few sites offer free papers sent in by high school to graduate students.

Qualities of the papers differ from paper to paper, not so much from company to company. A few concerns will actually write the paper to order instead of reaching into a bin of much used papers. These tend to be somewhat better in quality. None, and absolutely none will get past the alert teacher, particularly if the assignment is more than general.[8]

A legitimate, although some would say questionable twist to college work came in late 1999 when *StudentU* appeared on the net (www.studentu.com). The firm hires students who each semester at major universities take notes in core courses. The notes are then posted on a central website. The notes are free, with the student organizer hoping to earn profit through advertising.[9]

ONE-TO-ONE ON THE INTERNET

"The Internet is not just an information repository; it is also a community. Thousands of discussion groups provide forums for the exchange of ideas and information. Both e-mail discussion groups and Usenet newsgroups are good places to read about valuable Internet resources."[10]

---

[7]Note that in some states, e.g., Massachusetts, for example, law prohibits the sale of term papers.

[8]Gregory Anderson, "Cyberplagiarism: A Look at the Web Term-Paper Sites," *College & Research Libraries News*, May, 1999, pp. 371–373. This is an excellent, short summary of the term paper scam. It particularly is useful for examples of "websites to surf" for papers as well as a good bibliography of articles on the subject.

[9]"Free College Notes," *The New York Times*, September 9, 1999, p. 1+.

[10]Laura Cohen, "Searching for Quality..." *Choice* Internet Supplement, August, 1998, p. 16.

Until the blossoming of the mass media (from popular magazines and newspapers to radio) in the early part of the twentieth century, *what* most people knew depended on *who* they knew. Information was passed from individual to individual concerning everything from politics to preparation of food and caring for children. What average people knew was largely a function of conversation. Only the educated, only the literate turned to books and a relatively few reference works for information. And in the mid-19th century this group was a minority.

Today gathering information on the Net depends on neither social class or education—although some typing ability is presupposed. As more than one wag has pointed out, the second party in a newsgroup could just as well be a bright dog as a dull person.

Usenet and Company

Newsgroups and mailing lists are where people talk to each other about special interests. A network of computers stores opinion and articles. There are an estimated 50,000 plus newsgroups with a probable readership of 20 million people.[11]

Newsgroups are extremely popular on the Internet because they are easy to access and provide a person to person approach to information. "Conversations—whether chat, conferencing, listservs, one-on-one e-mail, even Internet telephone—...is the driving force behind many late adopters' desire to get online." Listservs and related services are important to librarians because they offer focus groups involved with specific areas of interest. Speaking of one topic, Reva Basch adds that "Listserv members took up the slack, providing eyewitness reports, analysis, and opinion. Lots of opinion...raw data, not always accurate, but delivered quickly, in detail, and without self serving spin."[12]

Special interests take in everything from spotting aardvarks to zoology. To become a part of the mailing list chain the user sends an e-mail to a listserver address, i.e., the individual or group that maintains the list. To read a newsgroup the user employs a Web browser that these days are part of most Net software. Simply type in the address or name of the group—i.e., if it is part of the group open to you. Usually easy to understand icons leads from one group to another or to information within the group.

The premise of newsgroups is that most of the information comes from individuals rather than reference sources. This can be an obvious drawback if the individual is mad or simply likes to chatter. Conversely,

---

[11]Newsgroups are often referred to by the umbrella term: "Usenet." Technically the newsgroups differ from the similar mailing list in that the latter comes directly to the individual's e-mail address. The former goes to a central computer that is open to anyone. There are advantages and disadvantages with each system.

[12]Reva Basch, "Reva's Wrap," *Online,* September/October, 1998, p. 96.

many are expert or near experts who are willing to share their knowledge—knowledge that can be of extreme value for certain types of information questions and problems.

Newsgroups are structured in a large group that gradually is broken down into more and more specific groups.[13] A large one may be concerned with libraries, a smaller one with the needs of college students to understand where to find answers.

After more than two decades of service, and a growing number of individuals and groups attaching themselves to Usenet, the "noise" is sufficiently loud to drive many to other sources of information.

> "Many of the newsgroups that have been popular among scientists have grown too noisy for those who used to frequent them. Everybody's given up on sci-physics, said Scott Dorsey, a computer system administrator who has been on Usenet since 1984. "It used to consist of serious discussions among physicists; then the U.F.O. people took it over.... If you're a specialist trying to carry on a discussion, it's hard to do that when people are popping up with totally irrelevant information, Mr. Dorsey said."[14]

Newsgroups for Reference Information

Given the reader is familiar with the fairly easy method of accessing newsgroups, how can they be employed for information, for help with reference work?

1. First and foremost, before turning to a newsgroup be sure the same information cannot be found more quickly by using standard reference sources discussed in this guide's previous chapters. Do not waste time and effort, for example, looking for biographical data on a President or movie star when an encyclopedia or the Net "Biography" can pinpoint the needed information in seconds. On the other hand, if seeking opinions on the arguments for or against stiff teenage jail sentences, or episodes in a well-known television program, the newsgroups may be the best place to turn.

In a sense, the newsgroup is the place of last resort—and yet the first if one specifically knows of a particular group, which is focused on the user's problem.

---

[13]In alphabetical order, some of the major hierarchies, root words in newsgroup addresses include: *alt:* alternative groups without benefit of censors or rules; *biz:* business; *comp:* computer information; *k12:* students in elementary-secondary grades; *misc:* a catch-all group which covers numerous topics; *news:* not general news, but news about newsgroups; *rec:* recreation from hobbies to mountain climbing; *sci:* science, and generally considered by professionals; *soc:* not sociology, but discussions of a wide variety of social topics, talk: the broadest of the group, i.e., any talk from the silly to the metaphysical is found here. For information purposes the most valuable of the hierarchies are *rec, sci, soc, comp, biz* and *k12*. Note that *rec* encompasses not only recreation but the arts and humanities. Under each of these addresses may be up to 400 to 500 subheadings.

[14]"Old Newsgroups," *The New York Times,* June 24, 1999, p. G10.

2. Always check to see if the newsgroup has an FAQ (frequently asked questions) division. This type of small, specialized encyclopedia may have the answer to a query right off.

3. When a group of interest is isolated, spend a bit of time learning about its interests, about its "experts." Read a few of the articles and opinions before putting a question.

4. Be sure the newsgroup is really the right place to post the query. The greatest error, and headache for all concerned, is to have someone ask questions of a group that has no interest in the topic.

5. Having located a likely newsgroup to answer the query, having searched the FAQ, and finally having gone through past records, what is to be done when nothing is found? Turn to a similar newsgroup first. Second, at least if time permits, post a query. Put the problem to the group, and hope for the best in the way of an accurate, timely response.

The Directory of Electronic Journals...and Academic Discussion Lists, (Washington, DC: Association of Research Libraries, various dates) (www.arl.org) has entries for about 2,000 newsgroups from one dedicated to "those engaged in the delivery of academic advising services" to the last entry, "Zyoga" which considers "Yoga related to Zen Buddhist practice and philosophy." Librarianship and libraries has about 80 groups, with a dozen involved in reference services.

Usenet "Search Engines"

The number of newsgroups and related chat groups found on Usenet casts for organization. There is no lack of attempts to reach this goal. The efforts are similar to the service performed by the more traditional search engines, who offer repackaged Usenet newsgroups as part of their service. An example of a much publicized unit (which makes its point primarily in large print advertisements), is *Talkway* (www.talkway.com). Working on the premise that most people have no more idea what "usenet" means than who is their Congressperson, the corporation has distanced itself from the descriptor—as has several of its rivals. Instead its homepage offers a wild variety of "exchange ideas," "join the discussion," and "find my group of people" to reach sources of information on the Usenet.

The first website to see the profit making possibilities of Usenet was *Deja.News.* With a change in name to *deja.com* (www.deja.com), the site by 2000 bills itself as "a consumer information exchange." Somewhat confusing, and filled with advertisements, it, as its competitors, is somewhat hard to navigate. Still, for the patient reference librarian it may be worth the effort.

Deja.com enjoys several major benefits for students. First, and foremost, it may be searched by Boolean logic, subjects, and key words.[15] This allows the student to narrow interests to specific study topics and to search one or a dozen newsgroup archives for the points of interest. Just enter, for example, "Nez Perce Indians," push "find," and material on this tribe will be posted. Second, one may do a "query profile" that turns up the newsgroup where the key words appear most often. This helps one to find the particular newsgroup of interest for further consultation.

There are, too, simple means of reading current news and browsing through the hierarchy of consumer interest topics from "which vitamins work?" to discount travel. Links are provided to online shopping, yellow pages and even Ebay.

Each subject group is weighed (100% to 7%) in terms of its probable usefulness. "The confidence rating indicates how sure we are that people talk about your query in the newsgroup." One simply clicks on the newsgroup name and under that appear all of the articles within the group that match the query.

This is a typical *deja.com* entry, in this case: Newsgroups where people talk about: *reference books*

"All the newsgroups in the following list contain *reference books* in some article. The confidence rating indicates how sure we are that people talk about your query in the newsgroup. Clicking on the newsgroups' name will show you all of the articles within the group which match your query."

CONFIDENCE NEWSGROUP

99%	*rec.arts.books.marketplace*
84%	*rec.antiques.marketplace*
75%	*rec.antiques*
54%	*sci.med.transcription*
28%	*schl.sig.lmnet*
23%	*comp.databases.ms-access*
23%	*rec.arts.books*
17%	*rec.crafts.textiles.needlework*
16%	*rec.music.bluenote*

[15]Newsgroup archives which allow Boolean logic have, too, a number of stopwords abbreviations to limit the search: *&* is the symbol for "and"; *&!* signifies "and not," etc.

"Reference books" produced about two dozen possibilities. Another 25 potential hits resulted from the highest rated newsgroup. The problem is that here as in other situations "reference books" is part of a larger database. The result: reference books on everything from depression glass to pulp magazines.[16] *Deja.com* points up the importance of having a specific address, a specific place to turn rather than hunt and hunt and hunt.

Listservs

Listservs, or mailing lists, are synonymous with newsgroups in that they carry the same type of information and tend to originate from the same sources. The essential difference really is a matter of technology and convenience rather than content. The user sends an e-mail message to a central computer or mail server. This then forwards the message on to only members of the particular group.

A mailing list differs from a newsgroup because one does not receive anything unless it is specifically requested, i.e., one "subscribes" to the mailing list. A discussion group, carried via e-mail, the mailing list goes to everyone who joins the list. Anytime anyone adds to the list it is sent to the individual's e-mail address. Questions can be posted, comments added, either to the group as a whole, or to individuals who are list members.

Subscribing to a list involves nothing more than sending a request to a list server. (There are two main programs: LISTSERV and Majordomo, with slightly different procedures.)[17] There can be problems, not the least of which is receiving too much e-mail from the particular group. For students it will pay to use the group for the length of the study or research and then drop it, i.e., send the message "unsubscribe [list name]." Usually when one subscribes there is a covering note about how to drop the service.

---

[16]These are a sample of the references when one clicks on "rec.arts.books.marketplace." Note: As sites change rapidly this is only an example and one may or may not find the specific site, i.e., "author" after mid-2000.

Date	Scr	Subject	Newsgroup	Author
96/07/27	061	*Depression Glass Referen*	rec.arts.book.mark	*e511@torfree.net*
97/01/02	058	*1997 multicultural refe*	rec.arts.books.mark	*stonegm@aol.com (St*
96/09/05	058	*Reference Books on Antiq*	rec.arts.books.mark	*accenter@biddeford.*
96/08/05	058	*Horror Reference Books f*	rec.arts.books.mark	*mametzle@vela.acs.o*

[17]The procedure to subscribe to a listserv: *(a)* Send an e-mail message to the listserv. *(b)* "subscribe [list name] [your name].* *(c)* For example, to subscribe to "stumpers-L," a listserv with questions and answers about tough reference questions put to librarians, one would enter *subscribe stumpers-L Jane Smith.* *(d)* This would be sent to the stumpers-L address: *listserv@crf.cuis.edu.* Remember: send to subscribe, send the message to the e-mail address, not to the mailing address. For a discussion of library oriented listservs see Michael Schuyler, "Listserv Redux" *Computers in Libraries,* February, 1999, pp. 28–31.

The "catch" is that one must know to which group to subscribe. While the problem partially is solved by mailing list directories, it can be time consuming. For that reason, many favor the direct newsgroup where sampling may be made, without e-mail, of what each group has to offer. Furthermore it is not necessary to have a subscription. It may be wise to regularly surf newsgroups to see what is available rather than enter a subscription for a questionable mailing list.

According to *Yahoo!* magazine, "mailing lists are one of the best things the Net has to offer."[18] While an exaggeration, it does make the point that mailing lists are extremely popular among people looking for sometimes banal amusement and wild discussions about everything from genealogical problems to dogs and cats.[19] In terms of down-to-earth study and research the mailing list does have a place. And that place primarily is to fill out an opinion about this or that event or individual. The judgments are no better than the source, and as long as this is understood, the mailing list can be valuable.[20] There are close to 100,000 public mailing lists. (A few are private and others charge a fee—as, for example, a newsletter on the financial markets.)

Where to Find Groups

There are scores if not hundreds of sites which list newsgroups, discussion groups, etc.

Laura Cohen, an expert on such matters, recommends three that seem particularly suitable for academic research:[21] (1) *The Directory of Scholarly and Professional E-Conferences* (http://n2h2.com/kovacs) which concentrates on academically oriented groups. (2) *Tile.net* (http://tile.net) which includes both e-mail discussion groups and Usenet groups. Also has search directories of FTP sites. (3) *Liszt* (www.liszt.com). A list with close to 30,000 listservers, this is updated regularly. While there are thousands of lists, the publisher limits any one search to 150 lists or groups. Actually, one is likely to come up with only one or two to a dozen, particularly in more scholarly areas of interest. Arrangement is by "main directory," i.e., broad subjects from business to social with the number of lists after each topic. A more efficient method is to enter the search keywords

---

[18] *Yahoo!,* May, 1997, p. 28.

[19] If the comment, addition or question seems to be of interest to every member, the response can be sent: *(a)* To the list server, which receives the message and redistributes to all of the group. *(b)* This is known, among other things, as a threaded conversation.

[20] Most mailing lists are made up of individuals and not corporations or educational or governmental units. This is fine as long as one knows (if it matters) the qualifications of the individual(s) sending out the data.

[21] Laura Cohen, *op. cit.,* p. 16.

or title and get a fast result, i.e., "your search on (reference services) produced two matches." And the names are then given along with a sheet, for each, on what is available on background material with the address.

Bulletin Boards

Closely associated with both newsgroups and mailing lists, bulletin board systems (BBSs) are synonymous with both. Sometimes "bulletin board" is used as an umbrella term for the newsgroups and mailing lists. Originally they were a separate service, usually from small businesses and individuals with servers who wished to reach out to a limited number of people. Today the typical bulletin board, as a separate entity and not as synonymous with newsgroups, is normally reached via e-mail. The greatest use of the BBS is commercial and by the government. Also, it is associated with online conferences.

Bulletin boards are set up as single point information sources and usually represent the interests of one of the 100,000 or so individuals who established the board. These may range from fan clubs for movie stars to professional discussions concerning health and medicine. Most of the boards have references to similar boards.

While for questions it is much better to use a newsgroup or a mailing list, bulletin boards can be of value. To locate type in the search engines box "bulletin board." When this is done, for example, on AltaVista the result is 40,000 sites. Obviously it is better to narrow this down by using Boolean logic, which unfortunately is not always an open path to success.

There are no acceptable overall indexes to bulletin boards. A happy exception is the paths to federal government material listed in order of preference:

Bruce Maxwell. *Washington Online How To Access the Government's Electronic Bulletin Boards* (Washington, DC: Congressional Quarterly, 1995 to date. Irregular). This is a book, *not* a website. The title is self explanatory. In the 300 plus pages there is a mass of information, with addresses and other data, about *all* federal government bulletin boards. Also clear information on how to access what sometimes can be difficult sites.

FedWorld National Technical Information Service (www.fedworld.gov). This gateway offers links to over 100 different federal government bulletin boards. Some of the BBS are closed to the public because they are closely involved with the Defense Department.

FAQs/Frequently Asked Questions

Associated with newsgroups and mailists, FAQs or Frequently Asked Questions serve at least three purposes: (1) They often answers queries about the technology of various aspects of the Net; (2) They will give answers to questions without the user asking; (3) They are a gigantic archive of information which can be tapped by subject.

Throughout this guide and chapter there are references to FAQs. Many are a major part of information sites where the user is asked to turn to the FAQs section first in order to save time by asking the same question which has been answered in full previously. The FAQs section serves as a type of small, one volume encyclopedia—either general or subject.

In addition to the FAQs built into a site, there are specific separate groups.

The subject FAQs usually have a table of contents or an informal key word listing that makes it possible to find the question and answer without going through the whole archive. Nevertheless this is an extremely inefficient way of finding information. The exception is where one is searching a highly esoteric area.

The broader the area of interest the more the number of FAQs, e.g., try "news.answers" to find what many believe are the greatest number of FAQs lists and similar matter on the Net. Anyone interested in striking out for FAQs beyond those built into a site, should turn to: *Internet FAQs Consortium* (www.faqs.org/faqs/index.html). This is a group of FAQs with an extensive archive and an ability to search for specific areas of interest. It is a springboard to numerous other FAQs sites and offers more than enough material for even the most complex search.

Chat Rooms

The chat rooms (sometimes referred to by technologists as IRC: Internet relay chat) is a great favorite on the Internet. It is *not* a great place to gather information.

Closely associated with newsgroups, mailing lists and even bulletin boards, the chat room differs in two important ways. First it can be "live, real time," i.e., a conversation can be carried on much as one would on a telephone or by e-mail. People literally talk to one another over the Net. Second, it is difficult to find chat spaces on the Net which qualify as information sources. *Yahoo! Chat* (http://chat.yahoo.com), for example, allows up to 10 people to speak to one another using microphones wired through their computers. One can talk online while still communicating via typed messages.

The chat room where one can speak to someone else or a group in real time requires a given type of software. There are numerous programs about, usually for free. Also access is offered by many of the online companies such as America Online.

Even a casual visitor will note two obvious themes in chat rooms. One is that the average age seems to be between six and sixteen with "chat" primarily about television, romance, and school problems. An expert on the commercial side of the Web observes: "You have ordinary people, millions of ordinary people, engaged in a narrative enterprise. Writing dialogue, crafting descriptions, setting scenes, and developing characters. You have real dramatic engagements. It's a new form of story, of the written word, of the way we communicate fantasies, desires, and aspirations. I'm serious."[22]

The majority of chat sessions are what some call "bull sessions" where talk is more valued than content. One could surf the Net for days and not find anything worthwhile—at least of valuable information content. And even when found, the conversation rarely is supported with anything but opinion. Only television rivals most chat rooms for a low level of discourse and inane conversation. There are exceptions (i.e., the ones the reader of this text joins), but exceptions to boredom are as rare as quality television.

Useful chat rooms move from health (www.hairtoday.com) to movies (www.moviefone.com). Note, too, that the Net vendors, such as America Online and Compuserve offer a wide group of links to chat groups.

This is not to say the chat group cannot be a useful source of information—in the future. Today, though, it is much more efficient and certainly much more time saving to turn to a newsgroup for information.

There are no reliable directories of chat groups, at least in total or even in subject areas. The best approach is the grape shot method, i.e., enter the term "chat room" in the search engine box and check the results. Most come up with the standard "this is a list of the chat rooms that are available at this site." Once a group is found which seems of interest, links are provided to the conversations, past and present. The "past" are listed by date with a word or two indicating content.

When looking for a place to chat there are numerous possibilities: (1) Check the thousands of sites from *Yahoo!* to *Wired* magazine that sponsor a limited number of different chat groups each day on current news and personalities. (2) Look to sites devoted totally to conversation where there are ongoing chat groups one can enter and leave at will. See, too: *iVillage* (www.ivillage.com). (3) Then there are moderated groups where a host is assigned to keep the conversation on a level field. Here try *Talk City* (www.talkcity.com) which claims to have about 1,000 moderated chat groups each week. (4) A few sites, such as *PeopleLink* (www.peoplelink.com) let one set up lists of friends and colleagues with whom they may chat privately. (Note: some chat rooms may require extra software, but most will allow movement with any standard browser). (5) Then there is *Amer-*

---

[22]Michael Wolff, *How I Survived the Gold Rush Years on the Internet* (New York: Simon & Schuster, 1998) quoted in *The New York Times*, July 2, 1998, p. E12.

ica Online (www.aol.com) which offers its customers chat forums. Several other of the commercial carriers have similar offerings.

There are several methods of having what amounts to a direct conversation or phone call with an individual or group of people around the world. The IRC (Internet Relay Chat) requires a program and access to a server. For the latter see *Servers and IRC Networks* (www.mirc.com/servers). Pick a name, join a channel or chat room and the one to one or one to group conversation can begin in real time.

Yack (www.yack.com) is one of scores of open highways to "chats and events. Our editors...rank the top event and chat choice." In addition, as the company points out on its Net pages, the user can move from music and book events to the latest on travel and parenting. Further divisions are by sex and age. There is even a type of dating bureau. As a tribute to trivia, mixed with some truly awesome gossip and facts, *Yack* is hard to beat. Scoff, but even this type of site has a place in reference work, e.g., for the latest on TV and films as well as rock stars it is a solid beginning.

SUGGESTED READING

Alison, Dee Ann et al., "Database Selection," *College & Research Libraries,* January, 2000, pp. 55–63. What major factors should the librarian consider before contracting to lease an expensive database? "This article describes a strategy for making delivery decisions that addresses local conditions, pricing, feature options, hardware costs and network availability."

Betcher, Audrey, "Strikeout or Home Run? Managing Public Access to the Internet," *Computers in Libraries,* April 2000, pp. 28–32. How does the librarian control traffic around the Net terminals? How does one cope with heavy public demand? What are the basic problems with free use of the Net in the library? These and related questions are answered in a practical guide to Net use by the public.

Burton, Paul, "Information Professionals and the World Wide Web," *Online & CD-ROM Review,* no. 2, 1999, pp. 103–104. A brief outline of what skills are required by librarians to use the new technologies for reference services. The skills are as applicable to public and school librarians as to special librarians.

Coffman, Steve and Susan McGlamery, "The Librarian and Mr. Jeeves," *American Libraries,* May 2000, pp. 66–69. Comparing the for free answering service with typical reference services in libraries, the two librarians suggest ways libraries may learn from Mr. Jeeves. They explain how a project (24–7 Reference Project in Southern California) takes over the better features of Jeeves and other similar services to improve one to one reference service online.

Cohen, Laura and Julie Still, "A Comparison of Research University and Two-Year College Library Websites..." *College & Research Libraries,* May, 1999, pp. 275–289. Two experts explain the right and wrong approach to evaluating and constructing library home pages. A superior article for anyone who wishes to know what to do to construct a practical library website.

Kleiner, Carolyn, "The Great Term-Paper Buying Caper," *U.S. News & World Report,* November 22, 1999, p. 63. The customized term paper over the Internet is discussed with an analysis of just how good such papers are to students as well as the harm they may be doing. In addition, the brief article considers how some lift articles, and parts of articles from reference books without a word as to their real origin.

Lynch, Patrick J. and Sarah, *Web Style Guide,* New Haven: Yale University Press, 1999. Assuming the reader knows the basics of the Web, the authors show step by step how to create a website. As one reviewer put it, the book is "sort of an Elements of Style," for Webmasters.

Rogers, Ali, "Planet Webcam," *Yahoo!,* October, 1999, pp. 117–119. Background on the use of more than a half million Web cameras sold in 1999 alone. One can find everything on the Net from office interiors to discussion groups. Just how this will be used in reference work remains to be seen, but it will be employed.

Stover, Mark, "Reference Librarians and the Internet," *Reference Services Review,* no. 1, 2000, pp. 39–46. A librarian studies data to find that attitudes of librarians vary about professional services using the Internet. Opinions and attitudes have much to do with the quality of that service.

Sutherland, John, "What Can Happen When You Make Contact in a MOO," *London Review of Books,* July 29, 1999, pp. 14–15. A well-known British critic reviews a book (Julian Dibbell, *My Tiny Life.* London: Fourth Estate, 1999) and in so doing examines the social and cultural aspects of online conversations and entertainment. The legal issues are considered, too. Both the article and the book reviewed serve as a good introduction to a wild, wild field.

Tomaiuolo, Nick, "Ask and You May Receive..." *Searcher,* May, 2000, pp. 56–62. In this examination of commercial reference services on the Net, the author concludes that while some sites are promising, "few have the necessary features to command the loyalty that they may desire." See, too, the short, well selected bibliography on the subject (p. 62). See, too, Chris Sherman, "Reference Resources on the Web," *Online,* January/February, 2000, pp. 52–56. He tests the efficiency of "Ask Jeeves and the Electric Library as well as Information Please, the online almanac.

Withers, Rob, "Foreign Language, Literature and Culture," *C&RL News,* May, 1999, pp. 361–364+. Students and scholars use the Internet for their "tutors." A sample of what can be found, from discussion groups to overseas websites is covered nicely in this short article. An ideal model, by the way, for anyone compiling a website finding device/bibliography/article, etc. for a narrow area on the Net.

CHAPTER FIVE
NETWORKS AND
INFORMATION COSTS[1]

In discussing the wider implications of the worldwide information super-highway, several comments regularly surface. (1) The highway repre-sents the most significant change in communication since Gutenberg invented movable type in the mid-fifteenth century. (2) Time and space are shrunk to zero. In a second all of the world's experts in any given sub-ject area can be located, as it were, in one room. (3) One can now be thousands or more miles from a laboratory, business office, or classroom without being intellectually isolated. (4) Collaborative efforts on a world scale are now possible because of rapid, almost instant, communication of twists and turns in research. (5) As it breaks geographical and time bar-riers, the computer network hammers away at social and professional roadblocks. Theoretically, at least, no one because of rank, position, wealth, or education has to wait for information until someone else sees fit to have it published.

A network allows people as well as computers to be linked together to produce harmonious short cuts to finding information. By 2000 net-working has expanded to a point where almost every reference activity can be put under the umbrella term "networking." Networks link libraries, individuals and organizations. They make it possible to send informa-tion to a friend down the block or to a hospital half-way around the globe. A network brings about a more efficient flow of information, greater con-tact between persons, better understanding, and greater knowledge.

[1]For an outline of the major networks, as well as vendors, see "The Data Dealers," *Library Journal,* May 15 of every year.

Networking creates a library without walls. A digital network, and that is today's most common use of the term "network," consists of two or more servers, that is, computers linked together to share information files, e-mail, games, and anything else that can be exchanged. Networking is made possible because a series of the computers are linked to a similar "protocol," that is, a common language and standard for exchanging data.

There are two basic types of networks, commercial and nonprofit. One processes information while the other communicates the data to the user. Some systems, as the Internet, are a combination of both. Beyond that there are main divisions:

1. *Bibliographical networks or utilities,* such as the ubiquitous OCLC. This is tied, in turn, to *(a)* regional or state networks linking libraries and their holdings. *(b)* community networks which serve to link two or more libraries to one another in an immediate urban or county area. All are nonprofit, but charge a fee.

2. *Information processing vendors,* such as DIALOG where the information is sent for a fee to the individual or to the specific library. Closely related is the consumer networks such as America Online which connects the Internet for the average individual. All are commercial.

3. *The Web* which has both commercial and non-commercial materials. Most of the data is free, but if the Net is used to carry (1) and (2) systems above, then there normally is a charge. Unless used for free in libraries, the individual must pay a charge to get on the Net via such consumer networks as America Online. The future of local and regional networks, as well as national and international systems, depends on how long it takes to integrate and develop the information superhighway, or, as many librarians now prefer to call it, the national information infrastructure. Close cooperation, if not amalgamation and merger, will be the pattern of state, regional, and local networks over the next decade.

NETWORK QUESTIONS

Networks present basic questions:

1. Who owns what, and how is ownership to be maintained when information crosses the world in seconds? There is the matter of "fair use" and royalties and, well, just about anything of concern in copyright.

2. How does one preserve electronic data, at least that which is used and generated for only a brief time? A simple example: the personal letter, which is a valuable source of information for everyone from corporations to social historians. Can e-mail communications be archived like typed or handwritten letters?

3. Who is to control the means of transmitting the information? This is an explosive social, political, and ethical issue. Should a national resource as important as health care and scientific research be developed and controlled by the government or by private interests?

4. Cyberliteracy, or computer literacy, is important if people are to make full use of the information highway. Who is going to be educated, who is going to be left behind? Are there going to be as many cyber illiterates as there are now text illiterates in the United States—in the world? Lack of this kind of literacy will simply widen the gap between the haves and the have not.

At the day-to-day reference services level, several major questions about networks have yet to be answered: (1) What is done best at the national, state, or local level? The plethora of networks—from state networks to Internet and OCLC—blurs the lines of discernment. (2) Who is responsible for what? (3) Will the access to such networks improve, make the flow of information from institution Y or Y to individual P more efficient and speedier? (4) Does access to such a network affect either the amount or the quality of research, particularly at the graduate level? The same question might be asked of teaching aids from the earliest grades through a four-year college. Most of these questions have yet to be answered, at least in a definitive fashion. Conversely, individuals will gladly tell anyone who will listen how helpful networks are to their quest for information.

The problems associated with the information superhighway offer an opportunity for the reference librarian. Faster and more efficient ways of delivering information require considerable expert navigation. The reference librarian is that navigator.

World As Library

Thanks to networks, electronic databases, and digitalization of information (from books and periodicals to reports and sound and motion pictures), a library is no longer a library unto itself. The world is the library. A great library is no longer the one with a million or two volumes. Today it provides services to allow users to make the maximum use of information available hundreds or thousands of miles away.

What will be and, in fact, what are the duties of the reference librarian in the world library, in the electronic age of information?

1. As always the primary duty is to answer questions, although now, because of wider access to information, both the query and the response is likely to be complex.

2. The reference librarian continues to be a mediator between the individual and information, but in a more refined way. A few years ago, the librarian pointed out the value of one or two citations in *The Readers' Guide to Periodical Literature.* Today the librarian indicates to the user what index would be best, how index formats (print, online, and so on) differ, where to find the index, how to locate the citations, and, often, how to search the electronic database. In an unlimited sea of resources, the librarian is the navigator who indicates to the user where to find what in the shortest amount of time.

3. Instruction in searching electronic databases, particularly on the Internet, is a major duty. Even librarians who hesitate to support the old-fashioned bibliographical instruction realize the importance of making information available to those who want and who need instruction.

4. Knowledge management, in the acquisitions, labeling, and storage of data—as well as skills in locating elusive facts on one or more networks—is a major professional duty.

5. In sophisticated situations, the reference librarian is part of the research team that may be seeking answers to everything from the key to cancer or the best transportation system to high-definition television.

Librarians attempting to meet the challenge of the new approaches to networking hold meetings and publish reports on every aspect of the network situation. Findings include what every librarian who works with electronic information sources knows: *(a)* The more the average user knows about electronic databases, the more use he or she wants to make of them, with the resulting higher costs for the library. This also leads to a stress on hard-pressed staff. *(b)* Moving back and forth from the print to the electronic reference work is not only a stress, but also requires considerable skills in estimating costs and the place of the new technologies. *(c)* Security and privacy on networks are growing problems, particularly with easy availability of e-mail and bulletin boards. To meet this, many encourage a "firewall" system of computers to monitor the flow of messages in a network.

COMMERCIAL NETWORKS

There are some 2,000 to 3,000 commercial vendors, or data dealers whom supply database information to libraries and individuals. According to Carol Tenopir, who each year reports on the database marketplace, there are 24 major companies which collectively distribute and produce information available through 44 separate online, Web based systems.[2] The major networks have been discussed elsewhere in the text, but in summary the largest of the group in terms of the amount of information supplied include:

DIALOG offers over 500 databases, primarily indexes. Of these some one half, or about 260, offer full text. It is available on the Net as well as directly from the company. And, of course, as with this entire group, there is a charge for the service, which varies, from a transaction pricing system to a subscription approach.[3] DOW JONES has about 140 full-text databases with an understandable emphasis on business. It is available on the Net and World Wide Web, and has much the same pricing approach as DIALOG. LEXIS-NEXIS from Reed is a combination of a legal database (Lexis) and magazines, newspapers and journals (Nexis) which gives it added value for the non-legal library. Some 140 sources are available in full text. Thanks to a generous library pricing program, it began to appear in many libraries during the late 1990s. Others, many of whom offer individual publications from indexes to reference works, would include: R.R. Bowker, EBSCO, Elsevier Science, Gale Group, UMI and Wilson.[4]

BIBLIOGRAPHICAL NETWORKS

While considered earlier in the text, as by way of a reminder a bibliographical network (or *bibliographical utility,* as it is sometimes called) puts a massive national-international catalog at the fingertips of the librarian. The librarian may locate 30 to 50 million books and a comparable number of periodicals, reports, recordings, and so forth. Over the past years the size of the international catalog(s) has been increasing. By the turn of the century it is quite possible that bibliographical networks will

[2]Carol Tenopir & Jeff Barry, "Database Marketplace," *Library Journal,* May 15, 1999, pp. 40–48. This annual feature includes short descriptions of the basic data dealers as well as what they offer libraries. See, too: Ameilia Kassel and Karen Drebes, "Dialog Alternatives..." *Searcher,* September, 1998, pp. 31–54. This is a detailed analysis of various commercial vendors with particular emphasis on the offerings of DIALOG.

[3]Purchased by Knight Ridder in 1997, DIALOG was sold to Thomson in 2000. The latter company has renamed DIALOG "Bright Station plc" (www.brightstation.com). See, too, *DIALOG Select* which is the company's lower priced operation with some changes in search process. It is treated here as part of the larger DIALOG.

[4]An excellent way to keep up with the rapidly changing commercial networks is to read Carol Tenopir's column in *Library Journal,* "Online Databases," e.g., "New Versions of Old Favorites," *Library Journal,* April 1, 1999 (pp. 30–31) considers the latest developments in several of the services outlined here.

give access to virtually all information in the world. Bibliographical utilities such as OCLC and RLIN are nonprofit networks which cross state and national lines. They are managed in a variety of ways and provide services in many different forms.

The Internet connects a group of local, regional, and national networks in such a way as to suggest a new approach to bibliographical reference queries. Traditionally the commercial online services employed their own carriers. No more. This is because the commercial online reference services now use the Web as a carrier. The changeover is dictated by layperson and librarian preference for the ubiquitous Web. Now no one has to sign on to individual carriers one after the other in order to use this or that index.

At a formal level, and one that offers countless approaches to data, there are two major bibliographical networks or utilities. These are OCLC and RLIN, which were discussed briefly earlier.

OCLC[5] (www.oclc.org). As of 2000, OCLC (Online Computer Library Center) has about 34,000 participating libraries (of all sizes and types) in 65 countries and gives access to some 42 million records. Impressive, although hardly up to what many librarians foresee for the "virtual university library." Here there will be access for anyone with a computer to 60 million books and 550,000 serials.

Among its services: *(a)* OCLC cataloging that allows libraries to catalog collections online; *(b)* Interlibrary loan; *(c)* First Search which serves as an access to 100+ databases, including *WorldCat* and over 1,500 online journals.

The OCLC records turn up some fascinating data. For example, what single book was purchased by most libraries in 1997–1998? Answer: *The Moral Intelligence of Children,* by Robert Coles (1,468 holdings by OCLC members), with *The Partner* by John Grisham holding the record for a fiction title (1223 holdings). Suitably enough near the bottom of the list of 100, at 99, was Peter Maas' *Underboss* (863) with Bruce Cummings' *Korea's Place in the Sun* hitting the 100 mark (862).[6]

OCLC also includes the important original cataloging of members and holdings of all major government libraries. In an average year the system carries close to 50 million interlibrary loan requests. Only rarely is it impossible to find what is needed on OCLC. When that does happen, the desired information is probably so esoteric (such as the

---

[5]Carried on the Web as well as commercial vendors, OCLC provides a "guided tour" of scope and purpose of its services (www.oclc.org/oclc/menu/fs.btm). This is free, but any search of OCLC must be done with a password. The normal procedure is to turn to the reader's library, which offers free OCLC searches both in the library, and often at the reader's home computer.

[6]*OCLC Newsletter,* March/April, 1998, p. 24.

morning prayers, printed, of the Tibetan monks) that an answer will be found only on RLIN, or a similar database which includes highly specialized information.[7]

RLIN (www.rlg.org/rlin). RLIN (Research Libraries Information Network) is an academic bibliographical network. It includes records of the major universities, and research centers such as The New York Public Library and the California State Library. Membership is limited to only the largest of systems. The small homogeneous membership has two things in common: (1) huge collections of materials, often with esoteric data; (2) comparably large staffs in reference, acquisitions, and cataloging. The assumption of some librarians is that the larger research libraries are more careful about their cataloging and that therefore the RLIN cataloging entries are more precise than found in other networks. This is not the case. Analysis reveals no statistically significant differences in accuracy or fullness between OCLC and RLIN cataloging.

The records include the "standards," that is, MARC tapes, National Library of Medicine holdings, bibliographical records of the Government Printing Office, and so forth. While the membership is limited to about 160 libraries, the actual number of records is over 40 million in 365 languages.

After OCLC and RLIN

Although OCLC and RLIN dominate the national and international library world in terms of both coverage and use, there are auxiliary bibliographical networks employed by libraries in the immediate region and larger libraries looking for special services.

The leading bibliographical networks outside OCLC and RLIN include:

1. *CARL Corporation,* (www.carl.org) is privately owned by the Library Corporation. It was begun in 1988 as a for-profit spin-off of the Colorado Alliance of Research Libraries. The system includes the basic bibliographical data found on OCLC and RLIN and in addition, some indexes. The primary "outsider" use of CARL is the UnCover system which offers almost immediate access to the text of some 20,000 journals held by CARL members from 1988. As with OCLC the service

---

[7]In addition to books, one finds pretty much what is on the MARC tapes: computer data files, computer programs, films, periodicals (but not individual articles), manuscripts, maps, musical scores, newspapers (but not individual articles), slides, sound recordings, and videotapes. OCLC constantly is updating and adding to its online search facilities, e.g., Connie Zuga, "A New First Search," *OCLC Newsletter,* January/February, 1999, pp. 35+. For a complete listing of OCLC First Searching databases see the frequently updated *OCLC FirstSearch Databases.* This describes each database with specific notes on how to find information. The guide is available from OCLC, 6566 Frantz Road, Dublin, OH 43017.

updates daily a listing of tables of contents from which articles may be chosen. Also a key word search is possible. When an article(s) has been chosen it can be delivered electronically or in other forms to the user for a relatively low fee.

2. *OCLC/WLN* (Pacific Northwest Service Center), (www.wln.org) located in Lacey, Washington, provides computer services to over 370 libraries in Washington, Arizona, Alaska, Idaho, Oregon, and Montana. WLN has a database of close to 8 million records, and is incorporated into the aforementioned OCLC system. The records represent what is available on MARC tapes and from the subscribing member libraries. The records cover books, periodicals, audiovisual materials, and instructional materials. The emphasis is on English-language works, and about 5000 records are added to the file each week.

3. *MELVYL* (University of California) (www.melvyl.ucop.edu) is available on the Internet and the University of California online facility. It has over eight million books, one million periodicals, and other materials available from the various University of California centers as well as Stanford and several other private schools.

The OPAC Directory (Westport, CT: Mecklermedia, 1993 to date, annual) offers a state-by-state listing of online public access catalogs and, where available, databases. This gives users a key to access virtually every major network and catalog in the United States. A typical entry includes the name of the institution, the number of volumes and number of title, subject strengths, personnel, and system data (along with the practical and technical aspects of networking).

REGIONAL AND STATE NETWORKS[8]

The average librarian thinks of networking not only as a way to access information, but also in terms of sharing. It is a formal arrangement whereby several libraries or other organizations engage in a common pattern or exchange of information, materials, services, or all three for some functional purpose.

Libraries for generations have found it advantageous to join consortia for loose confederation to share resources and conserve budgets. Why buy or access online an expensive subject encyclopedia in each of 10 libraries when all are within easy distance. The consortium purchases

---

[8]For a complete list of the local "networks, consortia, and other cooperative library organizations," state by state, city by city, see *American Library Directory* (New York: R. R. Bowker, annual). Each listing includes a brief description of the activities of the organization.

the one set and makes it available to all members. On a larger regional, even national scale, there are joint efforts to deliver and access journals; increase the speed and efficiency of interlibrary loan and document delivery; provide new avenues for distance educational students; and in some cases even centralize administration and consultants.

The regional network, which may be only a handful of libraries in the immediate area or spread out over several states, is important to reference librarians. This type of network differs from the National-International Network in that it has many purposes, not simply bibliographical services.

There are different methods of defining and determining what a regional network is: (1) It acts as a broker for bibliographical utility services (such as OCLC) directly or indirectly to libraries within the group. (2) It provides training and skills in services not likely to be found in member libraries. This may range from building union lists to assisting with financial problems. (3) It is of no particular size, although this is not much of a test, as networks may have as few as a half dozen or more than 3,000 members. (4) It has a small staff which may include only one or two employees or as many as 50.

An amalgam of regional networks was founded as the Alliance of Library Networks. They represent 9,500 libraries and information centers throughout the nation. The alliance formulated several key goals. The goals are indicative of the hopes and the actions of regional libraries, both in an alliance and working by themselves:

- Strengthen the capabilities of alliance partners to provide high-quality, cost-effective services and support to member libraries and information centers; Contribute to the development and evolution of a sound, equitable information infrastructure in North America;

- Sustain and enhance a strong partnership with OCLC and other suppliers through cooperation for the benefit of member libraries;

- Collaborate in arranging joint agreements that will enable alliance partners to provide member libraries and information centers with the greatest value per dollar spent through economies of scale and through concerted negotiations with suppliers; and

- Develop and carry out joint operating and research programs for the benefit of member libraries and information centers.

Regional Networks

The number of regional networks crossing state lines are limited. They tend to be of assistance to reference people in that they make available shared cataloging (usually via OCLC or RLIN); lower rates for online searching through DIALOG and other vendors; better interlibrary loan systems, and technical help with any of numerous problems. Among such better-known networks:

AMIGOS (a Texas system) with over 170 members.

CAPCON is a multiregional library system with 150 member libraries in Washington, DC, Maryland and Virginia.

FEDLINK is about 1200 libraries and information centers contracting with information from the Library of Congress.

MLC (Michigan Library Consortium) with over 320 libraries.

OHIONET serves the needs of well over 200 academic, public and special libraries in the Ohio area.

SOLINET (Southeastern Library Information Network) is one of the largest of the systems, with a membership of some 730 libraries.

Network members use a turnkey computer system to cooperate with one another and to facilitate interlibrary loans. Examples of this type of networking can be found in most systems listed above.

The networks appoint managers whose staffs make most of the day-to-day arrangements for service. Each member of the system has a voice in governing, and there are regular meetings to discuss problems.

Nonreference services vary, too, but they generally include: (1) Arranging contracts with the major bibliographical utilities, and in so doing, acting as a director in negotiating terms between the utilities and the individual members of the regional network. (2) Holding down the cost of services made possible by a large membership base. (3) Providing for the training of librarians and consulting with libraries that wish to modify existing database services. (4) Arranging new services for members and developing those services at the local, regional, and national levels. (5) Determining the authority control of records for the members and improving circulation and acquisitions databases. (6) Helping members to change or even drop bibliographical brokers who serve the local system.

State Networks

The earliest networks, for everything from interlibrary loan to cataloging, were organized at a state level. Many of these continue as a middle unit between libraries and national and international networks. And several, such as CARL (Colorado Alliance for Research Libraries) and The Washington Library Network (WLN) and the California Library Authority for Systems and Services (CLASS), go beyond state service to regional and even national importance. They link cooperative collection development to interlibrary loan and resource sharing, as well as national information networks.

Statewide networks are cost savers, particularly among universities and larger public research libraries. The purpose is to cut duplications of low-use materials so the individual libraries can expand collections of much-used items as well as more esoteric titles that will be used across the network. For example, libraries on primary campuses of the State University of New York, as well as the libraries in the City University of New York system, share catalogs, indexes, and other commercial digital databases. This means one may search basic databases at the various campuses, although the primary home of the service is at one center; for example, SUNY-Buffalo provides both PsycInfo and ERIC, while CUNY provides Newspaper Abstracts. Delivery service, with a two-day turnaround, is available for articles and books located in and through the network.

A typical pattern of state reference networking connects the smaller libraries in the state to the central state library. When a person has a question the local librarian cannot answer (usually because of lack of materials), the reference librarian sends the request to the central network headquarters by teletype, fax, telephone, or in writing. If the request is not clear, the central service may talk with the librarian or the patron. Today the service is likely to involve a computerized system giving access to databases. Thus the individual may receive (1) simple citations, (2) citations and annotations, and (3) in rarer cases, the documents and articles themselves.

The New York State Education and Research Network (NYSER Net) is an example of a superior, ongoing state network. It literally offers electronic gateways for libraries throughout New York State. A five-year plan will see a hundredfold increase in the network's technological ability to carry information. Working jointly with telecommunications companies, the founders of the network have set up services that range from access to online databases and library catalogs to a ramp onto the Internet.

Local Area Networks (LANs)

The local area network, or LAN, is normally located in an urban center which draws upon the resources of libraries within a larger governing unit, such as a county. LAN differs from other networks in that the members are literally neighbors. Most are within walking or driving distance from one another. This establishes what some call a "natural information network."

The locals rely upon one another for advice and assistance in all aspects of management and reference services. There may be mutual pooling of funds for a given project or service or monthly meetings to discuss current problems. Normally the librarians serve the same type of audience and meet much the same needs.

Electronic local area networks, complete with access to the Internet, and other sources of databases are a much heralded feature of modern university life. The terminals are scattered throughout the campus. They may be in an individual teacher's office, a dormitory, a classroom, or, of course, the library. In a way, it is like connecting telephones throughout the campus to a central operator, but in this case the central operator is the library computer.

While the electronic aspects of the LAN are dramatic, the administrative purposes are more usual. Most activities occur by informal arrangements, usually at the local level, without any sharing on a regional or statewide basis.

Typical business includes:

1. Informal meetings between public and school librarians to address mutual concerns
2. Exchange of lists of collection holdings
3. Joint compilation of community resources
4. Joint material evaluation, selection, acquisitions, and processing programs
5. Placement of public library book catalogs in school libraries
6. Reciprocal borrowing and lending of materials
7. Provision of the public library with school curriculum guides and units of instruction
8. In-service programs designed around topics of mutual interest and concern
9. Production facilities for materials
10. Preparation of union lists or catalogs
11. Access to specialized and computerized databases
12. Joint film cooperatives

Community Networks

Community networks, unlike the conventional library network, are places where people may look for employment listings, participate in political discussions, use e-mail, and a number of other things associated with the more mundane activities of Internet fans.

Free-nets, sponsored and financed by local governments, are another type of community network. They may give access to the Internet. They will not open up all of the Internet features, particularly the costly ones, but they do afford basic services such as e-mail. The only expense for the user is a phone connection.

INFORMATION COSTS

Anyone who remotely follows the fortunes of the stock market realizes the tremendous profits and losses of Net stocks. This swing is based on business hopes which are not all that clear, but important as they decide the fate of information sources—at least free ones—on the Net. Viewing the business side of the Internet, a commentator admitted: "Nobody knows what's going on. The technology people don't know. The content people don't know. The money people don't know. Whatever we agree on today will be disputed tomorrow. Whoever is leading today, I can say with absolute certainty, will be adrift or transformed some number of months from now." He concludes: "It's a kind of anarchy. A strangely level playing field. The Wild West."[9]

If Internet oriented reference librarians sometimes feel they are characters in the last episode of *Gunfight at the OK Corral,* it's probably true. The financial-news expert Michael Bloomberg sums up the dilemma of business and the Internet: "I'm uncertain about the business model of many of the Internet companies. They either give away information and hope for traffic and revenue from advertising, or hope to earn a small commission from electronic commerce...I do worry that most Internet companies have very low profit margins—and an enormous amount of competition, so their margins will get even lower. The competition is great for consumers, who get a better deal, but I don't see how most of these companies will ever make an appreciable amount of money.[10]

There is another path to profit in addition to advertising and product sales online generated from those ads. Pay for the information service. As all reference librarians realize, current, reliable information—whether it is via a commercial index or a standard online reference work—costs money. Laypeople, too, are beginning to understand that easy paths to the same data will not be free. Either they have to wade through masses of advertising or go directly to the information source. The first is "free," the latter is at a fee.

Advertising now underwrites virtually 90 percent or more of commercial websites. But as consumers begin to realize the truth of the old adage, "you get what you pay for," the free content argument looks increasingly irrational.

The movie critic Roger Ebert offers a proposal called "micro-payments." Subscription sites where one has to pay a set monthly or annual fee for information, are, as indicated, not likely to be popular. Why? Because there are so many of them, so much duplication and, most

[9]John Sutherland, "The Browse Function," *London Review of Books,* November 27, 1997, p. 6.
[10]"Net Trading Skeptic," *Yahoo! Internet Life,* July, 1999, p. 81.

important, who wants to pay a set fee for something which may not be used often. The micropayment solves that by simply charging a small fee (two cents to a dime) for the answer to a given question as found in an encyclopedia, index or other reliable reference source. "Micropayments would be an incentive for publishers to put entire libraries and databases on the Web. That wouldn't hamper book sales, because before I'd search for—and pay five cents individually for—dozens of different [answers], I'd buy the damn book. Micropayments are the obvious future economic foundation of the Web. They add up to macropayments. I ran into an executive from Citibank who promised me that Web micropayments were coming my way sooner rather than later."[11]

Pricing Practices

What does an online for a fee (via a commercial or Web carrier) database cost?

That is the question which continues to baffle librarians. Publishers, carriers or anyone else involved in the cost-profit chain are reluctant to simply state a given price. Unlike standard magazine subscriptions or the cost of a bound reference book, the online reference source is an enigma in terms of real cost. This is not so much a plot on the part of vendors and publishers as their confusion as how to make a profit with a new technology. The countless variables result in almost as many quotes.

One aspect of pricing is obvious: it is high. For example, the cost of searching DIALOG on the Net is the same as searching on other online platforms—and this can be expensive, from $5 to $40 to several hundreds of dollars per search time involved.[12] Translated into student, teacher, layperson use, this means it is a prohibitive service except when used in or through a library, public or private.

Today (2000) there are several basic pricing options for online databases:

1. *Number of users.* Favored by most libraries, this is a complicated schedule, which is based on how many readers are using a given database. Rates go down the larger the number of users. Fine, but the problem is that almost all prices are negotiable and the best rates are achieved by hard hitting consortium members and/or the size and prestige of the given library. What it comes down to is the library enters a figure of the

---

[11] *Yahoo!,* September, 1998, p. 66.

[12] "Search time" varies from service to service, but generally includes the print/downloading time as well as the actual search time and telecommunication charges. On the other hand the time it takes to decide which database to use and compiling a search strategy normally is free. At any rate, the charge system is complicated.

population likely to use the service, which can be about $2 per person. The database producers calculate profit because only a small portion of potential users (say 500 out of a student body of 5,000) will ever go online, or use a CD-ROM. There is much, much, much more to the formula than indicated here, but it seems to work for libraries.

2. *Flat fee.* The next most popular approach is the fixed rate. The library, as it would for periodicals, pays a single one time yearly subscription for X or Y database. While more common for CD-ROM networks, it is used for online as well. The problem is the "license question." Usually the flat fee is based on a single user at a single computer. It then costs more for two or three thousand users. And in that situation, the flat fee is not so flat. It rises quickly.

3. *By the hour.* Originally, and to this day some vendors charge a fee based on hourly (i.e., minute by minute) use of the database. This pay-as-you-go system adds up not only the hourly charge for viewing documents, but also so much more for each citation viewed, printed out, etc. This is preferred by many special and some public and academic libraries for databases that are used only infrequently and do not warrant an annual user or flat fee schedule. The problem is that the fees are high and can add up quickly.

Other "wrinkles" in charges are based on the size of the library, the type of library and a number of other variables which may be used as the base of the charge, or worked into one of the basic approaches outlined above.

Concluding a study of pricing systems, Carol Tenopir sums it all up:

> Librarians in public and academic libraries want pricing options that they can control and budget for (flat fee and simultaneous use). Many academic and public librarians recognize that cooperation with other libraries is essential to achieving the best prices in an electronic era. Sometimes this is the only way to get affordable prices with desired pricing options...A wide variety of pricing options is a reality for all libraries no matter their size or type. No one pricing option will satisfy every situation in any library. Complexity will remain.[13]

Prices are brought down by sharing the databases among libraries, i.e., consortia contracts. Examples: "In Ohio forty institutions will receive all of Elsevier's periodicals electronically over a period of three years for the tidy sum of $23 million. The state of Georgia supports a $9 million project [which] sends multiple databases to libraries of every kind across

---

[13]Carol Tenopir, "Pricing Options," *Library Journal*, September, 1, 1998, p. 132. For actual examples of different pricing schedules see the chapters on Indexes. See, too, Bill Carney, "Internet Flat Fee Pricing..." *OCLC Newsletter*, January/February, 1999, pp. 46+.

the state. In Texas we receive the two major UMI databases that normally would cost us $30,000 to $40,000 for a mere $5,500. Smaller libraries get them for even less."[14]

Fee Becomes Free

The concern of how to profit from Net information may be academic. Soon, some believe, all Net data will be free. Lawyers are only now beginning to wrestle with another major aspect of copyright and for-a-fee online databases. And their opponents are the idealists (or realists?) who believe all information on the Net should be, and will be free. To this end they are developing programs which will make it impossible for publishers to protect fee databases via the usual passwords, scrambling of data, use of special servers, etc. They expect the programs to be so ubiquitous in the years to come that for fee information sources no longer will be feasible. Everything on the Net will be free. One can only say: let's wait to see.[15]

SUGGESTED READING

Bambrick, Jane, "OCLC's First Search," *Searcher,* March, 2000, pp. 36–41. Statistics are given from a study of First Search as well as a report on the good and bad points of the by now universal online search system. A useful model for study of similar systems.

Hirshon, Arnold and Barbara McFadden, "Hanging Together to Avoid Hanging Separately," *Information Technology and Libraries,* no. 1, 1999, pp. 36–44. Turning to the new technologies, the authors explain how librarians can organize consortiums as partners with information providers. There are four basic types of library consortia which the authors examine, pointing out the good and bad points of each.

Oder, Norman, "Consortia Hit Critical Mass," *Library Journal,* February 1, 2000, pp. 48-51. An overview of the major consortia and what they do. The problems, particularly of the "buying club" role are explored. There is likely to be more combinations of libraries to share resources and to save on expensive purchases.

Rabogliatti, Denise and Marsha Fulton, "Round the Clock, Round the Globe Customer Support: Are Vendors Ready?" *Searcher,* June, 2000, pp. 40–45. The authors analyze services offered by Bell & Howell (i.e., ProQuest), DIALOG, Factiva (i.e., Dow Jones Interactive), the Gale Group, and LEXIS-NEXIS. Most vendors meet service requirements of customers about basic

---

[14]Curt Holleman, "From the Field of Dreams," *Against the Grain,* April, 1998, p. 18.

[15]John Markoff, "Cyberspace Programmers Confront Copyright Law," *The New York Times,* May 10, 2000, pp. 1 & 23. This is a short discussion of progress towards (and away from) free Net information which is now for a fee.

questions. But there are numerous variations and these are spelled out by the authors. A good snapshot of what to expect, and not to expect from the major vendors.

Saffady, William, *Automation for Libraries*. 4th ed. Chicago: American Library Association, 1999. This is the basic, easy-to-understand guide on how to bring technology into the library and/or update what is there now. In this completely updated new edition (and these come out every three or four years), Saffady moves from computers and videos to catalog systems and computer based reference services. The jargon free approach makes this fundamentally a guide for those who may not know the first thing about automation. Highly recommended, particularly for students.

Sanville, Tom, "A License to Deal," *Library Journal*, February 15, 1999, pp. 122–124. An expert talks about how groups of librarians can tackle rising costs by taking an active role in licensing. "All factors point toward expansion and long term use of consortium based licensing."

CHAPTER SIX
THE TIME OF FULL TEXT

Exercise helps to keep librarians and their readers slim, happy, and healthy. A good deal of exercise is a given for any reference librarian. Dashing from reader to reader, meeting to meeting, reference source to reference source, guarantees a maximum amount of conditioning. One aspect of the days of in-house exercise are about over.

Not too long ago, and to an extent today (particularly in underfinanced libraries) one had to go to a print index, or other similar reference sources, find something on hunting grouse and then trip about the library looking for the book or the periodical in which the article was buried. No more. Today many sources are available at a computer. Tomorrow (give or take a decade) and they are likely to be *all* there from an elusive 14th-century manuscript on hunting grouse in Scotland to a modern treatise on grouse itch, caught by grouse killers over 75 years of age. One only need move the eye and hand muscles to find the texts. Welcome the age of the electronic full text and one suspects much chubbier librarians and readers.

The full contents of most world libraries, from articles and books, to recordings and photographs will be available at the movement of a mouse, the touch of an icon. Such commercial indexes as those published by LEXIS-NEXIS, the H.W. Wilson Company, IAC, EBSCO, or UMI today offer numerous articles in full text online. Books, too, can be downloaded cover to cover. Frequently a magazine or newspaper article will discuss a report or study and at the end or beginning of the piece refer the reader to its full text, i.e., "The article is available at http://www....on the Internet."

As of 2000 the picture of full text online is blurred. Just how much is available out there is a guess. Standard guides are of some help, e.g., the *Directory of Electronic Journals, Newsletters, and Academic Discussion Lists* (Washington, DC: Association of Research Libraries) in its latest edition has about 3,000 items. Also online: (www.arl.org) *The Fulltext Sources Online,* (Medford, NJ: InformationToday) another guide which is updated semiannually, lists some 8,000 titles, of which about 10 to 15 percent are journals. Numbers change constantly. One certainty: the numbers will grow.[1]

What is Full Text?

Digital full text is not necessarily the complete contents of a magazine or newspaper page. There are several basic forms of full text: (1) The so-called ASCII (American standard code for information exchange) means *only* the text. (2) "Full image" or "scanned image" includes everything on the page from text to graphics and photographs. (3) A combination of ASCII and scan allows some material, some graphics to be deleted. (4) Finally, and often found as part of popular multimedia electronic reference works, the publisher not only includes the full text and illustrations, but adds sound, moving images, and animation—in other words, offers a multimedia approach.

In most situations it is best to have a system that has the text plus the option to include the illustrations. This way one may search the text, download only the text, or call up only the graphics, etc. As this is so much more desirable than the full image page, most systems are offering the "text plus illustrations" option.

Just what is included and excluded in so-called full text journals online is explained in great detail by a group of Rhode Island librarians. In a detailed study of database vendors (EBSCO, UMI, Wilson, etc.) and their claims to have the full text of journals running parallel with citations, the researchers found: (1) Often only the full-length article is included online with the citation. "This means that letters to the editor, short columns, book reviews, and so on may not be included in the database, or may be indexed, but not available in full text."[2] (2) When participating librarians asked whether the online database adequately replaces the print copy, only UMI drew a 50 percent satisfactory response. A loud "no" was sounded for

---

[1]The digitization of most, if not all printed material will take time. Major companies have made a start. Bell & Howell (UMI) has made the claim it plans to create the largest digital collection of printed works in the world. How? By converting their already impressive microform library to a form that can be read online. This will take (as of 2000+), about three to four years to scan 5.5 billion page images.

[2]Patricia Brennan, et al., "What Does Electronic Full Text Really Mean?" *Reference Services Review,* vol. 27, no. 2, 1999, p. 25.

EBSCO (77%) and IAC (90%). This, as similar studies, raises the obvious questions of how much full text is needed online and whether or not print copies of journals should be kept in parallel to the digital.

Problems

The numerous problems and hurdles to having all, or most of the world's print material in digital form are enumerated below, but this is not to say the problems can't be solved. They will be eventually, and in the meantime there will be scores of efforts to put this or that type of print online. Why? Because publishers, vendors and, yes, authors see that eventually this is the only way to go for both access to the printed word and profit for all. The "profit" extends, too, to the readers who will have the world's information at the PC. With that, on to the difficulties.

The difficulty with full text online is that it is elusive. There is nothing to bind, nothing to view in whole, nothing to rely on as being continued from day to day, year to year. This is hardly a problem for the typical search where someone wants only yesterday's facts and events. It is difficult for research when there is no insurance about backfiles online.

The librarian dreads indexing services that suddenly drop full text titles for more than a year or two back. "All of the vendors loudly proclaim that they have no intention of voluntarily doing so…but no empirical evidence is available to either support or disprove such assertions."[3]

FULL TEXT ON THE INTERNET

The free magazines and journals on the Internet rarely cover more than current issues, or at best two or three years back. There is little or no provision for maintaining archives. Read it today. Gone tomorrow.[4]

Three types of publications are on the Web. First, are those exclusively published electronically. They have no print or, for that matter, CD-ROM equivalent. This is the majority of free online magazines.

The second type is primarily newsstand, popular magazines (from *Time* to *Popular Mechanics*) which are online editions of the print works.

---

[3]David R. Majka, "Remote Host Databases…" *Reference Services Review*, Fall/Winter, 1997, p. 32. The statement is as true in 2000 as it was three years before.

[4]In addition to the UMI and similar projects (see Reference No. 1 above) retrospective issues of for fee periodicals will be available online, e.g., see in this chapter the discussion of JSTOR. Both individual and group efforts will result in both the full text of back issues, along with indexing, in the next decade or so. One example of a single publisher: *TLS (Times Literary Supplement)* of London announced in 2000 the availability of this international book review service "in full facsimile online, 1902-1990" available via the Gale Group.

Usually these are modified versions and do not include all of the text found in print. At the same time the Net version has added features from up-to-date news breaks to links to similar interest sites. The daily newspaper from New York to Seattle to Mandan, North Dakota are included in this group.

All of these, and this is worth emphasis, are free.

Why do publishers make their magazines free on the Net? Twofold answer. If it is an individual or small group, it is a way of getting a message over without costly print and mail distribution. This accounts, in fact, for the majority of only online magazines.

Why do hard headed business types give away valuable information on the Net? Why, for example, can you read most of the contents of *Time* or *The New York Times* without paying a dollar or more for the privilege? There are many "answers." The truth is no one really quite knows how this has come about. Commercial heads justify the massive information giveaway as part of the subtle Research and Development plan. Another parallel explanation is the firm wishes to maintain market share on the Net so it is not crushed there by competitors also working on R&D and market shares. "Well, it's new, and who knows?" is another response. Some try to fight the tide and charge. It is more boast than profit, i.e., *The Wall Street Journal* brags it has subscribers to its online edition, but it charges only $49 or so a year for what in print they get three times as much.

For-a-Fee Titles

The third type of online periodical is for a fee on the Web. Here the library pays a standard rate, just as it does for the print version. To date these are primarily scholarly journals from both commercial and university presses. Because the full text of such titles is expensive, most are available only with a password issued by the library to students, faculty or a select group of employees. On the other hand, all may be read online in the library itself.

Major publishers charge a subscription fee for their online prestigious, better known journals.[5] They, too, tend to be more substantial in terms of number of articles as well as authority of the authors. Subscription schedules vary, i.e., one publisher may charge only for the online version, another may have a free online journal if the library subscribes to the print edition, while still another will offer reductions on both formats

[5]Here one has to differentiate between newsstand major publishers (e.g., Time-Warner, Ziff-Davis), and scholarly publishers. The former, as indicated in this text, put their popular magazines online free for a number of reasons. The scholarly publishers charge.

when the library subscribes to the two editions. The one thing they all have in common: none are free.

Among the leaders in offering their journals online, in full text and often with all of the illustrations, include a growing number of publishers. Some of the better known, more representative of the group will suggest various patterns:

The *Academic Press* publishes technical and scientific works and has about 176 titles on the Net beginning with the first 1996 issue. Anyone can look at the table of contents of individual issues as well as abstracts of articles at no cost. The full articles are only available to subscribers. In this same area of interest are: *Blackwell Science* with 225 journals. Here charges are based on a formula: 90 percent of the cost of the print edition for an online only subscription. For a combined print/electronic subscription the price is 130 percent of the combined cost of the two. *Elsevier Press* with over 1,200 scientific titles has an equally complex scheme of subscriptions.

The Scholarly Publishing and Academic Resources Coalition, made up of the libraries of the Association of Research Libraries, is trying to help fight the high cost of commercial scientific and technical journals by encouraging, among other things, "rebel" personal journals online as well as in print. These are put out by well-known individuals with the experience and the credibility to warrant charging a fee for the journals—although considerably less than requested by such publishers as Reed Elsevier. Whether this move will check the rising cost of journals in the new century remains to be seen.

Nonprofit For-a-Fee Titles

Turning to nonprofit academic journals one of the best known is "Project Muse," from *Johns Hopkins University Press* and M.S. Eisenhower Library. The leader is: John Hopkins University Press (http://muse.jhu.edu). But in addition 11 other universities which publish journals are part of the "Project Muse." Some 120 to 150 periodicals are on the Net that cover a wide variety of topics, not simply the sciences. The subscription rate is almost as complicated as operating a VCR.

The JSTOR Project is truly independent, and an experiment established by the Andrew Mellon Foundation. Unlike the other systems the concentration is not on new issues, but on finding ways to preserve older periodicals. The focus is on pre-1990 issues of core titles. These are available in full text including everything on the page (i.e., from notes and book reviews to advertising). The files go from issue no. 1 to 1990. Also, few of the journals are indexed retrospectively. JSTOR, to some extent, solves that problem. Here searching is more sophisticated than other systems. Not only can a contents page of an individual journal be examined, but the user can search all of the journals collectively by key word.[6]

The real hope is that in time archives may be built up so that the library will not have to store and bind individual magazines. They will be able to find their full content online.

Another avenue to full-text archives is via the large bibliographic utilities. For example, OCLC has what it calls the "Electronic Collections Online" that offers not just one publisher's titles, but some 2,500 titles from several different publishers. The goal is really to construct a large archive of back issues. Note, too, that a search by key words can be conducted across all of the journals.

How well does all of this work?

It is much too early to say. There are too few scholarly journals online (either for a fee or for free), and hardly any effort to catch up with back files. In time, and this is almost a sure bet, all periodicals will be available in some type of electronic form from the first issue to the current number. Whether or not they will continue to publish parallel print editions remains to be decided. It is likely, though, that only journals with a large circulation will be able to afford the two formats.

Then, too, there will have to be much better coordination between commercial indexing and the scholarly publishers with journals online. It seems fruitless for the publisher to devise in-house indexing or software when it is available in a more sophisticated style elsewhere.

CrossRef (www.crossref.org) offers another approach to gaining full text access. Rather than the user going first to an indexing service (EBSCO, Wilson, etc.) to find an article in full text, he or she goes to *CrossRef.* The user usually is looking for the full text of a footnote or bibliographic reference found in reading. Given a citation, more than 30 publishers' journals are open for full text online. Some three million articles from thousands of journals are available. About half a million articles are to be added each year. The member publishers do much of this through *ScienceDirect* (www.sciencedirect.com) which sets up links from bibliographic records and footnotes to the full articles. Most of the emphasis is on scientific journals, but in time this will broaden to include other fields of scholarship. It is not free. Payment is by subscription.

Problems

Problems, which are bound to be overcome in the next decade or so, include: (1) Most researchers and teachers who contribute to journals

---

[6]For a listing of some two dozen similar sources of archived journals, as well as ongoing titles in full text, see: "Access to Electronic Journal Content," *Against the Grain,* June 2000, p. 42. See the detailed review of JSTOR and its use online: "Database & Disc Reviews," *Library Journal,* March 15, 1999, pp. 120–121.

prefer the old-fashioned tried-and-true print copy because (as of today) it is more prestigious. A nicely printed journal is physical evidence of publication that can be stored and displayed. Also, citation indexing and circulation figures indicate the relative importance of the print journal and, by implication, the importance of the contributor's paper. In time, when more writers are accustomed to electronic databases (and those who evaluate them), this stumbling block may be removed. (2) Editorial standards, or so it is argued, disappear when the author can go directly online with an article. There is no one between the contributor and the reader. Actually, for an acknowledged online journal this is not true in that no matter what the format there is an editor, and often a board of referees, to check the article before it is available in any format. Still, the feeling persists that producing writer-to-reader material electronically destroys the editorial superstructure that protects high standards. (3) Cost of the electronic format is usually much lower than print, but here the assumption is that all potential readers have invested in PCs or have free access to PCs and other hardware and software.

Despite doubts and drawbacks to the electronic online journal, few question that in the decade or so ahead, many, if not most, standard and sometimes little read scholarly journals will be converted to this format. The saving in trees alone is a fine argument. The journals, when properly edited, will be reliable and considerably more current than the present print versions. The obvious advantage to the scholar who is able to search across a wide range of journals, instead of through the full text of only one or two journals at a table, is impressive. From the library point of view there is a tremendous saving in space, binding, cataloging, and the like. As teachers become familiar with the new format, electronic journals will be as prestigious as their print cousins. Overall cost will be lower for publisher, library, and individual. Eventually copyright problems will be solved. The publisher is likely to agree to an annual sale to a library or individual, such as a subscription, and then let the journal be used online as it is in libraries today.

With that, though, it should be understood that more popular journals and magazines will retain the print format. As with the printed book, the magazine with a circulation of over 20,000 or well into the millions is simply easier and more profitable to publish in print. And the print version reaches many, many more readers. The major hurdle is how to attract advertising dollars to online magazines. With no promise of the success of the printed magazine, the online title is less than attractive to necessary advertisers. It is a problem that Madison Avenue has yet to solve.

A working reference librarian points out other problems with full text indexes that are not usually considered. Full-text searches are more sophisticated than the average citation search, and as such require more supervision by the overworked librarian. Then there is the matter of the

Internet and the problem of downloading information, the slowness, the sometimes crashes, and the impatience of the typical user. Another more obvious difficulty is that the typical layperson will call up too much information and print out or download more than needed.

If volume of material is a potential problem, a more subtle one familiar to anyone working with patrons and indexes is the impatience of the searcher. He or she is inclined to accept the first few citations for what is needed. Given full text, the temptation is even greater to print out what is available rather than wait for an interlibrary loan or some other form of document delivery of more relevant, but not at hand articles.

BOOKS ON THE INTERNET

When discussing the availability of books on the Net, the librarian must consider several points: (1) There are now (mid-2000) about 150,000 to 300,000 digital books, most of which are out of copyright and thus avoid the difficulty of arranging payment to publisher and author. *Books in Print* includes close to 1,800,000 titles. Scanning titles to put them online takes time, and just how much is to be digital depends on time and money involved. (2) Given these statistics it will be many years before even a small to medium sized library can claim books are available both in digital and print form. Meanwhile print will dominate. (3) Few want to read a whole book, or even a chapter at a computer screen, so provision inevitably is made to print out what is needed. At this point the institution or vendor makes a profit. Most concerns charge a few cents to print out a page which otherwise can be viewed free and/or for a subscription fee for the whole system. (4) The catch, as indicated throughout this chapter, is how to make money, or just break even with digital books. Advertising, subscriptions, charges for printouts and other services are part of the package.

What follows are some typical examples of the *online* book. The e-book is discussed later. It is only the beginning.

The Library of Congress has a program to make all of its holdings (from periodicals and books to recordings and films) available in digital form online. Under the banal name of National Information Infrastructure the revolutionary project's potential for document delivery is quite beyond most people's imaginations. Essentially, though, any book one wishes to read, where the Library of Congress has access, can be called up on a computer screen, read, downloaded, or whatever. The whole world, then, is a personal library.

Another example is the Vatican Library. Working out an arrangement with IBM, the Vatican will make not only printed works, but also manuscripts available online to the world—in full text and with the illustrations and other graphics.

On the Internet, the by now famous *Project Gutenberg* (http://promo.net/pg) is attempting in a more limited way to make 2,500 books available online—at least those where copyright and royalty demands are not about. The founder at the Illinois Benedictine College in Illinois has hopes of increasing the number to include all of the classics. The immediate objective is to have 10,000 books in electronic format.

NetLibrary (www.netlibrary.com) is a commercial effort to make available both classics and current books online. These can be read on the monitor or downloaded—but unlike Gutenberg, at a price. (The exception: "public collection" "are public texts, i.e., not in copyright, that are available to all netLib free of charge). The site claims it has over 16,000 titles (as of mid-2000) which may be read as a book and/or "search every word in every book" when looking for a particular subject. The copyrighted titles the company claims is putting online at approximately 2,000 titles per month. (As of mid 2000 it had 18,000 copyrighted books and 4,000 public domain titles). Searching can be done by author, title and broad subject. Considering the millions of books now available in libraries, the online text progress of the company is far from impressive—but at least it is a start and will invite much competition in the years ahead. Primarily a service for libraries, netLibrary charges a subscription fee to libraries for its use.

Questia Media (www.questia.com) offers 50,000 titles with plans to have 250,000 books online by 2004. The emphasis is on "core" titles chosen by qualified librarians. The books are the ones most called for in academic research, usually by students working on a paper. Free searches by keywords, etc. are available, but only subscribers to the system may actually see the pages and print them out. The subscription fee varies with type and size of library.

Ebrary (www.ebrary.com) follows what they call the photocopier method. Searching of online titles is free as is simply reading a page or two. The cost is to print out the pages—usually from 10 to 25 cents per page. The company claims it has 130,000 volumes (both books and periodicals) available and will work to 600,000 in a few years. The choice of title is governed in part by the availability of digital forms already available from the publisher.

With the claim "every book written can now be published and made available in printed or electronic form to any reader on Earth at no cost to the author."

Xlibris (www.xlibris.com) goes a step further. Sponsored in 2000 by the internationally known publisher, Random House, this site promises to print out or otherwise make available the author's book. According to numerous advertisements (and see their online Web page): "Here's how it works. You upload your manuscript. We process it, format it, design the cover, assign it an ISBN and register its trade paperback publication...Your book is then available from any retailer and from the Xlibris website to any reader who order it—printed on demand." The probable catch, without too much definition by the publisher: "Xlibris fulfills book orders, manufacturers copies, and you can earn a fair royalty on every sale. This core publication service is free, unless you opt for additional services."

Xlibris offers 1,700 titles (as of mid-2000) of which about one-half are fiction. The company hopes to be publishing 100,000 titles a year by 2005. This is about twice the number of titles now being published by all American publishers each year. While jolly for the authors, the question is whether or not anyone except he or she's relatives will read the online books. And who will review even a small portion of the online books? No matter, by charging authors for editing and galley proofs, the publisher will make a profit even if it sells nothing on the Net.

Collections of rather esoteric materials—out of copyright, and therefore free to package publishers, but not free to libraries—will become more popular in electronic format. For example, Chadwyck-Healy has pioneered the "giant" literature database. Three examples, some of which are discussed further in this text: *(a) The English Poetry Full Text Database* includes the work of 1350 poets from Anglo-Saxon times to the end of the nineteenth century. Search is by subject, poet, title, phrases, and so on. One may search the texts. *(b) English Verse Drama* covers verse drama from the Middle Ages to the early twentieth century. It has more than 1500 works by 450 authors. *(c) Patrologia Latina Database* is the full collection of extant Latin prose with, again, full-search capabilities.

The technological miracle goes beyond the traditional reprint. A local bookstore, library, or even individual will be able to reprint a book as needed. The file will be encoded by electronic data, downloaded from online, CD-ROM, or files supplied by individual publishers. The day will come when one may simply order an item from among, say, the 100 million individual titles at the Library of Congress by having it downloaded and printed (or held online or on a CD-ROM, etc.) at a key command. The long-term results of such storage and retrieval by individuals and by librarians are still to be evaluated. Meanwhile, the concept of the coursepack and the quickly printed book to order is an indication of what lies ahead for all reading matter, and for that matter, multimedia from television to CD-ROMs and recordings of music.

Online Textbooks

Online customized textbooks, with a wide selection of everything from typefaces and grades of paper to binding, are now available on many university campuses. Locally produced texts, often made up of judiciously selected articles and bits and parts of other books (sometimes along with some multimedia materials) are known as *coursepacks*. Copyright is cleared by receiving standard approvals from publishers and authors.

While few reference librarians are concerned with textbooks, it is obviously important to have a record of what coursepacks are currently being employed. Furthermore, the concept has implications for reference publishing. There will be little to stop a library or an individual from ordering an out-of-print book or other unavailable materials in much the same way a student gains access to a home textbook. The publisher will reprint as few as a dozen books on request, and while the unit cost may be higher than printing, say, 5000 copies, at least it is reasonable and within the library budget.

E-Books

The most publicized electronic book is precisely that—a device that weighs from 12 ounces to more than two pounds. It looks like a printed book but is a reader with a television/computer-like screen. Printed books, from bestsellers to classics, from textbooks to biographies, can be downloaded into the electronic carrier. Most people prefer paper, but this should not underestimate a new generation of young readers who may have different ideas about what constitutes the physical book.

Carrying such brand names as Rocket eBook, Millennium E-Reader, and Softbook, they range in price from $100 to $500. Eventually, like cellular phones, they will be given away to entice customers to buy and download books, newspapers, and magazines.

The Rocket eBook is typical. It is priced at $199 in early 2000, and offers over 2,500 titles online, which may be downloaded at no charge into their reader. Also, those lacking the reader may view the books on their computers. (The software is reasonably priced and, to be sure, available from Rocket eBooks).

The "catch" to all of this is that the majority of books, including over 150 reference titles, are out of copyright, e.g., quite dated. This is fine for the classics, but a distinct drawback for most reference works. In time new titles will be available, although at a fee. Other services offer current works for a price. To get a notion of what is involved with this form of reading try the Rocket eBook web site for detailed information (www. rocket-ebook.com/enter.html).[7]

[7]"In Maryland, the state library just bought 24 Rocket eBooks, one for each library in the county." This story began in mid-1999 and critics now believe eBooks will be a common feature in most libraries. "E-Books: Coming Faster Than You Think," *Library Journal,* July, 1999, p. 75.

By mid-2000 all of the national bookstores were offering and widely advertising e-books. For example: *Barnes & Noble* (www.barnesandnoble. com) observes that "the future of reading is here" in their ebookstore. "Our ebookstores offer e-books to be read on PCs, laptops, or handheld devices." About 100 out of copyright titles are free, i.e., *Jane Eyre* to *Tom Jones*. Those who want current titles pay to download. Other features, worked out in cooperation with Microsoft which supplies the Microsoft reader software free, include the ability to read one chapter from the book without cost as well as reviews, comments from the author, and related titles. There is a list of "smart" features from the ability to make notes to looking up words in a built-in dictionary.

Stephen King garnered publicity for both online and e-book publications when he put his work online, e.g., in late 2000 *The Plant* was put up for download chapter by chapter. King asked readers to send him money each time they read a chapter. This may be a sign of the joys and profit in self-publishing, but one wonders how successful others would be who were not as well known as Stephen King. Publishers prefer to be the leaders in this field, not the authors. Random House, for example, in early 2001 will offer best-sellers for online and e-books. Similar plans and offers are available from Borders to Amazon and you name it. In an effort to stir up enthusiasm some publishers now offer current titles at low prices online. The catch is that these are all best sellers. Normal run-of-the-mill books come at a much higher price than the lost leader popular titles.

Will this catch on? No one knows, but as of now the possibilities seem dim as real readers, i.e., those who read more than one book a month, are quite content with print.

Print on Demand

"Print on Demand," the term used to explain the process allows the publisher to make very short runs (as few as a single copy) on both esoteric and out-of-print books. The book can be computer printed and bound for each individual order. UMI has been offering such services for generations, but usually from microfilm copies of the original. Today, they too, use a computer. In addition individual publishers have joined the technological turn. For example, Macmillan includes over 1,000 out-of-print titles on order. Simon and Schuster have more than 10,000 books similarly available.

When a library or individual orders, there rarely is any indication it will be filled with a "print-on-demand" order than regularly printed volume. Publishers, of course, claim the PoD is indistinguishable from the original. While this is a great help, it has its drawbacks for authors, e.g.. problems of copyright reverting to the writer when a book goes out-of-print, for example. (With PoD the publisher can claim a book is never o.p.). Also, the cost of the PoD usually is higher than the original.

DOCUMENT DELIVERY

There are several dozen commercial suppliers of documents, and particularly articles from periodicals. The major document suppliers include EBSCO, Engineering Information, Information Access Company, Fax Research Services, UMI, and LEXIS-NEXIS. Each has its own peculiar system, but they share in common the ability to deliver in hours or days (depending on how much the library wishes to spend for the added speed) the given document(s) in full text and/or in full-text image.

Ordering is usually done in one of two ways: (1) The librarian finds a citation to a wanted article (which is marked with the information concerning full text) that is available, say, from UMI. A click of a mouse and the push of a key send the order on the way for the full article to UMI. It may arrive from UMI in hours by fax or a laser printer, or be sent by mail.

When using a bibliography, index, or whatever, the decision as to which document is needed is made at a computer terminal. The greatest number of documents are specific articles from journals. When X article is required the document must be located. This is done in several ways:

1. The logical approach is to combine the process of searching with that of the request. The most advanced method is to simply press a computer key, or click a mouse, which will bring up the article for viewing or make it possible to order it from an outside source or print it out at the terminal.

2. Some systems indicate whether the library has or does not have the article, that is, periodical. If it does not have the periodical, the user may automatically place an order—usually routed through the local interlibrary loan system—for the article.

3. Where there is no indication at the terminal of who has what, and it is not found in the library, the usual procedure is to turn to the interlibrary loan office. ILL checks to be certain the needed item is not in the library and then orders the document from a nearby library or a commercial or nonprofit service.

4. Depending on the sophistication of document delivery, when the request order is received at point Y, where it is to be filled, several things may happen: *(a)* Incoming electronic requests are matched automatically with files of, say, periodicals in the library or the document center. *(b)* Once the request is validated, the required item is taken from the shelf and the article is photocopied, faxed, or reproduced in some fashion so it may be sent to the point of request.

The increased use of electronic databases with accompanying full texts online has encouraged the user to expect almost instant access to materials. Networks, from the Internet to OCLC, opens up avenues to a vast area of information that the library does not have on hand. The material must be ordered, and document delivery is simply more efficient, often even less costly than traditional interlibrary loan. Staff cuts and reduced operations of ILL offices have made the appeal to commercial suppliers of documents even more appealing. The commercial firms take care of such sticky problems as copyright clearance, and the need to have the latest issue of this or that periodical.

Delivery Problems

The drawbacks to document delivery are obvious: First is the cost. This varies widely with the amount and type of material needed as well as the source from which it is ordered. In 2000, if an average can be reached (and this is really impossible because of so many variables), costs average between a low of $6 and a high of $30 per document. Second, most users, and particularly those who have grown accustomed to free (if somewhat slow) interlibrary loan services, balk at paying such high charges for documents. Third, if the library decides not to charge, then it must absorb the high costs in an already tight budget.

The faster the article is sent, or if an article with full illustrations and not simply text is requested, the higher the cost of transmission. Whereas a photocopy by mail may cost no more than a dollar or so for postage, an electronic transmission can run much more.

Today the problem is not finding a method of document delivery, but which vendor, which system to consider for both general and specific needs. Some vendors specialize in given areas, others are supermarkets for almost everything from general periodical articles to specialized reports. The common-sense approach to selection includes these points:

1. What do readers need? Libraries servicing high school and college students will concentrate on popular material, while a library with an engineering clientele will turn to technical suppliers. Parenthetically, one thing is certain about the users and document delivery. The more it is offered, the more it will be used. Furthermore, in time they will expect the article to be delivered quickly (whether it comes from next door or half way around the world) and for little or no cost.

2. What will it cost? Where the library meets the expense of most documents, this is a major consideration. Also, it figures into the equa-

tion where the person is expected to shoulder the expense, in part or in whole. Note that the cost inevitably is divided between the price of reproducing the article and the fee due the copyright holder.

3. What is the best route? Today it is difficult to beat the speed, low cost and general satisfaction of online documents. Interlibrary loan to be better for delivery of books and large files. On the other hand where specific articles, reports and smaller pamphlets, etc. are required the fastest route may be a non-profit or commercial document supplier. A major consideration as to which path to follow depends on the date of the needed item. Current articles are available almost anywhere, but material before the early 1990s or mid 1980s normally are not available from commercial organizations. Here one must turn to libraries.

4. How fast? Delivery speed is important to everyone, although for some it may be a matter of hours, even minutes while others are willing to wait for a week or more. Actually, the cost and best route have speed pretty well built in as a major factor; but it is worth considering as a separate element of choice.

5. Can the eligible reader order his or her own document without sending the request through the library? The user finds what is needed in the catalog, the index, the bibliography and then at the same terminal, the same place requests the needed record or document. It is then routed through a preselected supplier.

Document Suppliers

In selecting a private or not-for-profit document supplier, the evaluative questions are almost self-evident, or certainly self-evident to anyone who has requested a document on interlibrary loan, or worked with interlibrary loans themselves. The questions: What technologies are required to place the request and to accept the document? Expensive hardware can cancel out any benefits. How long does it take the dealer to fill the order for the document, that is, what is the turnaround time? Is copyright compliance met by the dealer? Does the dealer have access to the needed documents, or have them immediately on hand? What subject areas are covered, not covered? Finally, what does all of this cost?

Once the field has been narrowed to a few choices for document delivery: (1) Test them by asking for a week or month's trial—either free or at a reduced subscription fee. (2) Test if orders can be placed and fulfilled easily, and with glitches from bad reproductions to errors in typography and spelling to poor citations. (3) Test the customer service and—i.e., are the bills clear and accurate, is there someone out there (besides a computer) to answer questions, to meet problems. Is the document delivery able to provide good troubleshooters.

All networks and most of the information vendors offer document delivery. Among the best, and representative of what is available:

OCLC full texts are linked to the FirstSearch indexing and abstracting services. Access is available through FirstSearch. Internet, dedicated lines, dial-up, and so on are other methods of establishing contact. The user may switch from a citation to the full text (i.e., any part or the complete text) where available at the computer keyboard. Key word searching of the text is not available.

RLIN's document delivery is similar to other systems. Online ordering of material is possible with several, although not all, of the databases. The individual or the library may place the order by interlibrary loan or directly. The user may pay for the service with a credit card; fax or the mails are used for delivery, which takes from 24 to 48 hours on average. If speed is necessary, RLIN offers the user the Internet.

Larger, research libraries offer fee based information services, e.g., they share and deliver documents at a fee to the commercial–business community locally and internationally. Not only will the library find what is needed for an individual or business, but, for a fee, search the needed item(s) in other libraries. One of the better known examples is the New York Public Library "Express."[8]

British Library Inside (www.bl.uk) allows the user to search, order and receive delivery of articles from the British Library's journal and reference collection. This is divided into two parts—the sciences and the social sciences. Updated daily the service covers 10 million articles from some 20,000 journals and 16,000 conferences. Costs of orders are displayed on the screen, and cover a 2 hour fax; an overnight fax, regular mail, or special mail—as well as the standard copyright fees.

The British Library Document Supply Centre is only one example of several efficient document delivery systems supplied by national libraries. The Canadian Institute for Scientific and Technical Information, for example, offers similar Web-based document delivery orders.

INTERLIBRARY LOAN (ILL)

The oldest, best-known system of moving material from one library to another (whether it be a book, a photocopy of an article, or an e-mail response) is known as *interlibrary loan (ILL)*. The term is self-explanatory, although today "loan" may not be quite that when a document is sent by fax; and "interlibrary" is often more than one library to another library. Still, it is a useful, well-known term for sharing resources.

---

[8]For a complete listing of such services see *Internet-Plus Directory* or *Express Library Services* (Chicago: American Library Association, 1997, irregular, to-date).

The benefits of national and international interlibrary loan library networking are numerous: (1) One may secure a book through interlibrary loan from another library in the same community, state, country, or, for that matter, from a library abroad. (2) An elusive magazine article may be secured in the same fashion. Thanks to modern technology one may place the order at a computer terminal and have the needed material within days—if not in minutes, where online or a fax machine is available. (3) As indicated elsewhere in the text, an individual may sit in her or his home or office and obtain much of the needed material without even going near a library.

Interlibrary loan has two complimentary purposes. The first is to aid the researcher in acquiring specialized material from other libraries. The second is to assist the general reader in borrowing material otherwise inaccessible because of lack of complete library resources. The interlibrary loan as a research aid is almost exclusively the charge of college and university libraries. The interlibrary loan as a boon to popular reading, and, to a lesser extent, as a reference tool, is usually a service of public libraries in cooperation with one another or with a state library.

The best-known subsystems for interlibrary loan are those operated by OCLC and RLIN. Somewhat similar services are offered by the other bibliographical utilities.

In a successful effort to cut costs, speed up delivery and in general construct a more efficient interlibrary loan process, several regional consortiums have more or less deserted OCLC and other bibliographic units for their own interlibrary loan system. Rather than turning automatically to, say, OCLC, they first search electronically the catalogs of their fellow members. In 95 to 98 percent of the time, they will find what is needed among the five to ten million titles owned by the consortium. Foreign language, esoteric data, reports, and hard to find materials are ordered, as usual, from OCLC, but this makes up a small part of the interlibrary loan traffic.

Five or more large research libraries may have resources in a consortium of 7 to 10 million plus volumes and other materials. Why go through a middle person, such as OCLC or a commercial document source, when the books can be borrowed one from another.

Interlibrary loan is made easier for readers by allowing them to request the loan at the computer terminal. Usually it is a matter of filling in blanks and then forwarding the request electronically to the ILL office where it, in turn, is sent electronically to the place holding the wanted information. Another method is for the user to skip the local loan office and send the request directly to the library with the article or book. For example, the OCLC "Direct Request" allows the user to send the query to OCLC who, in turn, acts as a local loan center, finds interlibrary with the data and instructs it to send it on to the lender.

What is borrowed?

Several studies indicate it is about evenly divided between books and copies of articles or other materials. A majority of the requests are for older works and particularly for items not available electronically. This, in fact, means almost anything indexed before the mid 1980s and not found in the local library.

What are the options for receiving the needed item?

The most evident is the ability to scan articles or sections of books, or what is needed and send the material online, usually via the Internet. Items may be faxed, as well. Still, the most popular way is to use the mails. What is different here, though, is the increased reliance on private delivery services rather than Uncle Sam.

Who operates interlibrary loan?

For the most part it is libraries. On the other hand there are an increasing number of commercial services that go around the library. For example, all of the major general electronic indexes offer the user (or the library or both) the opportunity to order the article(s) online. These then are sent by the commercial service via post or private carrier. More likely the order will be fulfilled by sending the data online or by fax. The catch: various comparisons indicate this method is no faster than library interlibrary loan and almost always is more expensive for both the library and the individual.

Who lends and who receives?

Most of the lending, from 50 to 60 percent is from large academic research libraries. This is hardly surprising as libraries go where the books are to be found. Smaller academic libraries lend about 20 to 30 percent of the materials, while the average public library comes in at about 10 percent. Typically, to turn the figures around, a large research library such as the University of California at Los Angeles will loan four times as many titles as they will borrow.

What does interlibrary loan cost?

It is impossible to generalize because of the numerous variables. At the same time larger libraries report a typical loan (in 1999) which includes the cost of personnel, office space, computers, etc., runs at between $25 and $30 per transaction.

In addition to supplying the material, a function of interlibrary loan is to supply the user with the material promptly. The user is normally in a hurry, and a common question is "When may I expect to receive X book or Y article?" There is no single answer to the question. The amount of time depends on how close the requesting library is to the source of the book— across town may take only a few hours, whereas across the country may take days or weeks. The actual processing of the request is another factor. Experience indicates that this varies from library to library and a safe guess is from 24 hours (exceptional) to a week (average within a state or regional system) to two or three weeks (average when one has to go beyond the state or region). Technology, such as OCLC and fax, has speeded [the interlibrary loan] process. Nonetheless, the biggest drawback continues to be the amount of time a patron must wait to receive a document.

Finally, and this may be forgotten in the network-technology excitement, one can simply refer an individual to another member library. If the library is near, it is much simpler for the user to read the article or book there than to use any of the above avenues. Thanks to reciprocal borrowing among network libraries, the individual may well take the material home.

When is it legitimate and practical to send a person elsewhere? One must take the person's added effort into consideration, even if it only involves walking or driving to another library. Consideration should also be given to what is fair to the other library, particularly if it is a common practice to send people to that library.

SUGGESTED READING

Albanese, Andrew, "The E-Book Enterprise," *Library Journal,* February 15, 2000, pp. 126–128. An interview with an E-Book company founder. The former banker explains the economics of the system—economics which may leave some breathless and wondering just how practical the whole system is, particularly in terms of average readers and libraries. Time will tell whether his company is hot air or the beginning of a major shift in how books are supplied. See, too, the editorial on e-books by the *Library Journal* editor, Francine Fialkoff, (*Library Journal,* March 15, 2000, p. 68) who announced the beginnings of e-book reviews in her journal. For another of countless views on this subject see Stephanie Ardito, "Electronic Books," *Searcher,* April 2000, pp. 28–39. Good bibliography and rundown of primary manufacturers.

Bartlett, Rebecca, "Back(list) to the Future," *Choice,* May 2000, pp. 1,599–1,603. A practical consideration of the ebook and how the new format may or may not be of value for reference and university publishers. Particularly useful in that it has a simple explanation, "How Does This eThing Work, Anyway ?" See, too, the e-book from a reader's point of view: Doreen Carvajal, "Judging a Book Without Its Cover," *The New York Times,* May 7, 2000, p. WK5. The reporter uses several versions of ebooks over a period of time and reports her judgment.

Bates, Mary Ellen, "In Search of the Free Lunch and No-Cost/Low-Cost Full-Text Archives," *Searcher,* June, 2000, pp. 55–59. The author discusses nearly free online information sources, i.e., the cost of an article from several sources (DIALOG to Northern Light) as well as "other low cost options" for full text. She ends with specific recommendations for the best sources for specific needs. As informative as it is pragmatic and a model of research of this type. In case you don't know: tanstaafl is an acronym for "there ain't no such thing as a free lunch."

Brennan, Patricia et al, "What Does Electronic Full-Text Mean?" *Reference Services Review,* No. 2, 1999, pp. 113–126. A consortium's experiences with so called "full-text" journals and databases are less than totally satisfactory. On the other hand the steps taken to evaluate the sources can be used in almost any type of size library. Note, on p. 119+ the valuable outline of services offered by the major general index services in terms of full text titles and how they are analyzed and made available to the user.

Brunette, Bette, "Quieting the Crowd: The Clamour for Full Text." *Online & CD-ROM Review,* October, 1999, pp. 297–302. Everyone who uses a reference work in a library online expects it to be accompanied by the full text of what is needed in digital form. The author discusses how to meet this need via the three basic models of full text. Each system is examined and the author points out the pros and cons of each.

Epstein, Jason, "The Rattle of Pebbles," *The New York Times Review of Books,* April 27, 2000, pp. 55–59. A careful study of the book business as it "stands at the edge of a vast transformation." Just what that change will be is explained in terms of both good and bad developments. On the whole the author is optimistic about the future, and sees the new technology as increasing both opportunities to publish and the number of readers. For another brief point of view by the film critic Roger Ebert (*Yahoo! Internet Life,* May 2000, p. 72) see his self explanatory titled article: "Don't you dare call me e-Roger. Why I'm Resisting the Very Idea of E-Books, and Taking a Stand for Real Pages." See, too: Roberta Burk, "Don't be Afraid of E-Books," *Library Journal,* April 15, 2000, pp. 42–45, and note the handy chart of e-book choices by brand on p. 44. In the same issue there are e-book reviews (pp. 127–128).

Fleck, Nancy, "Interlibrary Loan, A New Frontier," *Library Hi Tech,* vol. 18, no. 2, 2000, pp. 172–176. Tracing the tremendous changes in the use and the techniques of interlibrary loan, an experienced librarian believes the system will grow rather than diminish. The technology to improve the process is explored in detail and several studies are reviewed.

Hafner, Katie, "Books to Bytes," *The New York Times,* April 8, 1999, pp. G1, G5. A discussion for laypersons concerning how "research libraries grapple with the task of preserving the digital present." Makes major points in an easy to understand fashion. An ideal opening article for students.

Kinder, Robin, ed. "Document Delivery Services," *The Reference Librarian,* no. 63, 1999. A survey of document delivery methods, this special issue includes a half-dozen articles on the subject. These move from an overview to fee based information services.

Kovacs, Dianne, ed. "Electronic Publishing in Libraries," *Library HiTech,* no. 1, 1999. An entire issue is given over to such things as "electronic journals and academic libraries" as well as "E-reference: incorporating electronic publications into reference." The close to a dozen articles are by working librarians and offer practical rather than pie-in-the-sky responses to the question of publishing and libraries.

Krumenaker, Larry, "A Dillar a Dollar...Where's that Online Article," *Searcher,* September, 1999, p. 3740. Advice on how to "get a particular article from a particular journal" online. Various services are described.

McDonald, John, and Jimmy Ghaphery, "Do We Have This in Full Text," *Against the Grain,* April 2000, pp. 28–30. Why should a library provide full text of electronic journals? Answers: Users expect this; it makes life easier for the library staff; and in the long run it may prove more economical than to have the full text only in print. These and other considerations are given a practical examination by the two experienced authors.

St. John, Warren, "Barnes & Noble's Epiphany," *Wired,* June, 1999, pp. 132-144. In addition to discussing the development of the bookstore online, the author considers various new paths for the electronic book and, by the way, a new approach to selling textbooks which gives the student more of a break than the publisher or bookstore.

"Special Topic Issues: Digital Libraries," *Journal of the American Society of Information Sciences,* Part I: February 2000; Part 2: March 1, 2000. A sweeping overview of the Worldwide Web, information access, and digital libraries. The two issues, and some 15 or so articles, cover all major issues. While much of this is technical, there is just enough here to help the average librarian understand the past and probable future of today's digital reference services.

Tenopir, Carol, "Should We Cancel Print?" *Library Journal,* September 1, 1999, pp. 138–142. A discussion primarily of types and numbers of full text journals online. The answer to the question: "Yes, but..." Ms. Tenopir wisely points out: "The decision should be made on a title-by-title basis."

PART III
INTERVIEW
AND SEARCH

CHAPTER SEVEN
THE REFERENCE INTERVIEW[1]

In Robert Musil's novel, *The Man Without Qualities,* there is a perfect example of the hedge as part of the reference interview. General Stumm wants to know "How do I find the most beautiful idea in the world?" He asks a librarian because, "this fellow lives among these millions of books, knows every one of them, knows where each one is, and so he ought to be able to help me."

The General does not want to put the question directly as it sounds like the beginning of a fairy story. "So in the end I resorted to a little stratagem. Oh, by the way, I began innocently, by the way, I mustn't forget to ask how it is you always manage to find the right book in all this endless collection...And sure enough, he began to purr and wriggle about and asked, very eagerly and helpfully, what it was in particular I was looking for...Oh, well, all sorts of things, I said, dragging it out. I mean, what question or what author are you interested in, General? he asked. Military history? Oh, no, not a bit of it. Something more like the history of peace...?" This goes on for three more pages and a baffled librarian and a helpful attendant finally enter the scene with the suggestion the General "should read Kant or something of the sort."[2]

---

[1]The less palpable literature of psychology and communications is heavy with citations on interview techniques. Most of this is either too technical to be of value to librarians or too gas filled to serve anyone except the author. Conversely, there are useful bits to be garnered for application to the reference interview in the library.

[2]Robert Musil, *The Man Without Qualities.* (London: Picador, 1979, Book 100, p. 193–198). Anyone interested in how librarians are pictured in fiction should see: Grant Burns, *Librarians in Fiction* (Jefferson, NC: McFarland, 1998). Here is a "detailed description of more

As a mediator between the General and the "millions of books" the librarian fails because, even after a lengthy conversation (reference interview) the General remains reluctant to ask the primary question.

In a familiar quote Gertrude Stein put two questions on her death bed, "What is the answer?" [Silence]. "In that case, what is the question?"[3] In one sense the average librarian dies at least several times a day and not once but many times responds to silence or confusion with "What's the question?"

Failure of the person putting the inquiry to make it clear to the librarian is the greatest road block to reference communication. And there are times, to be sure, when the librarian simply does not understand even the clearest question because of lack of knowledge about the language employed to put the query. Still, most of the "fault" is with the innocent individual seeking an answer.

This side of knowing where to find answers, there is nothing more important than mastering what some like to call the "reference interview." It is usually less formalized. The average "interview" is simply a matter of chatting, no matter how briefly, with another individual about his or her wants.[4] Most questions hardly need a long discussion between the librarian and the client. At the same time, the ever-growing masses of information require someone who can help the user find what is needed. The reference librarian as mediator is synonymous with the interview. Also, the interview represents a broader issue—that of communication between the librarian and the user. The librarian should be concerned with communication rather than with the particulars of a one-to-one interview.

One may discount the importance of the reference interview, but even critics realize it is important the librarian understand the patron's needs. It becomes more complex when the new technologies literally cry for explanation. The poor user who cannot get the terminal to function desperately needs to talk with the librarian. Conversation, inter-

---

than 350 novels…short stories, and plays teaching including at least one significant character employed in a library." The witty, descriptive annotations consider just how important and accurate the librarian's role is in the work of literature. See, too, "secondary sources" for several pages of citations on the same subject. Actual passages, some several pages in length, about librarians are found in Alan Taylor's *Long Overdue, A Library Reader* (London: Library Association, 1993). Both fiction and nonfiction is included such as poet librarian Philip Larkin's consideration of libraries as well as Kingsley Amis on renewing a library card.

[3]*Bartlett's Familiar Quotations,* 6th ed. Boston: Little, Brown, 1992, p. 627. This is from Alice B. Toklas' *What Is Remembered,* 1963.

[4]"Reference interview" is used throughout this chapter and this text as a convenience. Granted, the discussion rarely reaches such formal heights, but it is a convenient way of describing what some might simply call an exchange of queries, opinions and statements between one individual and another.

view, discussion—no matter how it is labeled—is as essential in today's library as any resource.

The reference interview, which takes place between the librarian with expert knowledge and the layperson in need of information, is a common form of communication. Obvious, to be sure, but consider the etymology of *communicate*. The word derives from the Latin to "impart," "participate." Other key meanings associated with communicate include "share," "convey," "reveal," "exchange," and "express." A person who fails to "participate" in a discussion is not communicating, unless it is in the sense of a nonverbal signal for disdain or stupidity, for instance. Communication does not necessarily have to be verbal.

A study produced for the Federal Department of Education found that managers think "attitude" is the most important factor, followed closely by "communication skills," when evaluating a potential employee. Much the same might be said in considering the reference interview. A successful interview implies an open attitude on the part of the librarian as well as sometimes extraordinary communication abilities.

Nothing quite ensures the success of the interview as much as experience. No article, no book, no bit of personal advice can be as instructive as an hour or two fielding questions. In the beginning weeks or months it is advisable to seek advice from others who have had the same experiences, the same frustrations. Not even the most practiced librarian is necessarily an expert on the interview, but at least she has been there and survived. Even the worse interviewer can give suggestions on how to succeed.

An Overview of the Interview

A discussion of the reference interview points up the true nature of reference service. It is an art form with different responses for different people, different situations. Granted, technology, logic, and a knowledge of history are involved; one does have to know information sources, understand the finer points of a given subject, and have an understanding of human foibles—including one's own. Still, when it comes to explaining how to conduct the reference interview or, in fact, when not to engage in conversation, there are no specific rules, no well-beaten paths, no completely sound response. Almost everything depends on the situation, the individuals, and the particular time and place.

Unfortunately or fortunately, depending on how one views such matters, the reference interview can be discussed, dissected, and deconstructed without making much difference for the individual involved in the process. Too often the rules and the suggestions are as broad as they are banal. Qualities that constitute the good interview tend to be inherent in the personality of the librarian who instinctively knows which move or word is appropriate, or whether withdrawal is suitable. A draconian personality is going to have problems with a well-meaning patron. Anyone ruffled by puzzles is not likely to be happy in the interview. On the other hand the self-confident, calm, and responsible librarian will search for opportunities to converse with people about their reference problems. Ostensibly one is born to be a good conversationalist, or not; but even the best and most self-sufficient interviewer can learn from those who have experienced the seduction and the horror of the interview. And that is what this chapter is about.

The average layperson is nervous about putting a question and/or uncertain how it will be received. Add to this a given amount of nervous anxiety by many people, particularly youngsters and those with limited understanding of information sources, and perfect paralysis is almost certain. The suffering individual will either fail to make the question clear, or put it in such terms that it has more to do with elephants than the real problem about putting down a lawn.

With typical American optimism, the usual response to patron hysteria is to advise the reference librarian to smile, extend a welcome hand and become a stand in for the welcome neighbor person. A friendly, welcoming continence will overcome the natural fear of the library and its hammering computers.

The smile, the pleasing personality does help, but don't do it unless it is natural. Otherwise the result often is similar to the welcome delight of the used car salesman or the funeral director.

Misunderstanding is the ghost, which haunts numerous reference interviews. A quick summary of how things can go wrong: Watch that definition: "I am looking for something on China." Real question: "I am looking for something on China, i.e., dinner services. Check that universal query: "Where can I find your books on art?" Real question: "I am trying to find information on Degas' interest in photography." Check that pronunciation: "Where do you keep the biographies?" Real question: "Where do you have the bibliographies shelved."

Why are so many overawed, overcome, and overstressed by a library? Answer: They have never been in a library before, or never in one this size, or never in one with so many computers. The librarian (actually the antagonistic circulation clerk) does not look friendly, or looks suspiciously congenial, or appears to be sleeping. Everyone seems busy, and unlikely to be interested in my inquiry about how to get my dog free of fleas. The librarian (this time the reference librarian) doesn't appear to have any knowledge of mousetraps, looks like Mrs. Grundy and no one to ask about safe sex, or seems to be as stupid or morose. Here is a special case of the person who knows so much she does not trust the librarian to answer any query except where is the library.

Whose fault is this evasive action on the part of the public? Possibly bad parents or drink. More likely, a past bad experience, or even reluctance to look for help. The latter attitude is prevalent among the same men who won't ask their way from X town to Y city for fear of disgust or laughter on the part of the service station operator. Actually, there are as many explanations as boring articles and tracts on the subject. The only real pattern is in two parts: First, when talking about readers and the inevitable mix-up, misunderstanding and mish mash of queries, the pattern is more anecdotal than universal. Second, inevitably the person talking or writing the treatise is a reference librarian without much sense of humor, and is easily annoyed. He should have gone into administration.

The satisfaction of the reference interview is its uncertainly. If every person was like every other person, self assured, pleasing to the eye and extremely affable and intelligent, as well as articulate, the distress of reference work might disappear. At the same time, bid good-bye to the capricious and the prodigious challenge to the librarian's imagination and diplomatic skills. Install a computer and take up another profession. The irresistible charm of the reference interview is the glorious public.

WHO NEEDS AN ANSWER?

To interview or not to interview more often than not depends on the individual's needs rather than on the type of overt question. Following are examples of the types of people who do or do not need assistance and an interview.

1. The individual who requires only a minimum of help, often to find the copying machine or catalog, and who is in the library primarily for pleasure, not for study. This person rarely, if ever, needs the assistance of a reference librarian.

2. The same person confronted with a computer, which may not be understood. Even a skilled hacker often is not at home with the databases available at the terminal. More and more reference interviews center around the computer and its mysteries.

3. The "moderate" information seeker who may have a question once or twice a year about a practical measure such as how to find stock market quotations or how to lay a tile floor. Here a reference librarian may be of assistance, if only in evaluating the probable level of difficulty of the material to satisfy the reader.

4. The student who, at any age, is involved with finding just the right amount and type of information to complete a paper, prepare a speech, or pass a test. An interview usually is desirable.

5. The parent, friend, brother, or sister asking a reference question for someone else is not unusual. The most common is the father or mother looking for information to help a recalcitrant child complete a school assignment. This type of query requires somewhat different approaches, e.g., one is dealing with an adult, but the information sought is for, say, a 10-year-old.

6. The serious researcher who needs specialized materials as well as specialized assistance in locating data for business, scientific or scholarly reasons. An interview is a major consideration, although in a few cases the researcher may wish to conduct the search (manual or online) without assistance other than directional help.

Satisfactory Service

Just how satisfactory is the reference interview in a library? The questions below set the stage for understanding what the average individual requires:

1. How difficult was it for you to find someone to help you, and how long did it take before a reference librarian had the time to discuss the problem with you?

2. Did you feel comfortable, or did you feel like you were imposing on the time and the good nature of the librarian?

3. Did the librarian seem to take an interest in your problem?

4. How much time and effort did the librarian take to understand precisely what you were looking for, as well as the type of information you needed.

5. At this point, did the librarian find what you needed, or did the librarian indicate how you could find the data yourself? Which of these two approaches do you prefer, that is, do you want an answer, or do you want someone to help you find what is needed?

6. Did the library have what you needed? Was there enough of it, and was it in the form you required, that is, a book rather than an article, an online citation rather than a photocopy of a print index page, and so on.

7. If the material you needed was not in the library, what steps were taken to help you either find alternative sources or obtain the material from another source?

8. Did the librarian follow up and ask if you needed more or less data? Were you asked if what you received was satisfactory for your particular purposes? Was the user encouraged, as a matter of fact, to continue to ask the librarian for clarification and help?

There is another aspect to this, and that concerns just how helpful the librarian is to the client in using the new technologies. Many people, and particularly those who realize help from reference librarians is limited, embrace online reference sources.

Is advice on which keys to push, or which clicks of the mouse are necessary, really a reference interview? The question is important for three pragmatic reasons: (1) Does the individual really understand how to get from the question to, say, an abstract on the terminal monitor? (2) If the individual has knowledge of the technology of searching, is there an equal appreciation of the various levels of searching sophistication? (3) Will the individual be able to objectively determine whether the first two or three citations printed out or viewed are what is needed?

If the answer is no to any of these three questions, then the reference interview, or some form of basic instruction and assistance is required. Where an online search is needed, the reference interview usually is built into the process—at least where the librarian is the mediator. Rapid developments of online searching by laypersons may seem to point to the elimination of the middle person. That is true when only an undifferentiated citation or two is required in a relatively short amount of time. It is *not* true when discrimination is the object.

THE REFERENCE INTERVIEW—STEP BY STEP

Years of experience, volumes of articles, and numerous books prescribe certain definite steps in the reference interview. Although it is a highly individualized form of communication, there are certain methods that many find useful.

The rule of the successful interview is in four parts: (1) Obtain the greatest, most precise information about what is needed. (2) Understand at what level the material is needed and how much is required. (3) Complete the interview, and arrive at the necessary key data, in as short a period as possible. (4) Maintain a good relationship with the person asking the question.

It is absolutely imperative that the librarian has all the facts necessary to answer the question. How is this done at the average reference interview? Three or four points will help: (1) Ask enough questions to make certain the user's question is understood in dimensions of what is or what is not required. (2) Try to keep the patron on the verbal track and do not let distractions interrupt the clear goal of clarifying the question. (3) Where appropriate use open-ended questions which encourage the user to expand on needs rather than respond with "yes" or "no." (4) Be sure to talk the language understood by the user. On one hand this may be simple street talk, on another it may be a conversation filled with technical jargon. (5) Where there is any doubt, be sure to ask questions about, for example, the length of the required response or the need to consult books or journals or both.

No question should be dismissed as trivial, soporific, or banal. There are a few occasions when a question does not deserve attention, although the librarian should make an effort to be polite or at least not to attempt to strangle the person on the other side of the desk. For example: "Do men who habitually wear a hat increase the probability of baldness?" "Can you find a book which will confirm that somewhere in a field in Northern New York State there used to be a sign saying 'Please do not throw stones at this notice?'" "Where can I find a biography of either Beevis or Buthead?" Actual questions, mind you; but can even these be dismissed as trivial or banal? There are times when the librarian must make critical decisions without help from textbooks.

1. What is the Question?

First, foremost, and always the purpose of the reference interview, even if it only takes a moment, is to clarify the question.

Infinite pains should be taken to understand the question. This implies, too, an equal effort to understand the needs of the individual and how much or how little information is required to satisfy the question.

Experienced reference librarians know that the original question put to them by a user is rarely the *real* question. Different people, with equally different needs, phrase their queries in different ways. The librarian who has a tolerance for ambiguities and vagueness will follow a simple, direct route to a possible answer. For example, when the query is vague, the librarian may not try to get more information through the interview, but will look for a basic broad subject approach which is likely to meet the needs of the user.

In a school or academic library setting, the normal reason for asking a question is related to an assignment. The student wishes to know where to locate a reference work or needs serious help finding material for a paper or talk. Teachers will want more refined sources, although essentially they are in quest of the same types of answers.

The greatest variety and type of queries are put to the public librarian. Clients are not only students and teachers, but laypersons, of different ages and backgrounds who may wish to gather information for practical purposes. Questions may range from how-to and self-help problems to business, scientific, or research decisions.

A distinct advantage of the e-mail request for information is the necessity for the user to write out what is needed, much as in a person-to-person interview with a librarian before an online search. The person with the question uses terms familiar to herself or himself and, if a subject expert, terms employed in the subject. Given this type of specific information, the librarian usually is able to make up for the lack of interpersonal communication. Also, of course, there is nothing to prevent the librarian from phoning or using e-mail to clarify this or that point.

2. Question Summary

In any interview, no matter how short, it is wise to summarize the question or the facets of the question. The client may then correct or modify the librarian's response. For example, "If I understand you correctly...Let's be sure I understand you correctly...In summary, you wish..." All these are openers for the librarian who then goes on to state the query as succinctly as possible. If the interview is lengthy or complex, it is wise to occasionally offer such summary statements to help clarify matters.

The art of restating and paraphrasing the main points of the interview, in order to achieve a maximum of mutual clarity, is difficult. It requires not only that one listen, but also that one use memory and common sense. The process will fail if the librarian too often summarizes, repeats, or forgets what went before.

3. Open and Closed Questions

In the analysis of the reference interview, one is confronted with the open and closed question. The *open* query is general and one which begins with a broad topic. The respondent replies in his or her own words. Example: "What do you consider the primary elements of a good reference interview?"

The *closed* question is restrictive and normally calls for an equally specific reply. Example: "Do you think that the reference interview is useful or not useful?"

One talks of open and closed questions both in terms of the person asking the question and the librarian's response. The patron may begin a discussion with a closed question: "Do you have Henry Smith's *Tropical Flowers*?" "Where is the *Readers' Guide*?"

The closed question may be answered in one of two ways. Either take the query at face value and locate the specific item or, in the reference interview, attempt to change it over to an open query. For example, the person looking for the *Readers' Guide* can be told it is on the second table from the left. End of interview. Changed to an open query, the question would go a step further. "Can I help you find something specific?" or "There are other general indexes which may help, too. Do you have a specific question?"

Also, where online searches are available, the librarian may wish to point out that the quest for material in the *Readers Guide* may be had electronically. If the user is interested, the librarian is then launched into another set of questions. The first is simply: "Are you familiar with the online system?" Here a "yes" answer should be opened up because there is much more than a yes or no reply to that type of query.

As much depends on the methods of the librarian as on how the queries are labeled. A friendly, open person can ask a series of closed questions, but by her manner imply that the user is free to counter not only with answers, but with questions, too. Someone less skilled may bring the interview to a disastrous end with closed questions, but have no better luck with the open-query approach.

No matter how the gambit is analyzed, the best advice in the reference interview is to turn a tight yes and no discussion into a relaxed conversation about the topic. If this can be done with either closed or open approaches, then that is fine. The result is what is important, not how one classifies the questions.

4. Isolating and Correcting the Question

The librarian next must be able to classify the type of question being asked. The exact nature of the query may be brought out by a few courteous questions. For example, if a user asks for airplane magazines, the librarian might point to the rack, or might respond with: "The airplane periodicals are over there, but we could give you more specific information about airplanes in some other online or print sources we have. Do you want anything in particular, or do you just want to look at the airplane magazines? Some of them are available on the Net."

5. Essential Information

When the question is clear, the last piece of essential information is whether the query needs a quick, easy answer, or requires a number of complex steps which may take from 5 to 10 minutes or longer. One judges this, at least after a bit of experience, almost intuitively. For example, when the librarian is asked the birth date of Mathias Grunewald, the answer may be found quickly in any general or art encyclopedia in print or online. (In this type of query, though, usually it is faster to use print.) The same query becomes complex when the person wants details on the painter's work, the *Isenheim Altarpiece*.

Beyond determining if the question requires a single, quick answer, or more of a search, the librarian wants to learn:

a. What kind of information is needed? For example, if the query is about flying saucers, does the user want a definition, a history, an illustration, a news story, a confirmation—or what?

b. How much is needed—a simple fact, a book, or a mass of material? How much information does the user already have about the topic? (It helps to know this in order to avoid duplication.)

c. How is the information going to be used—for a talk, to answer an idle question, as a beginning for research?

d. What degree of sophistication is required—a beginning article or an advanced monograph?

e. How much time does the user wish to spend (1) finding the information and (2) using the information? Obviously, if each is a short amount of time, then one ends with a small amount of essential data.

f. When is the information needed? Is there a definite deadline?

6. Wrong Clues

Often the patron may confuse the issue and give the wrong clues about the information needed. For example, in seeking an author, the user may have the name spelled incorrectly, or in seeking the source of quotation, the user may misquote the passage. The librarian must then hope that the quotation is accurate at least in terms of subject matter so that a subject search may be launched. The librarian may recognize an error in information, a wrong spelling, a misconceived notion about a subject. He or she may then suggest other possibilities, while trying to discover, through courteous cross-questioning, another approach to the query. Often a single clue obtained this way will give enough information to correct the mistake in the query.

When working with students, the librarian sometimes finds it helpful to ask to see the teacher's question in writing or to see an outline of the material. The librarian may have enough personal knowledge of the subject to make mental corrections of user errors and to go on with the search for materials.

INTERVIEW TECHNIQUES

Everyone has his or her own personal approaches to the reference interview and, if they work, this is fine. On the other hand there is a consensus that certain attitudes and feelings can be useful, even for the most experienced librarian. Among the most frequently mentioned:

1. Listening

Listening is a major consideration in the interview. Nothing is more important than to pause, listen, and look attentive. However, doing so is *not* all that simple, and aside from making a genuine effort to listen, the reference librarian should be aware of a few of the subtle, but vital, aspects of the process.

There is a difference between *passive* listening and *active* listening. The former requires no skill. One simply lets the other person talk, interjecting at reasonable times an affirmative sign that one is indeed listening. Active listening at the reference desk includes not only hearing what the other person says, but evaluating and summarizing the message so that it can be acted on.

2. Approachability

One circumstance, which is neither special nor unique, but all-important in the reference interview, is the matter of approachability. The librarian should appear willing to give assistance.

Essentially one must be sensitive to the needs of others, open to relaxed and free discussion about a problem, and able to overcome sometimes subtle conflicts between oneself and the person asking the questions. One should have a strategy for dealing with the arrogant and shy persons. In order to do this, one need not be a saint but only aware of the positive and negative aspects of one's own communication patterns. This can be learned in numerous ways, from workshops, to maintaining a diary of a day's activities, to asking users what they consider the positive and negative aspects of a given interview.

The personality of the librarian is the major variable in any discussion of the reference interview and the larger matters of communication and approachability. Although there is no definitive superperson profile available against which to measure the average librarian's degree of personality and communication skills, common sense tells one that the ideal is somewhere between the stereotype (little old gent in tennis shoes) and the twenty-first-century information robot. Short of intensive psychoanalytical help, someone who is naturally shy is not going to be the best reference librarian, any more than the person who is confident to the point of arrogance. The average "social animal" will do nicely, particularly when he or she brings a glimmer of self-understanding to the mastering of the reference interview. Also, recognize that exposure of personality is fraught with danger for both the patron and the librarian. That danger cannot be avoided, but it should be recognized.

There is even a test to take to determine one's approachability. The test, somewhat tongue in cheek, asks the respondent to gauge such things as facial expression and methods of handling negative comments. One of the 29 test queries might be enough to reveal a librarian's true personality in relation to reference work: "Do you look toward each potential library user as a: (1) new adventure? (2) learning experience? (3) pain in the neck? (4) service which must be rendered?"

A good interviewer will keep out of the foreground—a lesson all too few professional interviewers of celebrities master. Fortunately, it is a better-understood maxim by reference librarians. The librarian should know as much about the subject as possible, but plainly try to shake off the urge to let the person with the question recognize the depth of his or her knowledge.

3. Verbal and Nonverbal Cues

Nonverbal cues are obvious in many situations. Gregariousness or being overly shy are apparent to almost anyone, and when either is recognized the reference librarian acts accordingly in the structure of the reference interview. Conversely, one can become too confident and assume it is possible to read subtle clues from an expression or gesture. For example, people who gesture a lot and look you in the eye are perceived to be dominant. But this is not the case. It's actually the reverse. Studies indicate most books on teaching nonverbal cues are worthless or, at best, of minimal assistance in the reference interview. None is absolutely required reading, and the librarian should do only what is natural. To act from a sense of duty rather than a sense of friendly interest is to undermine the whole process.

Gestures should be kept to a minimum, and one should not mimic what the user is doing, for example, putting a hand to chin when the user does so, and so forth. The tone of voice may also be considered a nonverbal cue, and it is wise to keep it even, although a little excitement when one makes a discovery is useful. Attempt to mask irritation or downright anger by keeping the proverbial "straight face," and, again, an even tone of voice. Look interested, and be interested, in what the person is saying. Do not turn away when it seems time to end the interview. Let the user make that decision, although subtle guidance is acceptable.

Other aspects of the nonverbal in the reference interview are obvious to almost anyone who engages in a normal conversation with a friend or even with a stranger at a party. A smile is a welcome, but a frown is enough to turn away all but the totally insensitive. One talks in a relaxed manner and does not rush headlong into the discussion or insert awkward stops so the other person is not sure whether to fill the space or to be quiet.

4. Dress

A hazardous, although subconsciously employed method of placing people in well-understood social and behavioral slots is to evaluate them in
terms of dress. Presumably, a person dressed as though from the pages of
a fashion magazine is more likely to be more receptive to intelligent
conversation and assistance than the same-aged person dressed like a
refugee from an MTV rock-and-roll band. Add to this judgment such
details as body odor, posture, height, and weight, and one becomes a kind
of amateur Sherlock Holmes. Fortunately, too many times the evaluation is wrong. Unless the librarian is omniscient a safe rule is to evaluate individuals in terms of their questions, not by the cut of their clothes.

Ideal Behavior

What is the ideal behavior of the perfect reference librarian? First,
include a quick, interested smile when the person approaches the desk.
Make eye contact, but do not try to stare the person down. Try to keep
gestures to a minimum and speak in a relaxed tone. Throughout the
interview, speak, listen, and clarify and above all else give the person
asking the question your full attention.

Generally, it is not appropriate to consciously use nonverbal gestures.
Still, in the course of a truly friendly interview a bit is appropriate. Again,
though, much depends upon the librarian and the patron. For example, an
admiring gaze will indicate to the patron the question is one the librarian
has longed to hear for years. Other appropriate cues, the tilt of the head,
a brief look of fascinated approval of the query and the way the person is
putting it to you, and a smile are guaranteed to establish the proper atmosphere. Where appropriate, the arm touch may give the person putting the
question the feeling that you are paying close and careful attention.

On the other hand another school considers any nonverbal cue a
danger, a bad sign, and certainly not in the best of taste. The librarian
should be approachable, but make no effort to alter his or her personality to suit the situation.

Primarily be yourself. If this self fits into the rhythm of the reference
interview, you are born to the profession. If at the end of a brief conversation, people rush away from you in horror, it might be better to turn to
another part of the library, possibly administration. A dash of humor and
a bit of perspective are the best preparations for the reference interview.

INTERVIEW PROBLEMS

In any discussion of communication in general, and the reference interview in particular, the participants are likely to split into two or three
groups. One is firmly convinced that most of the rules can be learned

through proper courses, workshops, study, and the like. This is a persuasive argument for anyone who believes in education, but indications are that more lip service is paid to this than to any real effort on the part of teachers, students, or working librarians to implement it. The normal approach is to dismiss the interpersonal communication experts with a shrug and point out the attitudes of the second group: that the interview is more of an art than a science.

The third group admits that both sides in the communication controversy are right; that the interview is both an art and a science. While this author is more inclined to bend toward the interview as "a performing art," this is not to discount the importance of a clear understanding of the research and findings connected with interpersonal communication.

If an interview is in order, and the subject appears to be relatively complex and requires equally complex sources, it is best to give a few moments over to friendly conversation about the subject as well as the individual's need for materials. This is both relaxing and revealing. It tends to put the user at ease and the end result may be a more cohesive statement of the question.

Interview Interactions

Most people who approach a reference librarian with a question expect to like the librarian, or at a minimum, not dislike the individual who is about to help them with a problem. Students in particular tend to be no more than indifferent, but even the most blasè can be at least focused if the query is more than a "where" or "what" ready-reference or directional query. The secret of rapport is the attitude of the librarian. One should appear relaxed, yet secure in the knowledge that an answer is a relatively easy matter. Interest and at least a dash of sympathy help, as does the occasional smile, nod and word of encouragement.

Even brief encounters require another person, and often the individual putting the question, to shape an interaction. Everything from dress, age, and tone of voice may encourage good or bad feelings by the librarian. While attention to both verbal and nonverbal cues are necessary, the wise librarian maintains a certain distance and neutrality. If the student, for example, complains about the "stupid assignment" (a common comment in all types of libraries), the librarian might comment: "Well, that can be a real problem," without actually evaluating the quality of the assignment.

It is not always easy to show even a shadow of empathy with an individual who, for a good reason or not, simply reminds you of figures from a Bosch painting or an MTV commercial. Here one of two moves is appropriate. Either shift the person to another librarian who may be a trifle more sympathetic, or respond as openly and as positively as appropriate. Unfortunately the world is made up of some people who are moderately or completely antisocial, and yet need assistance. It is moments like that which test the librarian's true professional self.

Difficult People

Otherwise calm librarians sometimes panic at the idea of the reference interview. There is no reason to be nervous. It is a ripping good exchange, which tends to be more pleasant than painful. On the other side of the reference desk it may be a different matter.

The difficult patron takes many forms. Still, there are common characteristics of types:

1. *Indefinite.* "I want something on whales" or "What's the value of property in this town?" Generalities, vague concepts, and sometimes just plain lack of intelligence accounts for the indefinite question. Conversely, patrons may be indefinite because they are not sure what they are seeking, more or less asking. At any rate, the best approach is to turn from open to closed questions. Force the user to focus. "Whales? Is this for a class paper?" "Yes." Do you want to know about all whales, or just those in the Pacific?" Whatever method is used, at the end the librarian should have a more specific notion of what is required.

2. *Anger and hostility.* Here the individual may be as angry with the need to ask the question (for a child, for a paper in school, for a mistake) as with the librarian for being there to reply. Tone of voice, attitude, and type of question give this away without much need for analysis. The best way to handle this type of hostility, at least in the reference situation, is to ignore it as much as possible. Also, one should take plenty of time to reassure the individual that the librarian is there to help, not to do battle.

3. *Lack of focus.* The questioner may be confused and unable to focus on what is really wanted. Unless a person is suffering from dementia, this may simply be another case of feeling indefinite about what is wanted. More likely, though, the person lacks a command of the language in general and a specific subject area in particular. The librarian should try to formulate the question in easy-to-understand language. At the same time the librarian should indicate there is plenty of time and the nervous user should relax enough to have a gentle conversation about needs.

Those are only three of scores of what might be termed descriptors of difficult patrons. Everyone has a favorite complaint. Possibly the worst is the totally removed individual who has no sense of other people, who believes the librarian is there to serve, no matter how foolish or long-winded the question. This type requires patience, and according to some librarians, a help to the exit.

Talkers, who refuse to listen either to themselves or to the librarian, are another common headache. Normally, too, the fast talkers are interested in everything except the question. Here, again, the way out is to try to rephrase the query with a closed question. "It seems to me you need something on automobile registration?" or "Am I mistaken in thinking you are really looking for a guide to automobile registration?"

Online

In the online reference interview, the role of mediator is as important as any assumed by the librarian. It is impossible to play the role unless a reference interview, with its follow-up, takes place. Those who argue that the reference interview at a computer is not necessary, or moribund, or even dead, are obviously unaware of the rapid developments in information which make that interview more important today than it ever was in the past.

One may applaud the triumph of the electronic network that brings the word of one person (i.e., through bulletin boards, e-mail, electronic journals, newsletters, etc.) to another without interference of a middle person (i.e., an editor) but a major difficulty remains. What is useful, marginally useful, and a total waste of time? Furthermore, among that which appears to be useful, what is current, objective (where necessary), accurate, and specific to a need? Out of the piles of printouts in any hour of a 24-hour period what is worthwhile, even entertaining to read? The person is entirely on her or his own. It may take more time to wade through the material than one has patience or hours in a day.

Some believe everyone has the right to publish, say, and read or view what is out there. One may publish anonymously or pseudonymously. The responsibility for putting out information is that of the individual. The catch of this information boiling up from the bottom is twofold: First, the responsibility to select and choose shifts from the publisher, the editor, the author to the reader. Second, lacking any checks on information, how can the reader know what to read?

The advantages to having someone filter out the garbage or the material of no interest to a particular individual is obvious. For example, newspapers, magazines, and books are directed to specific audiences. This process relies on editors (i.e., mediators) skilled enough to recognize what is needed by X or Y.

Experience teaches the reader which magazine, newspaper, or for that matter television broadcast is of appeal. The individual may discount a good deal of what is printed or reported visually and orally, may even mistrust the media as a whole, but will inevitably, at a minimum, rely on mediators to filter out what is not important.

Need for information mediation is apparent. Recognition of this may come slowly to the library profession, but not to people anxious to make money from the process. A partial solution is to develop software that will filter out what is not needed. All major and some lesser-known search machine firms are at work on such projects. Some are in place, as an e-mail screen to put priority tags on the messages and a program to select by subject certain types of news stories for the computer reader.

SUGGESTED READING

Baker, Lynda M. and Judith J. Field, "Reference Success: What has Changed Over the Past Ten Years?" *Public Libraries,* January/February, 2000. The authors consider the history of the reference interview over the last years of the twentieth century. They find "little has changed. Yesterday's practices are no longer sufficient in today's information environment. Reference staff members must strive to develop more client-oriented service." Another interesting point of the study: "Our clients perceive that all information is obtainable through the Internet."

Isaacson, David, "Freudian Dream Interpretation and the Reference Interview," *Reference & User Services Quarterly,* Spring, 1998, pp. 269–272. Deconstructing the reference interview via Dr. Freud, a working reference librarian painfully explains the benefits of delving into the user's dreams to find out what really is wanted. Sessions take place in the privacy of the librarian's office. Only a careful reading of this major breakthrough will explain why constantly answering queries may drive librarians themselves into the arms of a Freudian.

Jennerich, Elaine and Edward, *The Reference Interview as a Creative Art,* 2nd ed., Englewood, CO: Libraries Unlimited, 1997. A handy summary of the basic points to follow in the reference interview, this is geared for all types and sizes of libraries. The stress is on the practical aspects of dealing with people who usually have problems making their needs known.

Owen, Tim, *Success at the Enquiry Desk,* 2nd ed. London: Library Association, 1998. A practical guide by a working librarian on what to do and what not to do in the typical reference interview. While published for an English audience, most of the advice is applicable equally to Americans. Common sense dominates.

Richardson, John, "Understanding the Reference Transaction," *College & Research Libraries,* May, 1999, pp. 211–222. After a definition of the reference interview, the author suggests an analysis of the "question-answering process...(with) fifteen functions requirements of the process." There are diagrams to assist the reader.

Ross, Catherine, Sheldrick and Patricia Dewdney, "Negative Closure, Strategies and Counter-Strategies in the Reference Transaction," *Reference & User Services Quarterly,* vol. 38, no. 2, 1998. A study of how reference librarians do battle with users. The latter wants an answer, the former is more concerned with ending the interview and getting on with the next question. The two experienced authors end with "recommendations" which are hard headed and sensible. They begin with "Let's stop kidding ourselves...."

CHAPTER EIGHT
RULES OF THE SEARCH

A mong trained reference librarians there is a simple formula. "It takes 20 percent of the time to get 80 percent of the information, and 80 percent of the time to get the other 20 percent." As one experienced librarian puts it "The question is: Are there better uses for the time being saved in being less than perfect. Successful [librarians] use their time for achieving priorities, not perfection."[1] The question: What is one librarian's notion of "perfection" and another's of "priorities"?

Simply put, there really is no formula for the perfect search. On the other hand, experience indicates certain truths about searching. In reference services there are two basic types of searches, both dictated by format. The first is the manual search, or the search of printed materials. The second is the computer-assisted search. The searches have much in common, and it is with the general rules of searching this chapter is most concerned. Once these are mastered, the librarian may use print, digital databases or serendipity to find an answer, to conclude a successful search.

Finding the needed information is more important than the process. And the process varies. One librarian may favor a type of "guerrilla warfare;" another may be more comfortable with a considered, logical plan; a third may use both approaches.

The search is an integral part of the reference interview. Despite efforts to analyze, chart, and teach by numbers, it can be as subjective and intuitive a process as the interview itself, and just as complex.

---

[1]Edward Stear, "Success Through Heretical Thinking," *Online,* March/April, 1997, p. 66.

An analysis of the search reveals that it may take one or two different, sometimes simultaneous, paths. The first concerns the thought processes of the librarian. The second concerns the actual steps the librarian takes once the thought processes have been triggered. For example, some searching is almost automatic in that the librarian knows from practice where to look. But sometimes considerable thought may be given to the question and to the source of its answer. Once the mental process has evolved, the actual search is then a matter of locating materials in given forms. Obviously, even the simplest thought process requires a follow-through to a source and an answer.

Given the necessity to concentrate on basics, the particulars of online searching are left to other texts, other articles. At the same time, the general approach concludes with a section on the basics of digital searching. For now, though, let's consider what makes a good searcher a true professional.

Attributes of Skilled Searchers

What makes a reference librarian a skilled searcher? More important, what attributes contribute to the ability to determine what is "best" or "better" information in a particular situation? What, in fact, determines success or failure as an information mediator, the person between the mass of data and the specific needs of an individual?

In general, the advice of a survivor of the Donner party (where most where killed by storms as they tried to cross the Sierra Nevada in 1846–1847) seems applicable: "Never take a cutoff, and hurry along as fast as you can."

Shortcuts and cutoffs in a storm, as in a search, can be useful, but normally they lead to disaster. It is far best to approach the search in a methodical fashion. The ideal search expert will have: (1) An understanding of details with an appreciation of logic and be blessed with a fine to excellent memory. (2) Enthusiasms and interest in what the search is all about. (3) An understanding of individual needs, which is another way of saying the person should have fine communication skills. (4) Self-esteem and confidence. This is important when the librarian comes to make decisions about what is or is not needed by the individual. The person with the question must sense that the librarian is knowledgeable. (5) Finally, an ability, like the survivors of the Donner party, to be able to admit a wrong trail was taken, and it would be best to go back and begin again. An able searcher is willing to admit an error and has the ability to make equally quick changes.

Aside from personal qualities, the individual must have: (1) A firm knowledge of a subject field(s). This implies constant reading, constant attention to new developments, and these days constant conversations, often over the Internet or similar networks, with others in the field. Only a subject expert—the librarian—can deal with confidence with another subject expert—the user. Here one is talking about users who are doing research, not students who may have wandered in from a recent class assignment. Both deserve similar attention, but the expert will make more demands. (2) A firm knowledge of technology—particularly where the search is conducted using electronic databases. Experience is most important. Constant reading and double-checking on new developments is equally necessary.

SEARCH STRATEGY

The search strategy a librarian employs depends primarily upon the nature of the inquiry. In its broadest terms, the inquiry and the search may be divided into two types. (1) If the inquirer seeks specific data, as in the case of a ready-reference query, the goal is predicted, and the search strategy can be laid out in a methodical, step-by-step fashion. A standardized pattern of routine movements can be prescribed, the purpose being to include, or exclude, certain alternatives. (2) A more in-depth inquiry, as in the case of a specific search-or-research query, requires an investigative type of strategy. Faith in routine must be replaced by faith in insight.

Consider the difficulties of the librarian assisting an individual to find information. Much of the search strategy is conducted by the librarian at a subconscious level; for example, while the interview is progressing, the librarian is matching needs with sources—rejecting some, accepting others. The librarian's fundamental effort is to match the query and the library system's resources.

The search process generally begins with an interview, no matter how short. Once the librarian has received the message and has understood the question, if only tentatively, the next logical step is to match that question with the source(s) most likely to yield the answer. If someone asks for information on Tom Jones and knows this Jones is serving in Congress, the librarian sifts through a series of mental signals: Congressman, important personage—*Who's Who In America*. If the question concerns the literary figure Tom Jones, the signals are different: literature, Henry Fielding—encyclopedia for Fielding; *Masterplots* for summary of *Tom Jones,* and eighteenth-century literary criticism. If the reference is to the singer, then the signal is to an appropriate index, which may be anything from an Internet search to more specific music sources and *Biography and Genealogy Master Index.* And so the process goes. Matching the question with the logical source is as complex as the needs of the user. Depending on the sophistication of the user's needs, one source may be used, or a more complex source, or even several sources may be needed.

The advent of numerous electronic databases and abstracting services has made the task somewhat easier in that one does not have to dash about the library seeking likely reference books. Still, sitting before a terminal and monitor, the same question remains: Which source is the best for the needed information? That question separates the professional from the amateur, and particularly young people who think no such question is necessary. Simply enter a phrase, word or name and let the computer do the rest, or so they firmly believe. Sometimes this works. Often it does not. But inevitably it is less satisfactory, both in terms of time and an answer, than knowing precisely where to go.

Search Process

Whether one turns to a printed almanac or an online full-text abstracting service, the basic principles of the search process are much the same:

1. The query is first analyzed and clarified through the reference interview. One determines the type of question asked, the parameters to be established (i.e., purpose, scope, time span, amount of material, level of material, etc.), and the source(s) or system(s) where the necessary information is likely to be found.

2. In the case of the majority of ready-reference queries, a source usually comes readily to mind. The source is consulted, and the answer is given.

3. In the case of search-and-research queries (and more difficult ready-reference questions), it is necessary to consider numerous sources. At this point, a likely source is usually one of two major possibilities:

a. Bibliographies, indexes, or the library catalog are consulted. These are not sources of answers in themselves but access points to answers. Thanks to online databases this is by and large the most favored path by today's reference librarian.

b. Form or subject sources are referred to, from standard reference books to magazines, newspapers, vertical-file material, and a given subject area on the shelves. In most situations, because the searcher is not entirely sure of the avenues for an answer, (a) will be a first choice as a source.

4. Generalizations about both the manual and the computer-aided search are in order. Where bibliographies, the catalog, and so forth, are to be searched it is best to determine likely subject headings or primary words, which may be located in an electronic database search. A helpful aid at this point is to list key words most likely to be appropriate for such a search. A choice of action must then be made. The searcher may

a. Broaden the search in terms of the subject headings and/or key words.

b. Narrow the search.

c. Select more specific, or less specific, subject headings, or key words.

d. Find more appropriate terms.

5. Through steps 3 to 4, there should be some type of dialogue between the user and the librarian. Or the dialogue may follow later when likely material is gathered. At any rate, adjustments in terms of which data can be used, which are peripheral, and which are useless, must be made throughout the total search process.

6. At this point other decisions must be made:

a. A judgment has to be made as to relevance of the data to the specific question put by the user.

b. If there is too little material, the librarian must decide in what order to search other sources.

c. If nothing can be found, the librarian must decide whether to try new or modified approaches, to give up, or to suggest to the user other resources (i.e., other libraries, interlibrary loan).

d. In any case, the librarian must determine how much more time can be given to answering the question.

Were the search process always this neat, the problem would only be one of finding specific sources or entry points to those sources. In practice, however, the librarian may decide that a given reference book or online service has the answer but not be able to find it; turn to another similar title but not find it; go to a bibliography but not find it; go to an online index, find it, but then discover the articles are too broad for the user; return to the index but not find additional materials; go to another print index—and on and on until the patience of either the librarian or the user has worn out. In most situations this does not happen, but it can.

THE SEARCH AND PROBLEM SOLVING

As stated before, the librarian is subconsciously clarifying questions and locating probable sources of information. In the average reference situation, each of these steps may be going on almost simultaneously. At any rate, rare is the librarian who consciously diagrams each step and moves neatly from square to square. Once the circuit of matching question with possible sources is closed, however, the librarian must have a strategy for finding the information itself. The strategy may involve no more than taking out a volume of an encyclopedia or looking up information in an online index or in the library catalog. On the other hand, it may involve a more extensive search that leads to dead ends and frequent returns to "Go."

The search process is strongly governed by the objectives and the philosophy of the reference service. If the service is minimum, that is, primarily one of helping the user find citations and possible sources, the librarian's search is really directional. The user will be advised to search X index or Y reference book or to look under P subject heading in the catalog. The user may even be counseled to try another department in the library or another library. These days the user may simply be urged to sit down at the computer terminal and try to figure out how to find a citation from an index online. Younger people, accustomed to such things, are delighted. Older people (say over twenty-one years of age) may be completely baffled. Even the minimalist reference librarian may have to help the user get started.

If the service is middling or moderate, the librarian will go to the index, catalog, or reference source and help the user find what is desired. If the service is maximum, the librarian will collect the information and follow through by gathering added citations and sources until satisfied that the user has enough material to answer the question. These days, too, maximum service means helping the user with the computer search, either through instruction or actually securing the citations for the user, or both.

Automatic Retrieval

Memory is one of the vital keys to a reference librarian's success. The librarian's memory may be filled with facts, but what is really significant is that the librarian has the ability to recall a specific reference work in terms of how it matches the question at hand. Librarians are capable of a considerable amount of this "automatic retrieval" of information. The automatic retrieval operates whenever the reference librarian knows (1) the solution or answers to a specific question or problem or (2) has an unvarying, simple rule for finding the answer.

In the case of (1), this may be no more complex than knowing the name of the mayor of the city or the population of the state. Obviously, there is no need to consult any reference aid except memory. In the case of (2), which occurs more frequently in daily reference service, the librarian knows a simple operation or procedure that is guaranteed to find an answer.

Both basic processes, memory and learning procedures, serve the reference librarian as they serve all of us, but for a reference librarian, learning the procedures is essential. And the procedures are more complicated than mastering the multiplication table. Some examples will suffice:

1. The same search procedure can be learned and used time and time again to find the answers to questions about prize winners. The technique for learning the Pulitzer Prize winner for 1999 is the same as that for finding the name of the Nobel Prize winner for 1989.

2. Once one learns to find the distance between New York and San Francisco, it is easy to apply the same procedure in finding the distance between San Francisco and Tokyo.

3. The procedures for finding the first line of a verse using "love" is the same as that for finding the first line of a verse using "hate."

4. The procedure for finding X book in the library is the same as that for finding Y book. Mastering a given search engine online will be faster than turning to one at random, or whatever is offered.

The same techniques or set of rules (sometimes referred to in the literature as "algorithms"), once learned, will automatically generate answers to the same set of questions or queries. The answers can be looked up or retrieved by what are essentially the same automatic techniques used when one masters any set of rules, from those for multiplication to those for boiling an egg.

Much—possibly too much—of reference work is no more difficult than any other automatic process, given these essentially automatic methods of deriving answers for certain types of questions. The librarian simply masters a group of rules and equivalent sources for finding answers. This becomes a subconscious process, almost a reflex action. If, for example, someone asks for the name of the secretary of the treasury, one would turn automatically to the *United States Government Manual*. Should the librarian suspect the post has been filled recently, the reference work would be *Facts on File* or an online check of a current newspaper. Matching the question with the probable source of an answer is no more difficult than knowing how to shift gears in a car, provided, of course, one is a trained driver.

In general, completely automatic techniques for handling questions are limited to answering directional and some ready-reference queries—and possibly some search queries involving no more than finding a group of documents. Research queries are rarely that easy to answer automatically.

The Trial and Test Search

In a very real sense, the search strategy is tantamount to making a hypothesis and then testing its validity through the search. For example, the answer to the question should be found in Y source (hypothesis). Y source is found, but the answer is not there. If it is not in Y, it is not likely to be in B, but it will probably be in C (hypothesis). A check of C proves the answer is there, and the hypothesis is correct. In initiating the search, the librarian can list all the possibilities, attach a success-probability function to each, and solve the problem by selecting what seems to be the best source(s) for the answer.

The formulation and the testing of any hypothesis presupposes a careful analysis, but in practice how often is this really done? If the librarian is left out of the search process, the average user is more likely to browse (or, as one student put it, "cruise") the print or online collection until something likely turns up. It may not be the best source, but it is a *source,* and it at least serves the purpose, no matter how poorly, of answering the question. Even the librarian may conduct a cruise. For example, a biographical query may simply lead the user to the biography section in the reference section or the general collection in the hopes of finding what is needed without further effort. A question about a quotation may take the librarian, with no other thought about other possible sources, to books of quotations or an online quotation database.

This is not to say that browsing, or surfing on the Net, is not beneficial; in fact, with proper direction it may be a very legitimate search process. It needs only a minimum of thought or planning, and it can be modified as it goes along to produce the desired results.

The ability to solve the problem, that is, carry on the search process, depends not only upon the librarian's existing knowledge of the online and print collection and the question, but on changes in that existing knowledge. The librarian begins the process by mentally testing and validating or invalidating given hypotheses and then accepting one hypothesis and testing it against the possible source. In a ready-reference question this may be quite enough, but if the source fails to provide an answer, the librarian learns to discount the hypothesis and, perhaps, the form for this type of query. Instead of an almanac, a yearbook may be more useful. This decision requires reorganizing the problem in terms of new hypotheses and building upon the state of knowledge existing when the question was first posed.

Throughout the search procedure the librarian is making decisions as to whether or not this process, this source, or this bit of information will be relevant to solving the problem of X question. One should not go "full steam ahead" on a request that has been translated into the terms of the information system without testing those translated terms first. After a partial search, it will be discovered whether the subjects chosen are adequate, or if there is a need for adjustment and refinement.

TRANSLATION OF THE QUESTION

Once the librarian has isolated, understood, and clarified the question, the next logical step is to "translate" the query into the form required by the available information system.

Form

Essentially, a basic step in translation is to isolate the form(s) for possible answers. The average television viewer or newspaper reader will translate the question, "Where can I find tomorrow's weather forecast?" in terms of form and find the answer by turning to the paper or switching on the weather forecaster or going to the Internet. In another situation, the question, "Where can I find the difference between the meaning of weather and climate?" would result in the translation of the query into the form of, say, a dictionary entry or an encyclopedia entry.

Of course, the translation of either question might be in terms of a human resource. "What's the weather tomorrow?" we ask the weather forecaster. "What's the difference between weather and climate?" the librarian asks the geographer.

Either question, too, might be translated in more depth. For example, the query changes if put by an airline pilot or by a geographer who wants a definitive explanation of weather and climate. In either case, the translation will be in more sophisticated forms, such as daily weather maps or scientific journal articles.

The most obvious type of translation occurs during a librarian's self-questioning: "Is the answer most likely to be found in a book, a pamphlet, a periodical, or a government document? Is an online database an even better source?" This decision is usually based on the depth and timeliness of information sought, as well as on the sophistication of the user. Another decision is based on knowledge of the collection or awareness of what is involved in obtaining materials from another library. For example, a library may have a good pamphlet collection, but the librarian who has not used the collection often may fail to consider it when a particular question is asked. Also, the librarian who realizes that technical materials on a given subject are well covered in a nearby library has the advantage of several options: go to the phone for an answer, or refer the user to the other library, or borrow the needed materials.

In the majority of ready-reference queries, as well as most search-and-research questions, the isolation of the form is probably the easiest bit of translating. And perhaps it is too easy. For example, a "typical" librarian who has grown accustomed to equating certain queries with biographical sources, or specific standard sources, often overlooks equally excellent or better forms.

Subject

The next most decisive and generally the easiest translation of a specific question to the library system is made in isolating the subject field. Queries about where to find information on "X member of Congress," or "Y American baseball player" will take little translation. The librarian will automatically go to the biographical section—print or online. The "where" or "what" query, by definition, inevitably leads to a subject classification. Queries such as "What is the cost of living in New York City?" "What is the formula for water?" and "Where is the capital of Alaska?" inevitably lead to related subjects, whether statistical data or chemistry handbooks or geographical sources.

All these queries, though, are at a simple, telegraphic level where a connection between query and subject is self-evident. Problems arise when the subject is not clear or, more likely, when the librarian's knowledge of the subject field is too general or too inadequate to translate the query into a meaningful source.

What happens when the question is clear enough, but the librarian is uncertain what salient part of a large subject area should be tapped? If, for example, the user wants material on the classical theory of unchecked population growth, the librarian, in an interview situation, might try to gain a more specific insight into the needs of the user. But if the needs cannot be expressed in any more definitive terms, what next? The obvious answer, if the librarian happens to know of Thomas Malthus, is to begin either with his works or with essays about Malthus. Lacking that subject knowledge, the librarian will move from the known, population and population growth, to the unknown.

The subject might be checked in a general encyclopedia for the historical background or in a subject encyclopedia. Inevitably the name of Malthus will appear. The librarian should then find subject material on Malthus and the Malthusian theory. If this does not prove satisfactory, a search of the encyclopedia (or for that matter, the catalog or any general bibliography concerned with population) will provide other key subject terms to consider. These steps follow the old tried-and-true principle of moving from the known to the unknown. Obviously, this presupposes an understanding of the general parameters and the vocabulary of the subject. Lacking this, the librarian should return to the negotiation of the meaning of the question with the inquirer.

Success depends upon a thorough knowledge of the library's classification systems, from cross-references in catalogs and indexes to storing and shelving systems. For example, the librarian may realize that a query has to do with the history of computers in business but be unable to make the association between the subject and the likely subject heading in the catalog or the place the material might be on the shelf—perhaps under business history, technology, or an important name in computer development.

The reference librarian must be able to move comfortably from the general subject to the specific subject. This presupposes a thorough knowledge of close subject classification, and the imagination to move about in related subject areas. For example, if nothing can be found about the history of computers in business under the subject of computers, the librarian should then move instinctively to the broader area of history or general works on technology. If the material is not available in the given library, the librarian must also know what bibliographies and union lists to consult in order to obtain it from another library.

A thorough knowledge of online sources and the general collection is presupposed here, primarily because the query may be answered not by scouring the usual sources but by looking in a standard biography, history, or manual in the circulating collection.

Time

The element of time as related to spatial situation is fairly well determined in the question "Where can I find the per capita income of America?" The answer is going to be from a current, not a historical, source. The question "What was the per capita income of America in 1860?" uses the same relation, but obviously leads the librarian to a different era. Sometimes, though, the time element is not clear. For example, when the user says, "I want something on the history of New York," she might be given a general history of New York City, but more likely something on a certain period. Once the time element is determined, it is relatively easy to move to corresponding sources online or in print.

Language

In the United States, in all but the largest libraries the collection is essentially in the English language. True, libraries serving Hispanic communities may have a number of Spanish titles, but by and large the reference section will be in English—as will, by the way, most of the electronic databases. In large libraries, though, the librarian obviously must know whether the inquirer can handle French before including an article from a French periodical among the sources.

The level of reading comprehension is another aspect of language that must be considered. The specialist will be satisfied with one source, the amateur with quite another, and the young student with a third. The difficulty arises with the adult user who may be better educated or less educated than the librarian suspects, and so the librarian should try to determine the comprehension level of the user first.

Availability

It seems obvious that the librarian cannot produce materials which are not in the library. But—and this is important—the right source may be precisely determined, although unobtainable. Everyone is familiar with the common situation of locating an article in an index and then going to the shelf and discovering that the library does not subscribe to the magazine, or, more likely, that the magazine is there but the particular issue is missing, or that the issue is there but someone has cut out the article.

A tremendous advantage of the online index is that the citation to a journal will usually indicate whether or not the library has that journal. Most important, the article (or one similar to it) will be available to read and/or download online. The "catch," as pointed out several times in this text, is that the student or layperson is more likely to settle for the article online than a better one, which requires finding the periodical.

Another approach is that even where the title is not in the library, the librarian may be able to order the article(s) directly from a vendor at the same computer terminal. The factor of availability is often more important than recognized. Ready accessibility, as countless studies have found, is a major factor in determining what type of information is used.

When the question is of the search-and-research type, and not the ready-reference variety, the emphasis tends to change. Here, instead of looking for a simple answer or an extremely limited amount of material, the librarian is seeking the highest-possible number of relevant and pertinent documents for the user's information requirements. This situation shows the importance of the use of bibliographical aids and adds the further challenge of matching the question with the access language of such aids.

ACCESS LANGUAGE OF THE INFORMATION SYSTEM

The librarian must know the control and access language of the collection and reference sources chosen. This means an appreciation of indexing and cataloging subject terms; it also implies a knowledge of the classification scheme of the collection, the location of reference books on the shelves, even the place where, say, the ERIC microfiche are filed. It certainly implies an understanding of how to find electronic databases. In this broader, more general context the language of the information system is more directional than conceptual.

The directional language is probably the most familiar one to the average library user, particularly the user who either does not want to bother the reference librarian or has little faith in the librarian's ability to locate needed answers and information. Usually such a patron simply finds a section of materials—books, magazines, documents, and so forth—which may answer his or her needs and commences to browse. In order to do this, though, the user must understand the language of classification or at least have learned through experience where the needed materials are located. That these materials happen to bear significant classification numbers may mean little to the user. The normal library-reference pattern of access via the language of the information system begins with specifics such as author and title, which, if accurate, afford exact entry through the catalog, index, abstract, or bibliography.

Here, in fact, there is really no translation. Lacking a specific entry, the librarian must translate the query into a subject form which the catalog, index, abstract, or bibliography will accept.

The librarian should not hesitate to confess ignorance of the meaning of certain terms. If it is obvious that the user cannot help (particularly true in the case of students who may be as puzzled as the librarian by a teacher's specific wording), the terms should be checked in a general dictionary, encyclopedia, or standard work on the subject. A dictionary will suffice for definitions, but an encyclopedia may be necessary for an overall view, especially when the question involves a matter of judgment. For example, in order to understand a request for material on hydrometers, a dictionary definition of "hydrometer" may be sufficient. However, if the question is "What is the dividing line between legislative matters of policy and executive matters of administration?" a dictionary definition of the terms will be of little help, and a quick check of an encyclopedia article on government may clarify the question.

Common failures at this level may come from misunderstanding and from failure to grasp the meaning of the terms. The user's mispronunciation may indicate one word, when the user actually had another term in mind; for example, the pronunciation "neurglia" for "neuralgia." Or the user may spell a term, name, or event, wrong and delay the search. This is particularly true when information on persons or places is sought. The difficulties of the situation are apparent in the cooperative reference service when a request is channeled to a central library for material on China or seals. The requester must clarify whether "china" is the country or the dishes, and whether "seal" is the animal or the signature sign. Context of the words may or may not make the proper selection apparent.

Searching Bibliographies and Indexes

About 50 to 80 percent of all manual or electronic searches of catalogs and indexes are by subject. Such subject searches usually lead to selecting books or articles or, in the case of the catalog, finding the shelf location of books in order to browse through the area of interest. Normally this search is limited to one place; that is, the librarian or user goes no further than a single subject heading.

The catalog is the starting point for many searches. Here one expects to find an author, title, and subject analysis of materials available in the library. The catalog limits the search to subject headings assigned by the cataloger. Linkage is indicated by "see" and "see also" references. This has its limitations, although it has the advantage of specificity.

Key Words

At any rate, to return to the librarian who is helping the mystified user, one excellent approach to subject headings that might be appropriate for the search, is to check the key words. When the key word is not found in the index or catalog, synonyms should be sought in the various subject-heading and authority lists, which are part of every library system.

The key word analysis is helpful when first writing down the question. This is hardly necessary for most ready-reference queries, but where it appears there will be some difficulty in translating, or where the search promises to be a relatively long or difficult one, the librarian (or the inquirer) should phrase the question, in writing, as clearly as possible. This obviously forces either party to think about exactly what is being sought. In this, one is not particularly influenced by the logical and linguistic constraints of the system.

RULES OF THE GAME

Over the years, reference librarians, through experience more than through scientific analysis or theoretical considerations, have compiled useful approaches to searching. Some of these are of the limited "how-we-do-it" type, but many others are of considerably more universal interest. Some applicable techniques are listed here.

1. When you know the answer is in a source, it usually is. There are times—and we have all had them—when after checking all the possible places for an answer, one source stands out as the most likely key to the problem. But a check of the source did not help. Take heart: The answer is there, it will just take some proper "page-shaking" before it falls out. Admittedly, this course will occasionally fail, but if it does, the fault lies not in the chance, but in your choice of source.

2. Depend on no one's prior research for accuracy or completeness. This involves fellow staff members. Although the staff members of your department are renowned "good guys" and have never led you astray, the moment one of them hands you a question and specifies that A, B, and Z have already been checked, believe them not. It may happen that they speak the truth; it will, however, not always occur that way. Of course if they have followed all the rules set forth here, trust can be extended—halfway.

3. Keep a list of where you have looked. On a long question it is folly to try to remember all the sources checked and the results of each search. It is doubly foolish to expect to transfer all of this negativeness to the next researchers and expect them to remember it too. So, mark, somewhere, the source checked and the result.

4. Take your time. One professional librarian twice selected the correct reference source but overlooked obvious answers because she was in too great a hurry. In another case, the key information from the patron was obtained but the librarian did not take sufficient time to examine it. Lack of time to interview and to consult sources appeared to be another major cause of professional failure.

5. Try various entry points. The subject approach is the most common, but consider the name of an author or an organization. Normally the author search is limited to those with some knowledge of the field, but it does no harm to ask the user (where appropriate) if the name of an author or organization is known.

Time to Reply

How long does it take to answer a query? There is no definitive answer. Some general replies can be made based upon experience and study. Most ready-reference questions can be answered in a matter of minutes, and 90 to 95 percent of them may be answered in under 5 minutes. Search and research questions may take from a few minutes to hours, or even days.

How much effort and time should the librarian take to answer a difficult question? A major constraint is the policy of the library. The library may have a written policy in which specific time limits are outlined, or there may be an unwritten understanding about the time per question.

An equally important aspect of the time element is what some call the "irritation quotient"; that is, just how long should the user be asked to wait for an answer? Potential irritation can be curbed at the beginning if the reference librarian indicates approximately how long the user should expect to wait for an answer.

In a related matter, everyone is familiar with the sometimes long wait for an interlibrary loan item, the necessary wait in line until the librarian is available, the wait which culminates at the reserve desk only to find the wanted item is gone, and so on, and so on. Not all of this, of course, is the fault of the librarian, but he or she should be aware that time is a very important factor in influencing the use or nonuse of the library.

When to Quit

Another major aspect of the time factor is deciding at what point one should give up the search. When the librarian concludes that the limits of the library's resources have been exhausted, the user should be referred to a larger library or to one with specialized materials. In smaller libraries the most frequent referral is to the state library; larger libraries may be part of a system or network that includes resources of public, college, or university libraries in the immediate area.

Search Failures

Other than those caused by lack of system resources, failures may be attributed to two basic flaws in the search process itself. The first, and most inexcusable, is a simple lack of the librarian's interest in either the user or the user's question; if an answer cannot be found immediately, a less conscientious librarian might call the search to a halt before it actually gets started. The second, and more common, failure is a lack of communication between the librarian and the user. At times the user cannot communicate in terms the librarian can translate into possible keys to an answer, and neither the librarian nor the user is sure what is being researched. The librarian may either misunderstand the query or accept the query at face value, without determining whether the user has given all the vital information or even the correct information. Another cause of search failure is the librarian who misses an obvious, but unexpected, answer.

THE ANSWER

Infatuated—some would say intoxicated—with the ability to retrieve online millions of facts, a librarian may forget the essential point to all of this: how the information is used. The average manual print search is not likely to turn up more than essential data. Harness the computer to the search, and the results can be overwhelming. This leads to essential questions about results.

It is not enough just to locate a piece of data, a source, or a document. There should be some kind of subsequent evaluation, interpretation, or clarification on the part of the librarian. This should be as much a professional duty as the interview and the search itself, although always with two considerations: (1) A user who does not want assistance should not have it forced upon him. (2) There are numerous times, as in most ready-reference queries, when the answer speaks for itself. One hardly need take time to explain, "Yes, the population of Zewa is truly 323,000."

Unfortunately, in the average situation the librarian only points out the reference sources (from online indexes to encyclopedia articles) and leaves the relevancy of the material to the individual. In the optimal situation the librarian helps determine the base relevancy. Several factors will help focus on the right answer for a particular individual's needs.

Level of Inquiry. The librarian is often able to determine the level of sophistication of the material required by weighing the age, experience, and immediate needs to the user. The judgment is made before the actual search is begun; the librarian is not likely to start looking for material on nuclear power for a scientist in the children's section. When the material has been found, the librarian, again in consultation with the individual, should be able to suggest what sources are too detailed or too technical and what sources are not detailed or technical enough.

Amount of Information Required. This is the quantitative side of the level of inquiry. The amount of information needed will depend, of course, on the proposed use of the materials. A student preparing a paper for a junior high school class in history will need considerably less material than a student on the graduate level at a university.

Dumping. The information or materials required cannot just be dumped in the user's lap, but must be introduced step by step as the patron goes through a certain pattern of behavior. A wide variety of potential sources should be offered wherever possible, but only in some logical, easy-to-understand order.

Where there is little or no control the user may suffer from the excellence of the search, that is, too much material is retrieved and dumped upon her or him.

Clarity. When citations rather than data or material are presented, how much does the user understand? In this situation it is important that the librarian follow through with explanations, as needed, of the different kinds of references (from books to articles and reports), of abbreviations of journal names, and of any unusual term or library jargon. In fact, the librarian should exhibit a general willingness to help with an explanation of any questionable matter.

Location. Where is the periodical or book located? It is not enough for the librarian to suggest the catalog. The librarian should help the user find the references, an act which in itself provides an opportunity to point out that material not in the library may be produced through interlibrary loan.

User-Anticipated Answers. An unhelpful answer may be anticipated, and accepted, by the user for a number of reasons. Thus, the essential question-negotiation process of the interview is negated. The odds are that the user will go away not with the *desired* answer but with an answer shaped by the anticipation of little or no real help from the librarian. In this case the patron's preconceived notions have cut short the reference interview.

The type of answer anticipated by a user is usually revealed in the phrasing of his question. Such phrasing is dependent upon a given situation or individual, but some good examples are found in these common situations.

1. *Time.* The user thinks: "The librarian has only a little time to help me." The user then says to the librarian: "I have to have an answer in the next five minutes."

Another version of this situation occurs when the user either believes the librarian is saying or actually hears the librarian say: "I have only five minutes to assist you, so please keep the request simple."

The result of this anticipated time difficulty is that the user either is confused or, more likely, frames a question to elicit a quick, simple answer.

2. *Form.* The user thinks: "The librarian is helpful when it comes to suggesting periodical indexes or magazines, but he is likely to refer me to the catalog if I ask for more extensive materials. The user then says to the librarian: "I need something out of a magazine."

One may reverse the thought process; that is, the user does want a book, but only a short, easy-to-read title. Rather than ask the librarian for an easy book, the user says: "I'd like a magazine article, not a book."

The result of this conflict is that the user may end up with nothing, or several books, or the wrong periodical articles.

3. *Clarity.* The user thinks: "In the past I have been able to get current material without waiting, so, while I would like some background material, it will be faster to ask for recent books or magazines." The result is a good current book which might not help her, although in the process of finding the book on the shelves the librarian may indicate where similar books of an older copyright date are located.

The solution to the difficulties is dialogue, which can build a mutual trust and understanding between the librarian and the user. Another solution is found in subsequent follow-up by the librarian. If a source has been indicated, the librarian should try to discover whether or not the source was adequate. Where the actual data or documents are retrieved by the librarian an effort must be made to determine if these materials are precisely what is needed or wanted.

The point is that providing information is not the final step. In the best of all situations the librarian is as involved with the answer as in finding the answer; and this concept is in need of development. The step after the information is located may be the most important phase of the entire search process, particularly when the librarian is working with a user who has only a vague notion of what is needed. This category, of course, includes almost any student or layperson who is involved with more than a ready-reference question.

Search Evaluation

There are many ways to evaluate the effectiveness of a search, not the least of which is the satisfaction of the user. In the early days a measure of satisfaction involved the focus on cost and how efficient the search was in terms of getting the maximum results for the fewest dollars. This remains a factor, particularly in terms of the abilities of the search analyst and the measurement of that person's skills. Other evaluative points include:

1. For the most part, the more citations, the more likely the search is to be a success. The catch is that one can simply give the user nearly everything on the subject which would introduce a swamp into the proceedings.

2. Librarians who spend more time in an interview and in preparing a search statement do better than those who are sloppy about such standard procedures.

3. The more manuals, guides, and so on, at hand, usually the better the digital search.

4. Practice makes perfect, that is, the more hours searched, the better the searcher.

5. Librarians who do something in a separate location away from the reference desk do higher-quality searchers.

Print or Electronic?

When does one turn to a computer or to a printed source for a reference response? In not too many years this may be a rhetorical query in that all, or almost all current reference works will be available *only* in a digital form. Still, for now, the question is appropriate, particularly in smaller libraries who may not have expensive access to sophisticated online searching.

Most ready-reference queries are answered more efficiently in a ready-at-hand printed work. For example, it is easier to determine the height of the Empire State Building in an almanac or architectural handbook than by searching for the answer in, say, a general online database. Where a simple answer is called for, the print source is usually best. One turns to a computer when the "simple" turns out to be complex.

Someone who needs one or two articles on a subject may find it faster at a computer terminal. Certainly, too, anyone looking for material in depth from an index is better served at the terminal. Unfortunately, laypeoples' love affair or hatred of technology helps make the decision. If it is love, it is the computer. If it is hate, it is the printed volume. All too often this simple answer is overlooked.

Given access to computer-assisted searching and a reasonably adequate hardcopy reference collection, one can arrive at a general conclusion about which medium to use: Where an online search is called for there rarely is need to augment it with a manual search. The exception is where retrospective material, not found in the database, is needed, or where another index is necessary but not available online.

ONLINE SEARCHING

Essentially the basic online search differs little from the print, manual quest for information. The technological differences are major, of course, but searching skills first have to be understood before the computer can be called into use.

The librarian decides what the layperson needs by listening and carefully modifying the query so that both the librarian and the person with the question have a clear idea of the dimensions of the answer. All of this can be made easy, and was so in the past, when the patron sat down with the librarian and filled out an online search request form. While this still is done in libraries where the query tends to be at the search or research level, for the most part the form has given way to the user simply using the computer on his or her own.

The reference interview for most questions is skipped. The layperson is content to follow the usual basic routine of entering a keyword and hoping for the best. Be that as it may, the remainder of this chapter is concerned with the ideal situation, i.e., where librarian and patron are working together to search. And, at least in the view of this writer, the librarian should be doing most of the searching.

An expert on Internet searching, Marylaine Block, points out that of all the misunderstandings about use of the Net, the difference between free and fee is most apparent. Laypeople "don't understand what they can and cannot expect to find on the Net—that some kinds of information are not free, that other kinds are more reliably found in books and journal articles."[2]

There is a widely held view that all information can now be found for free on the Net. Well, held by numerous laypersons and almost all students who avoid the traditional print. They do so as much from a misunderstanding as from downright laziness. The same student who may be able to turn up a likely citation at a computer has no notion it can be more efficient to use a printed source. And even if print is suggested, too, many have no idea how to use, say, a print index.

Given the print–electronic confusion, it is little wonder that almost no one this side of the librarian can differentiate between not only online reliable information, but the difference between for fee and for free.

Almost all for fee information databases now are found on the Net. They vary drastically from the free sources (the government and insti-

[2]"Marylaine Block: A Librarian with all but Walls," *Searcher,* June, 2000, p. 67.

tutional free sources aside) in that each has refined, distinctive patterns of search than normally associated with the millions of free sources. Hardly news to anyone who has managed to read the first book of this text, but it is worth stressing. Discussions of Net searches must be separated in terms not only of the best and better search engines for a particular free database quest, but for the best of the fee databases as well.

DIALOG, OCLC, the Gale Group, the H. W. Wilson Company are only a suggestion of the thousand for fee sources of information which now use the Net as a carrier. The trend is towards an increase in such databases, particularly among individuals who may have one or two valuable methods of presenting information which simply is not economical or possible for the larger database producers and vendors.

The for-a-fee databases offer search patterns more specific and for that reason faster and more efficient than the normal free source. That is why the reference librarian and well-informed layperson inevitably chooses databases for which there is a charge. You get what you pay for, and in the case of free vs. fee, it is the latter almost, although not always, which emerges the winner.

Selecting the Right Reference Source

This side of the usual rules for print selection of a proper source(s) to answer a question, the online database offers other possibilities. An obvious advantage here is the database has numerous searchable fields not available in print. The trick is to learn just what points of search in a particular database will assist the user beyond subject matter and the time period covered, e.g., language; document type (periodical, report, book); type of abstract, if any; index terms, type and number; free text search capacities and so forth.

Another aid available primarily from commercial type sources is the grouping of related databases by subject. The display shows how many entries are in each for a given topic. DIALOG, for example, has DIALIN-DEX, which lists the number of items found in each related database. Hence, if one is searching for "common-place books," it would indicate 15 items in *Books in Print;* 40 items in the *Modern Language Association* index; 5 items in *Art Index* and so on. The most useful files would be the one with the greatest number of citations. Oh? The catch is obvious. The one item needed might be in the index or reference work with the fewest citations. Still DIALINDEX and numerous varieties of the same form offered by all the major database publishers and vendors is at least a major filter.

Basic Searching Rules

As with the manual search, the online query must be matched to a likely source, at least if the librarian is dealing with for-a-fee databases. The point needs to be stressed that it is much easier, more direct and economical to go to a for fee periodical index than simply to float about on the Net hoping for something to come up in the subject area. Once the index, directory or whatever is matched to the query, then the online search follows the usual patterns: (1) Within the limits of software of the service the librarian looks for likely terms and tries a sample or two, usually employing Boolean logic, to widen or narrow the number of responses. (2) One then calls up a few citations, or in many cases the full text of an article to see whether this (or several) match the needs of the user. If yes, the path is opened to closer evaluation. If no, then one goes back to modifying the search terms. (3) In any case, the counterpoint of the search is to refine, revise and recast until satisfaction is obtained. All of this can take a few minutes to much longer depending on the difficulty of the question, the match of the source and a dozen other variables from time span covered by the source to availability or not of full text online.

All of the process ends, again as with the search for print answers, by evaluating the results with the user. Is more searching required? Has too much (too little) material been found? And so it goes with both online and print.

Search Engines

The primary vehicle for searching the Net, fittingly enough, is the search engine which was discussed earlier. There are in mid-2000 about 3,200, of which a dozen or more consistently are used by the majority of reference librarians. The layperson search patterns are well suited to the search engines. Those looking for popular terms which often are called up such as Pokemon, Britney Spears, Dragonball, or Pamela Anderson (all among the most popular key words used on Lycos) gave no problems. Conversely, esoteric terminology can quickly narrow the search and find usually what is wanted. The catch is that to enter a single key word, one may end up with hundreds if not thousands of results, none of which seems to meet the user's need. Engines attempt to get around this dilemma by listing results in probable order of importance. A good idea, but unless the number of results is less than 20 to 30, the listing is too ambiguous to be worthwhile, particularly after the first two or three entries.

A major misunderstanding about search engines, particularly among those who do not often turn to the Net, is explained by Marylaine Block: "Many users assume that if they don't find what they're looking for on the only search engine they try, it doesn't exist, and if they don't think the answers exist, they won't persevere. They don't understand that different search engines will find different things, and that the way they ask the question matters."[3]

[3] *Ibid.*

Pulling out what is needed from the ocean of possibilities normally is left to crude to sophisticated software usually referred to as automated crawlers. But even the most refined system can't compete with the slower, yet considerably more reliable human. The use of human searchers to evaluate citations varies from engine to engine. As of 2000, Yahoo! is not only the heaviest user of individual evaluations, but for that very reason, one of the most popular. Close behind are such engines as Google and Northern Light which rely on software to scan and index the Web, but call on human judgment as part of the search. At Northern Light, for example, trained librarians help to sort out the best websites and rid the system of the chaff. The greatest difficulty, as has been in the history of library classification, is to establish and sort out categories. For example, "alternative lifestyle" might be entered in the ubiquitous engine search box. The search might then turn up everything from sites on that subject to college fraternities and country clubs. The term is not specific enough. One response is to use "cultures and lifestyles" instead as a way of balancing what turns up with the software search. Still, as any working librarian knows, even the best classification system breaks down and some argue the entrance of humans into the computer-software approach may do more harm than good, at least as the Web increases in size and possibilities. Scientists work for the day when a computer will analyze a Web document and, without any human interference, instantly understand what that document is about. Some have been trying to build systems that try to understand the searcher as well. Most reference librarians know better. In this century it is not likely machines will do it all.

Search Techniques

There are numerous differences between print and online searching. One of the more obvious: almost complete shortage of subject headings at the free Web sites on the Net. All structured reference aids online have assigned subject headings usually drawn from the Library of Congress. In addition, the more sophisticated boast a thesaurus which serves much the same purpose but is more specific to the database. (For-a-fee sites, to be sure, are little more than migration of the print index, directory, encyclopedia, etc. to electronic format. As a result all do offer subject headings.) The for-a-fee sites lack, too, real indexing.

Given this lack, a good deal of filling in the search engine search box is an educated guess. If a proper name, there is no problem. If a narrow subject area, ditto. But when one comes to broad subjects which are nicely divided into subsections when one uses a controlled vocabulary, then difficulty arises. Try, for example, to enter "Greek poetry" or "telescopes" or "street crime" in a search engine. Without further specific subheadings, these simply call up hundreds, if not thousands of not so relevant citations. Experienced searchers use Boolean logic to narrow the field, but this is no real substitute for a specific subject heading.

Possibly the primary advantage of online vs. print searches is the use of the free text search, i.e., looking for key words in the title, abstract and/or text. Here one escapes the shadow of the assigned subject heading and can launch searches by using words familiar to the librarian. Key word searches particularly are useful when the subject is new and has not been considered by those who determine subject headings. Also, it has the advantage of being broader on the one hand, or more specific on the other than found in the assigned subject heading. When the assigned heading fails to turn up something, or only a few hits, one may wish to try for more by using free text. Finally, the word search saves the librarian the trouble of first going to a subject heading or thesaurus list.

There are scores of techniques for searching free text, and each for-a-fee database or series of databases has its own approach. That is why it is useful to read the manuals which accompany the various online for-a-fee sources. (Note: once again the free sources lack free text searching. Search engines do this to a certain extent, but lack entirely the on target methods of the structured fee database.

In a general way, all fee databases follow free text methods. For example, proximity operators or words allows the librarian to enter a search with qualifications, e.g., only in the title, only in the abstract, only in the text, etc. Search "reading(w)adults/ti," i.e., search for articles about reading applicable to adults, but key words found only in the title. One can broaden this to the full text. Note that in some systems the "w" may be "adj" and in others still another term. Still, they achieve the same end.

SUGGESTED READING

Bach, Reva, ed., *Secrets of the Super Net Searchers*. Wilton, CT: Pemberton Press, 1997. The search is all, claim the 35 experts who explain the various aspects of finding information on the Net. While the articles vary in interest, in total they give an excellent notion of the shortcuts to the electronic quest for information.

Boughanem, M. et al., "Query modification based on relevance..." *Information Processing and Management,* no. 35, 1999, pp. 121–139. The authors show by careful research how important it is to stress relevance rather than simply "the search and selection of unstructured full-text documents." Relevance feedback is considered of major importance in the process. The authors describe a model to obtain such assistance.

Walker, Geraldine and Joseph Janes, *Online Retrieval,* 2nd ed. Englewood, CO: Libraries Unlimited, 1999. A clear manual for those who wish to learn the basics of searching. What makes it valuable for both beginners and experts are the chapters on not only searching (excellent), but on such topics as database construction and structure and running a library search service.

PART IV
INSTRUCTION AND
REFERENCE POLICIES

CHAPTER NINE
INSTRUCTION IN
INFORMATION LITERACY

Pick up almost any magazine dedicated to libraries and there will be an article about "Computer training for patrons." (Distance learning is another parallel interest which is discussed later in the chapter.) Computers dominate much of the writing concerning the interaction of readers and technology in the library. There is a long history of what is still known by many as "bibliographic instruction." Today it is given the added label of "information literacy" instruction, or "online" or "computer" instruction.

Predicated on the democratic notion that everyone, whether they wanted to or not, should be able to navigate a library information system, well-meaning nineteenth-century types launched library instruction. This moved from simple explanation of the then card catalog to more complex matters, such as analysis of the best and better books.

The theory worked its way out of the public library in to the school libraries and later into academic centers. It never had much of an audience unless it took the form of a special class with sought after credits. Laypersons and students seemed to appreciate that the librarians should be about to answer their problems. This assistance from a librarian is much more acceptable than taking a five-minute or five-hour library instruction course. Bibliographic instruction rarely caught fire except where required (elementary and some high schools) or when instruction was needed because there simply were not enough librarians about to do anything but point out the bathroom.

Today expediency makes at least informal library instruction an absolute necessity. Lacking enough professionals to guide the user in manipulating data at a computer, librarians are forced into instruction. "Forced" is used advisedly. Even those, such as this author, who gently oppose the old fashioned type of bibliographic instruction, realize new technologies, new methods of searching and an increased number of people tramping about the library required users to master the fundamentals of the computer search.

In an ideal library there would be a librarian to answer any query. Usually, though, a librarian is *not* available. Therefore, two avenues are open: (1) Hire more reference librarians. This financially is rarely acceptable. (2) Lacking librarians, give the hapless user enough instruction in the use of the library to at least better the odds that he or she will make at least some right choices.

Most users, it can be argued from experience and observation, wander in and out of a library and rarely need assistance. Given a notion, for example, where the periodicals are located, or where to find biographies they will do fine on their own with or without a catalog or, for that matter, a librarian. Many are capable of making at least an elementary search at an online terminal, just as they are able to search for basic materials in any printed general index, such as *The Readers' Guide to Periodical Literature*. The majority of people require only a minimum of help because they need only a minimum of information.

Librarian as Technician

The real, all too often unexamined, argument is that most people need a minimal amount of information *only* because this is all they expect. Having learned they must dig out their own answers, they have little reason to address a librarian.

Much of this is going to change in favor of more service for the client. As electronic retrieval becomes widespread, as searching becomes more sophisticated, as greater amounts of data become available, more help will be required by the layperson. Both as a technologist, who understands hardware and software, and as an information expert, the librarian will become increasingly necessary.

Once the client understands that he or she can turn to the librarian for explanation of everything from the best software, say, for a home computer to the best article from a popular magazine the librarian will fulfill a necessary role. Technicians, particularly in America, are honored. Librarians working with computers have become those honored technicians.

Service and Education

Those who favor library instruction have a basic argument. They claim it is a necessity, and is important to the overall education of the individual (particularly in school and academic libraries). They follow a historical tradition. Librarian as educator is, simply put, a key part of being a professional librarian.

The other group, including this author, opposes formalized instruction, but certainly agree it should be given *if asked*. Opposition is based on the familiar argument that you cannot even begin to teach someone enough to make correct decisions about complex information sources. Information mediation cannot be taught to an indifferent student or a layperson who has an extra 5 or 10 minutes while wandering around the library. Nor can it be mastered even when there are formal courses for laypersons on the use of the library and its resources. It is as foolish as it is unfair to laypersons to believe one may elucidate, explain, and otherwise teach a skill of such depth and importance in a matter of minutes or over a few single credit course hours. To think this can be done is to deny the profession. It is to substantially cheat the individual who walks away firm in the knowledge that he or she knows the library and its resources.

Journal editor Gail Schlachter puts it this way:

> "Reference is in flux, but the emphasis is not on answering the stuck client's question, but on teaching in groups and in-depth consultation by appointment. The irony is that at a time when we are in a position to provide the ideal in reference service, we're making moves to abandon the service. It's as if there were an underlying premise at work that if we teach the new information literacy skills, our clientele won't have questions. Of course, it's more complicated than that, but the signs are pointing to a trend in mediated reference service that, if put on a graph, its projected future would be a downward slope to oblivion."[1]

False Battle Lines

There is no need to draw a battle line between those who advocate bibliographical instruction and those who say it is impossible, and not even advisable. No matter what a librarian may believe theoretically, action is dictated as much by the librarian's personality, willingness to help (or not to help) and a conviction that every situation is different.

If it appears that a patron might benefit from instruction, then it should be given. If not, normally it is simpler to find the answer for that individual. For example, a bright student with a need for background reading on the common cold, may appreciate a brief lesson on how to use the *Readers' Guide* or the *Index Medicus,* probably online. One with less interest or less apparent concern about sources may prefer simply to be

[1]Gail A. Schlachter, "From the Editor," *Reference & User Services Quarterly,* Winter, 1997, p. 127.

given a popular magazine piece or an encyclopedia article. Questions prompt different responses. Few librarians are likely to launch a lesson on use of the *World Almanac* when they can quickly find the answer to how many Americans go to college by referring to the *Almanac.* Ready-reference questions usually do not require bibliographical instruction.

Much, too, depends on the type of library. Academic and school libraries put considerable emphasis on bibliographical instruction. They see it as part of the broader education of the student. Public libraries give little time to instruction because few laypersons really want to be told how to use an index. The exception is the teaching of how to search at a terminal. This requires basic understanding of technology and search patterns. With computers in public libraries, the role of bibliographical instruction has taken on an added dimension. The librarian should be as familiar with the technology as with the electronic databases themselves. Ideally, the librarian should be able to help and advise on hardware and software—both in the library and at the user's home.

In the course of a day the reference librarian will answer questions about where this or that is located, or how to use this or that index, or explain the process of digging out this or that piece of information. No working reference librarian is against helping the patron master basic library procedures. Knowledge of how to use the catalog and how to search an index is useful for those who are interested. This type of help, (or call it instruction) is as much a part of being a professional librarian as a doctor's explanation of a test to a patient, a mechanic's display of a damaged part and how it was replaced, or the carpenter's reassurance about need while adding up a bill. Conversely, doctors, mechanics, and carpenters are not compelled to teach the layperson their professions or trades.

There is much to be said for allowing the user, no matter what age or position, to determine whether (1) information is wanted, or (2) instructions are wanted, or (3) a combination of both is desirable.

Instruction Benefits

Anyone who wanders into a library for the first time realizes whether it is "user friendly," or "detached," or "hostile." Librarians claim the first descriptor, while students often turn to the last two. There are as many reasons for these attitudes as libraries and librarians. A basic one is misunderstanding about the goals of the library. The historical, theoretical purpose is known to everyone; but the average individual with individual needs is more concerned with how easy it will be to find X or Y book, an article, or, these days, a computer terminal. At this point a friendly face, a gentle smile, an appearance of authority can ease the situation and can, indeed, turn what was until that moment a hostile place into a friendly spot.

Instruction, it might be argued, is offered to persuade the individual that the library is there to help. Assistance will be given gracefully with an appreciation for particular needs. Even the most vocal foe of instruction will agree on the necessity of making the library hospitable.

INSTRUCTION METHODS

Most instruction is turned towards explaining a different library resource, usually with the catalog coming first, followed by exercise on how to find and read citations and abstracts from indexes. The usual next step is to familiarize the user with much-used reference sources. This may be little more than to point out where they are found in the library or they may be rather extensive exercises in searching.

Libraries have several traditional instruction methods:

Computer-Database. Unquestionably the best argument for instruction is the need for people to at least learn the basics of making a computer search. There are as many different ways to offer instruction as libraries. The literature is filled with both theoretical and pragmatic "battle" plans to make the average user a near expert in online searching. While all admit this is impossible, at least an effort should be made, in fact has to be made.

Essentially, the programs break down into two parts. First, there is the so-called "hands on" lessons. Here the unsuspecting reader is confronted with a source of all answers, but has no idea how to turn the computer to his services, more or less insert paper into the printer. The benevolent, often frustrated librarian then gives the user a brief rundown on what is to be done.[2]

The second approach, and one favored by both librarians and users, are the short "courses." These may be no more than an hour or two, or an actual for credit course. The lessons cover all aspects of searching and are tailored for both the beginner and the near expert. Of course, this assumes the poor reader has the time, the inclination to get that familiar with the computer. The enrollment, then, depends more on the given situation than on any generalization about what is the best approach both to teach and to lure the user into the class.

Orientation Tours. Certainly the most familiar type of library instruction is the orientation tour of the library. This may or may not be directly

[2]In larger libraries the usual process is to have a trained student or clerk sitting near the computer terminals. This person, rather than a professional librarian, gives instruction and basic help when needed. On the other hand, for instructions on the skill of searching, most libraries even today rely on the professional rather than a clerk.

involved with reference services, although traditionally a reference librarian is likely to be in charge of such a program.

In academic and school libraries the instruction is established along set patterns. The librarian, at a given time(s) each year, indicates the major points of interest, explains the rules and regulations, and leaves the library groups with the feeling that, when in doubt, one should ask the librarian. This may be supported by audiovisual programs and printed guides. The printed guides, which may be general (i.e., "A Self-Guided Tour of Your Library") or specific (i.e., "Selected Resources of Anthropology"), are normally prepared by reference librarians. If the library is large, some type of floor plan or map should be supplied. The presentation should follow a logical sequence, usually along geographical lines from the time the person walks in the front door until he or she walks out.

The public library may have the same type of aids, but usually more modest goals. Instead of giving detailed instructions, there will be simple, easy-to-follow notes about how long a book may be kept out, where the circulation desk is located, and the like. The tours are more likely to be informal and held on a one-to-one basis when someone requests information about the library. Some public libraries work closely with schools, hold planned tours, and do have specific material for elementary and secondary school users.

The obvious problem with the orientation tour is that it tends to be superficial since it is brief, and therefore often is forgotten. Despite the fact that the tour does not seem to provide any lasting educational experience, it accomplishes at least three goals: (1) The tour makes the individual more comfortable in the library. (2) The tour encourages the individual to ask for help. It should at least make the patron realize that the librarian is a cooperative human being. (3) The tour allows the librarian to have some concept of the problems and difficulties faced by those who first enter a library. If used properly, orientation may do much to improve library service, such as placing the reference desk in a better location, putting up directional signs, or making circulation practices a bit easier to understand.

Exercises on the catalog, that is, OPAC (online public access catalog), are common. They range from a handout for the student and a 5- to 10-minute lecture on the catalog to structured small-group activities with specific problems and explanations.

Formal Courses. There is little question that the most effective type of bibliographical instruction is tied to a teaching program. This may be done formally with short courses of a general nature, or in lectures tied to the specific research needs of the would-be historian or social scientist. Depending on the situation, the course or series of lectures may be the jurisdiction of the teacher or the librarian, or a combination of both.

Today it tends to be the latter. Where possible, the formal courses should be required. If not required, two things may happen: (1) Instruction will not reach the very ones who need it the most and are not motivated to use the library. (2) The librarian, often uncertain of the size and interest of the class, may take a less-than-enthusiastic interest in preparation.

COMPUTER INSTRUCTION

Explanation of basic computer technology, which most students and at least a majority of laypersons now understand, if only in a rudimentary fashion, is no longer stressed in online instruction. The focus now is much the same as decades ago—the best sources to find the answer. Confronted with thousands of possibilities, the layperson wants guidance in finding the single best digital resource.

At the same time the reference librarian must keep up with the new sources. This has always been the situation, but never has the number of possibilities been so great. Add, too, the ever increasing number of print reference works and the average reference librarian's workload has been a matter of rapid addition. It brings on stress, but it is a rush which seems to increase the intellectual thrill of the game rather than bring it to a crashing halt. Electronic resources have lifted what sometimes can be a boring job to one often of excitement. The bonus: more respect for reference librarians, more acknowledgment that a professional really can save time and effort.[3]

There is a drawback, too. More and more users expect to be able to find everything online, full text. Technology lets us do much more, but it also increases expectations. The biggest change has been "more service, with greater expectations that a service does exist that will answer the question and that it is available immediately. Readers expect they will not need instruction and do not want to use Help screens either."[4]

Online Instruction: Problems and Solutions

Thanks to a shortage of staff and particularly those trained in the skills of retrieving digital information most computer instruction is minimal. There are several factors which makes this less than desirable approach feasible.

Many people, and particularly those under 30, are familiar with computer basics, know the general paths to finding data on the Internet

---

[3]One librarian explains: "Electronic services probably make reference librarians look more knowledgeable in the eyes of the patrons because a librarian can flee to online searching while trying to think of the right way to find an answer." Carol Tenopir, "Plagued by Our Own Successes," *Library Journal*, March 1, 1998, p. 40.

[4]*Ibid.*

Worldwide Web. Even people who are introduced to a computer for the first time in a library can grasp the simple paths to finding information, particularly if they are set on them by a helpful librarian.

In either case, thanks to simplified menus and layperson tailored software, a good many sites on the Net, including the databases to which libraries subscribe, are relatively easy to search. Granted the quest for information may be pretty senseless, but a minimum of data can be found.

There are three methods of overcoming the shortage of staff, the need of people to move to a computer and the usual dire results of amateurs seeking information:

1. Live with it, and hope the good fairy will one day solve the problem. Less by choice than by necessity, this is too often the case, particularly in underfinanced libraries (the majority) where the last big effort was to get a computer, to purchase online indexes. No money has been put aside for their proper use.

2. Do not live with it. Find the money, the time to offer computer training to staff and to readers. This, to be sure, is the solution most librarians hope to find. And it is the stuff of a good 90 percent of articles these days on bibliographical instruction. More on this later.

3. Forget the good fairy, forget instruction. Answer the question for the reader, whether it takes seconds or hours. This eliminates the necessity of training the user, which never really works anyway, and assures at a minimum of effort, although at some cost for more staff, sound, reliable answers.

It is worth stressing that anyone who wants instruction should be given that privilege, whether formal or informal. The third, and in this author's opinion the only rational solution, assumes the majority of people are more interested in the answer than how it is found.

Teaching Readers How to Go Online

The majority of librarians favor instruction of laypersons on how to search for information online. This solution may be by choice or by necessity, but it is the dominant one. In that case, what are some of the procedures for proper teaching of online searches? A few are outlined below. A cursory glance at journal articles will reveal scores more.[5] Still, they all tend to follow a basic pattern.

Instruction is formal or informal. The emphasis, again for lack of staff, is on the latter. Here a well-trained reference librarian goes through logical steps or questions. How much does the reader know about the basics of operating a computer? How much does the reader understand

[5]See the "Suggested Reading" section for methods of instruction.

about how to find information, how to conduct a basic search? Answers come out in the reference interview, or more likely an informal conversation. Given that perspective, the librarian will work with the person at the computer. Here instruction is in terms of a specific question with a specific, usually easy to find short answer. As time is limited, the success is dependent more on how quickly the individual masters basics than the particular skills of the librarian in teaching.

Aside from search problems, the librarian should be handy to answer queries about the computer terminal, software, and any other technical aspect in which the user is interested. Normally, this is no more than helping clear a paper jam, negotiating how to print out a citation, or, more likely, explaining how to turn off or on the computer terminal monitor. Rarely, for example, does the librarian explain the technical aspects of a network, or what computer the user might wish to purchase for home use in order to best tap information facilities. Even more unusual is to have someone call from home for assistance in a program that failed, a disc that won't operate properly, and so forth. Granted, this type of information is available at computer centers and from manufacturers, but one suspects it might be better offered by the experienced librarian.

Given a single short period with a person, the search techniques may be understood, if only vaguely. If a follow-up is allowed, then, of course, the teaching results are improved. Most importantly is repetition. The individual who masters the simplest of searches and who comes back to the library time after time for more instruction, for more searches, ends up an A plus pupil. (Of course, the same experience may be garnered at home if the individual has a computer.)

The classic "one-shot" lesson plan inevitably fails. Paradoxically, often the layperson is quite content with this result. In blissful ignorance, he or she has learned how to print out or download two or three citations from an online index or encyclopedia. Add a dash of full text and there is enough for a paper or a short talk.

The garnered information may not be precisely on target, but at least it was found at a computer terminal. As one young friend puts it, "Cool."

Formal Instruction

Formal instruction is preferable. Typically, where more than minute-to-minute help is offered, a formalized approach to mastering online is given in three or four steps. First, there is a lecture and a demonstration. The latter often involves the students as well as the instructor with simple searching and problems. Next, there may be visual, videos, and other suitable methods of demonstrating the search process. Finally, there is the computer tutorial where the individual student, or a group of students, is given hands on instruction.

Basic instruction and continued reiteration of basics are important. In addition, the teacher must give continued reassurance that the beginner is doing the right thing. Generally, only time and experience will make the layperson truly comfortable at the terminal. Beyond searching mechanics is the content. Content is more important, at least for the average person, than either the how-to-do-it and theoretical aspects of searching.

There are almost as many online instruction exercises as teachers, librarians, and students. For example, at random from several articles: (1) Exercises in Boolean logic, with particular emphasis on the use of "and" and "or." Rarely do the searching techniques become more complicated. (2) A sheet on which the student explains the question and then attempts to outline key words for searching. More advanced groups become familiar with controlled vocabulary, subject headings, and so forth. (3) Search strategies at the computer terminal. All students are given a single question and then asked to deliver the printouts of three to a half dozen "best" citations.

INSTRUCTION EVALUATION

How good is formal or informal library instruction? No one quite knows. There are a few objective studies. Too many of the reports about instruction are anecdotal, based on the joys of a single library in teaching the uninstructed masses on how to find a book at a computer terminal. With that, there are typical methods of analysis. They may be limited in scope, but they can be of some use to the reference librarian who is seeking better ways of telling people how to get from point A to B in a library without stumbling.

(1) Query graduating students, regular readers. "Graduating" and "regular" have to be stressed as this assumes the person has been given instruction over a period of time and not just ducked into a five minute course. Usually the answer is a resounding affirmation of instruction. The "catch" is that if the people did not learn they likely would not take part in the study, and/or would not "graduate" or certainly not be "regular" library people. Then, too, there is the factor of good will. It takes a mean individual to downgrade the efforts of a well-meaning librarian. Difficulty with evaluation involves lack of time and, to a lesser extent, lack of skill. The result tends to be specific evaluations of narrow areas of instruction and, as often as not, is only a step or two above the anecdotal.

Efforts to evaluate the effectiveness of library instruction indicate that there is some value in the process. Inevitably, success is tied to an academic credit-bearing course on library instruction and not to informally structured encounters between the librarian and the user.

A time-effort-efficiency study would be of value to answer one recurrent library-patron problem: Is it, indeed, faster and more economical for the librarian to search the needed material online, on a CD-ROM, or in print for the user? Or is it wiser to show the user how to find his or her own information, even when this consists of basic instruction in the use of online retrieval at a computer terminal? If, for example, 300 people a day have questions which can be answered at a terminal with access to a dozen or so general and specialized online abstracting and indexing services, would it cost less simply to have librarians at many terminals finding proper responses? In most cases the client would ask the question, leave and return in an hour, a few hours, or a day for the printed responses from the online source.

No matter what the justification, from philosophy of reference service to lack of staff, laypersons and students will be finding their own answers for years to come.

One may argue that the librarian should offer to find the necessary data, and at a minimum serve as a mediator between the data and the user's requirements. This is the goal, but meanwhile the librarian must make do with what is available. Facts conspire against the ideal: (1) Inadequate budgets, limited staff, and new technologies cut back on good service. (2) Given the situation where the user must, at least sometimes, find information, then it is absolutely necessary that some instruction in library use be given—if only a printed map of the shelving arrangement. (3) The new technologies require considerably more. Without assistance the novice at a computer terminal will often produce myriad value-zero citations.

Could it be that the close tie between instruction and the reference service has given users the wrong notion about reference services? Could be—and that may be why so many turn their backs on the library. Is the effort to instruct doing more harm, at least in the long run, than good? What do you think?

Is Nanny Necessary?

On the opposing side of the instruction argument is a group that deplores what Michael Gorman dismisses as a "terribly nannyish attitude" by reference librarians. The user who wishes to use a terminal should be free to do so. Incomplete or otherwise flawed searches must be determined by the individual, not by the librarian. "As librarians, we should be rejoicing in the fact that technology has brought us systems that are so well received and so heavily used...The best systems are those that can be used by the reasonably intelligent, if uninstructed, user...Many [bibliographical instruction] programs owe the existence and success to the 'user hostile' nature of the systems about which they teach. Replace those systems with others that are truly 'user friendly' and the whole purpose of [instruction] is called into question."[6]

In calling for the dismantling of all bibliographical instruction, Gorman strikes an optimistic note: The library "will be service oriented and will strive to provide the services that users want rather than the services that we believe they ought to want."[7] The catch, of course, is that few people have any idea of what they want or need until they want or need a solution to a current problem.

DISTANCE LEARNING[8]

Instruction in the use of the library no longer is confined to those who wander in and out. Computer patrons may ask for help at home. And these same people, too, may be taking part in distance learning of which the library is a major factor.

Distance learning is one answer to university and college shortages of funds, teachers, and classroom space. Students, or "remote users" as they are called by many librarians and educators, may take classes at home whether they are a few miles or a continent away from the home campus.

The key to successful distance learning is technology. Today this translates into computers and video. It includes, too, radio. In fact, the earliest great contribution to distance learning is the English "Open University." Established in the late 1960s, using both radio and television, the system is now in the top ten of British schools for teaching quality and superior students. Professors give standard lectures to the remote user who then takes examinations and prepares papers to pass the course. Interactive educational elements are made possible by telephone and, these days fax, e-mail, and websites.

The "Open University" now has a growing reputation for research. Furthermore, it has served as a pattern for nearly 50 similar efforts worldwide. A dozen of these are distance learning mega universities with enrollments over 100,000.

American universities were quick to pick up the concept of the Open University. The National Center for Education Statistics reports: Between 60 and 65 percent of four and two year colleges offer distance education.

[6]Michael Gorman, "Send for a Child of Four or Creating the BI-Less Academic Library," *Library Trends*, Winter 1991, p. 355.

[7]*Ibid.*, p. 357.

[8]Distance learning is carried on by "virtual universities," a term accepted by governments and bodies such as the World Bank. There is a large literature on the subject. A helpful collection of essays on distance learning will be found in: Arant (see Suggested Readings); and Carolyn Snyder and James Fox, *Libraries and Other Academic Support Services for Distance Learning* (Greenwich, CT: JAI, 1997, 334 pp.). See, too: recommendations on distance learning on the Web, as well as ongoing documents in ERIC.

Usually this is accompanied by computer technology as well as video and audio methods. In the next five to ten years a reasonable forecast is that 75 to 85 percent of the universities and colleges will have distance learning courses.

The concept of distance learning is likely to take many new forms. According to World Bank estimates, a new university campus should open its gates every week. Impossible, to be sure. But distance learning programs open the gates for hundreds of thousands otherwise denied access. Why not a virtual university just as there are virtual libraries and bookstores? Those who favor remote digital learning say it will bring education into every home.

A superior example of well coordinated distance learning appeared in 2000: This is *Fathom* (www.fathom.com) made up of six of the world's leading educational and cultural institutions: Columbia University, the London School of Economics, Cambridge University Press, the British Library, the Smithsonian Institution's National Museum of Natural History and The New York Public Library. The group will draw together the resources of the various institutions to help individuals with specific course work, as well as answer specific questions. Precisely how it will function is yet (mid 2000) uncertain, but there is every reason to believe the joining together of such groups will do much to legitimize and help distance learning.

Private corporations are aware of the potential profit in distance learning. Barnes & Noble University offers online learning courses generally which are free. Profit is tied to books which, of course, Barnes & Noble sells in conjunction with the free online service. The bookstore operates in conjunction with *notHarvard.com* (www.notharvard.com). This firm joins business concerns to offer specially tailored courses for their employees, at a fee. On the other hand it offers free pretty much "how-to-do-it" noncredit courses to laypeople. These cover a wide range of interests from baby care and creating Web graphics to "a beginner's guide to home repair." The authors of these "texts" are paid about $1,500 per course. More information on this aspect of the business world may be found at www.notHarvard.com. Other "universities" which have different methods of profit through free courses to individuals include: *Hungry Minds* (www.hungryminds.com); and *CodeWarriorU* (www.code warrioru.com).

How valuable are these courses? It is difficult to say as most are little more than online versions of self-improvement sections in a bookstore or library. As they are free and as they give no education credits, the user may "join" or not join a class at will, try it out for a bit, and then go on or drop it. At this point it seems such companies offer much at no risk to users.

Success of distance learning depends on four major ingredients: strong support by the university for students who are not on campus; a profound commitment to the program, not simply chatter; efficient technological approaches; and, from the point of view of the librarian, access to excellent learning materials.

Access to Reference Services[9]

There is only a small leap or hop and skip for reference librarians to reach distance learners.

Most of the necessary technology and reference points are established and used by on campus students. They can be extended to students across the city, state, country or continent. And basically all that takes is access to websites in general and expensive database indexes and reference works made available free by the university to enrolled students.

Beyond the obvious existing information paths to a degree offered by the library are:

1. Interlibrary loan services which are particularly valuable for a student otherwise cut off from a large library.

2. Access to local and often other library holdings through remote access to the library catalog(s), i.e., OPACs.

3. Remote access to books, papers, etc. which are on reserve for a given course, but until recently available only in the library.

4. Library Web pages not only offer standard reference service but select links to help the student find additional, often more current information on the Net. This type of guidance and selection is invaluable for the student who is working a full day and taking a degree in spare hours. He or she has no time to waste cruising the Net, and looks to the reference library for the best, basic sites.

The reference librarian constantly is called upon to develop new, more efficient methods of moving information to the individual user. This involves more than by now traditional approaches. All of these (i.e., mail, telephone calls, and e-mail) "lack the important element of visual contact that can be crucial for conducting a reference interview."[10] Here a reference librarian comes up with a response, a reply which is typical in the literature when a difficult problem presents itself to those involved with distance learning. Aside from the point made by the librarian—he or she solves the problem via video conferences and related technologies—there often are other resolutions, other paths which lead in turn to better methods of offering the remote user reference services.

---

[9]Elizabeth Lindsay, "Web Watch," *Library Journal,* July, 2000, pp. 32–34. This is an evaluative descriptive listing of sources of information on the Web about distance learning. A good place to begin any study of the subject. For an excellent discussion of what off campus users expect and how to gain knowledge of those expectations, see: Rosemarie Cooper, et al, "Remote Library Users: Needs and Expectations," *Library Trends,* Summer, 1998, pp. 42–64. Note the extensive bibliography.

[10]Robert McGeachin, "Videoconferencing and Remote Application Sharing for Distance Reference Service," *The Reference Librarian,* no. 65, 1999, p. 51.

Helping the Remote User

It is not enough simply to throw open existing reference gates for the remote user. The reference librarian has to tailor certain services for those specific users.

The first question: who are they and what are their special needs? The answer: the historical user survey, although this time aided by new methods of polling and study. The conclusion: one must do more than look at the figures and move them into a report. The data should be used to improve library service.

Beyond the general, the librarian must get down to specific paths to just as specific courses. If x or y course has certain requirements which require library use, can the remote user meet those requirements? The reference librarian must know what x or y course requires from the library and be sure the student has access. Beyond that type of support, equally important is bibliographic instruction, no matter how limited. In other words, the student should be able to find what is needed, usually via a computer, in the library for the given course.

SUGGESTED READING

Arant, Wendi and Pixey Anne Mosley, eds., "Library Outreach," *The Reference Librarian,* no. 67/68, 1999. Well over 300 pages and more than a dozen authors contribute to a better understanding of how the reference library fits into the distance education programs. Every aspect of the subject is covered from electronic databases to marketing and expanding the learning community. The emphasis is on a practical approach to the subject. Highly recommended as a basic text in the field.

Balas, Janet, "Online Training Resources," *Computers in Libraries,* January, 1998, pp. 28–36. A regular columnist for the magazine suggests various resources, many of them online, which will help the librarian in an instruction course. Also the sites are set up in such a way that an average layperson can master at least basics without help from the librarian.

Cohen, Laura, "The Web as a Research Tool: Teaching Strategies for Instructors," *Choice,* Supplement (August), Vol. 36, 1999. An expert on helping others to use the Web, an experienced librarian outlines the steps and basic principles of instruction. The article is as clear as it is comprehensive. One of the best available in a field of opinion and advice. Highly recommended for anyone contemplating Net instruction on a one-to-one basis or in groups.

Fonseca, Tony and Monica King, "Incorporating Internet Into Traditional Library Instruction," *Computers in Libraries,* February 2000, pp. 38–42. Comparing traditional ways of library instruction with a "template for incorporating the Web," the authors blend the two into a practical outline for teaching everything from online searching to various teaching methods.

Geffert, Bryn and Beth Christensen, "Things They Carry," *Reference & User Services Quarterly,* Spring, 1998, pp. 279–285. A survey of 521 college students indicates few have any real understanding of how to use a library. High school bibliographical instruction usually is less than useful. This is a challenge to the authors to construct a worthwhile bibliographical instruction program. A good profile of typical beginning college students.

Grassian, Esther and Susan Clark, "Information Literacy Sites," *C&RL News*, February, 1999, pp. 78–81, 92. The authors point out there are some 9,000 Web items regarding "information literacy." Which are the best, the ones most likely to assist the librarian? They are dutifully listed and annotated here. Particularly useful for details of use and pointers to related materials from magazines to articles. Practical, considered help for almost anyone.

LaGuardia, Cheryl and Christine Oka, *Becoming a Library Teacher,* New York: Neal-Schuman, 2000, 120 pp. A practical guide for librarians who are involved with library instruction, this is written by two experienced experts who are as practical as they are astute about what constitutes good instruction. The chapters cover everything from class preparation and outlines to anxiety on the part of the teacher.

"LOEX (Library Orientation and Exchange)…" *The Reference Services Review,* vol. 27, no. 3, 1999. Celebrating 25 years of determined policy to educate library users, this special issue of the *Review* is turned over entirely to the subject. There are some 18 articles moving from "Instructional Design and Student Learning" to "The Creating Evolution of Library Instruction." An excellent overview even for those who may not be that enthusiastic about the subject.

Rader, Hannelore, "Library Instruction and Information Literacy," *Reference Services Reviews*. Various dates. This is an annual "annotated list of materials dealing with information literacy including instruction in the use of information resources, research, and computer skills…" It appears usually in the Fall/Winter issue. It is by far the best annual bibliography on the subject, and is a necessity for anyone involved with instruction. See the special double issue of this journal (vol. 26, nos. 3–4, 1998) for close to 20 articles on "Library instruction for the 21st century," as well as Ms. Rader's roundup.

Roth, Lorie, "Educating the Cut-and-Paste Generation," *Library Journal,* November 1, 1999, pp. 42–44. "Now, students sit at their computers…" And with that bibliographic instruction has changed both in direction and definition to "computer literacy." The need for such teaching is stressed by the author, an administrator in the California State University system. She looks over the present situation and gives sound advice on what is to be done to make the Net a more productive place for students.

Slade, Alexander and Marie Kascus, *Library Services to Open and Distance Learning,* Englewood, CO: Libraries Unlimited, 2000. This is the third annotated bibliography by the authors, and it is updated regularly. Under detailed subject headings the list by year published more than 750 works from books and articles to reports and dissertations. There is a particular focus in this edition on websites.

Young, Rosemary and Stephen Harmony, *Working with Faculty to Design Undergraduate Information Literacy Programs*. New York: Neal Schuman, 1999. As one review put it, "this is a timely guide for librarians in academic libraries to plan, implement, develop, and evaluate information literacy programs." The reviewer sums it all up, and is correct in that the manual is a practical approach to bibliographic instruction from two experienced librarians.

CHAPTER TEN
REFERENCE SERVICE POLICIES
AND EVALUATION

Decade after decade, librarian after librarian, there are published reports about the success rate of answering questions. The average person in the average library is likely to leave with what is wanted only 50 percent of the time. Conversely, some libraries may have a success average up to 70 to 90 percent.[1]

No wonder evaluation of reference services is necessary. Something is wrong in many libraries. Checking out the possible potholes on the information highway helps both librarian and reader. For example, what factors dictate the success or failure of a reference query, i.e., the quality of reference service? It hardly takes a survey to find that out, at least in a general way. Success depends on:

1. A superior reference collection. This ranges from the basics found in *Guide to Reference Books* to the latest electronic reference sources.

2. More important than a collection is the superior reference librarian. An expert can mine answers from almost any source. An amateur may have 20,000 databases and printed volumes about and still come up with nothing or the wrong answer.

3. Time. The librarian should have a required time for the individual, whether this be a ready reference query or, at the reader's request, how to find information in an online database. Unfortunately, enough time is rarely the case.

---

[1]See a summary of the argument in Jo Bell Whitlach's *Evaluating Reference Services* (Chicago: American Library Association, 2000).

4. Floorplans. There should be adequate space for the printed works, the computer terminals and rooms where the librarian may discuss in private—where necessary—the patron's query.

There are numerous other factors, which mean failure or success in an adequate response to a question. Specific analysis differs from situation to situation, but there are generalities and formulas which are appropriate in not one, but most library evaluation situations. That's what management is all about.

Library Management

Traditional reference service depends on good library management and planning. The administration's policies must provide for everything from adequate new reference works to the latest computer systems. Without such aids, reference questions cannot be answered.

Reference librarians are usually not involved with daily administration. But they are concerned with the many policies and administrative goals that include aspects of personnel, professional development, and hiring of new employees. These are normally in written, sometimes published, policy statements prepared jointly by staff and administrators. The policy reflects the day-to-day activities of the library staff.

The individual library's written policy statement should incorporate certain basic considerations:

1. A *statement of purpose* which includes goals and objectives, not only of the reference process but of the library (and the system) as a whole.

a. The goals and objectives must be discussed in terms of the reality of budget, political process, staff, space, and so forth.

b. More important, the goals must be understood by all; that is, the librarian should be able to explain the purpose of the proposals, and if they are not practical or logical, the goals should be reexamined.

2. A *statement defining the broad strategy* that will be followed to reach the goals and objectives.

a. There should be a thorough analysis of "time present," that is, precisely what is going on at the current time in the reference process.

b. There should be a plan, with due consideration of cost, personnel, overall library goals, and so on for future development and growth.

c. Finally, there should be periodic evaluation of the movement(s) toward future time. And in the light of the evaluation, the general and the specific strategies should be modified or even dropped in favor of new approaches.

Purpose of Policy and Procedures[2]

The purpose of the policy and procedures is to state guidelines for providing reference service in order to ensure a uniform standard of service of the highest possible quality consistent with available resources. Reasons for having a policy are almost as numerous as the librarians who draw them up, but essentially:

1. The drafting or modification of a policy requires some appreciation of the overall goals, purpose, and direction of reference service. The systematic analysis of service given, or not given, helps to formulate these necessary objectives.

2. Standards are established, not only for service but also for such things as building the collection, handling of interlibrary loan materials, and preparation of correspondence.

3. A better view of the audience served (or not served) is achieved by considering objectives and standards. Obviously, neither can be analyzed without a careful study of library patrons.

4. Levels of service must be considered, that is, just how much assistance is to be given to help the user in finding information or in actually finding the information for the user?

5. Without a view of the world beyond the scope of the reference desk, services may become less than ambitious, locked more into routine and daily expediency than addressed to long-range needs of the individual and community the librarian hopes to serve.

6. Policy statements are developed to resolve controversies such as why the microforms staff cannot do all the threading of film readers or why advance notice of class assignments is necessary.

7. The policy serves as a touchstone of continuity for new staff and helps refresh the memory of veterans who may need a guide for rarely occurring problems.

8. Since there usually are not enough staff members for ideal service, the statement establishes priorities in the hierarchy of services.

9. And this leads to probably the most useful aspect of the policy statement: It serves to clarify, if not always answer, nagging queries about the limits of service that the librarian faces daily. For example, a good policy should consider (to name only a few) such things as: *(a)* What type of material is considered "reference" material and what does this mean

---

[2]Judi Downs, "Is it Time for a Policy Checkup?" *Library Talk*, vol. 12(2), 1999, pp. 12–14. A short piece on what points to cover when developing or overhauling a library policy statement. Most of the focus is on policy review and the precise steps to take in such a check.

in terms of use, circulation, storage, and so forth? *(b)* Who is served first? The person standing at the desk or the person with a question on the phone? *(c)* What should be done when a person wants legal, medical, or consumer advice? *(d)* Are the rules different for children, young people, and adults?

Why No Policy Statement?

Not all libraries have such policy statements and, in fact, these policy statements are probably rare in small- to medium-sized libraries with equally small staffs. But even in larger libraries there is some opposition to written policies. There are numerous reasons, both expressed and unexpressed, for the showing of less-than-enthusiastic interest in a codified policy. Commonly expressed reasons are:

1. Formulation is a time-consuming and sometimes costly business and, in a period of short staff and small budgets, the time and money are better spent elsewhere.

2. Often even the most detailed statement will not answer *every* problem.

3. Procedures and policies must change in response to need, technology, and so on, and there is little point in trying to codify them.

4. Even with a procedure on policy statement, few staff members will bother to use the statement and will rely primarily on experience and advice from peers to solve problems.

Even with written policies, there are decisions that librarians must make throughout their careers. It is with some of these concerns, from ethics to gaining professional status, that the remainder of this chapter is concerned.

ETHICS AND THE REFERENCE LIBRARIAN

Many years ago one critic summarized the proper attitude of the reference librarian toward everything from war and peace to the proper way to lay a kitchen floor: "No politics, no religion, no morals."[3] A reference librarian should be objective, and while assisting an individual to find information, should make no judgment on the advisability of answering the query.

Over the years librarians have come up with ethical problems. The "Statement of Professional Ethics," which is the guideline of the Ameri-

[3]D. J. Foskett, *The Creed of a Librarian...* (London: Aslib, 1962), p. 10. The piece may be dated, but the creed goes on and on and on.

can Library Association, helps answer some ethical problems. The following should be found in all reference policy statements. The guidelines cover the major points of ethical consideration:

I. Librarians must provide the highest level of service through appropriate and usefully organized collections, fair and equitable circulation and service policies, and skillful, accurate, unbiased, and courteous responses to all requests for assistance.

II. Librarians must resist all efforts by groups or individuals to censor library materials.

III. Librarians must protect each user's right to privacy with respect to information sought or received, and materials consulted, borrowed, or acquired.

IV. Librarians must adhere to the principles of due process and equality of opportunity in peer relationships and personnel actions.

V. Librarians must distinguish clearly in their actions and statements between their personal philosophies and attitudes and those of an institution or professional body.

VI. Librarians must avoid situations in which personal interests might be served or financial benefits gained at the expense of library users, colleagues, or the employing institution.[4]

Library Record Confidentiality

Confidentiality and privacy are of growing concern to reference librarians now that the Internet, and all it implies, is in place. Also, the daily use of electronic databases often requires logging in and logging out, which may be necessary but is a danger to confidentiality. Often there is a managerial conflict between the necessity of keeping records and the expectation of the user for protection of his or her privacy. At the same time, the American Library Association, among others, has gone on record in favor of privacy of reference transactions.

The question may be more theoretical than real. Very few outsiders ask for a user's records. At the same time while students do not expect confidentiality, faculty members assume as much. Much the same situation seems true in school and public libraries, that is, younger people

---

[4]"Statement of Professional Ethics" (Chicago: American Library Association, 1991). These are often incorporated into other guidelines by the ALA. (The ALA encourages the wide distribution of the guidelines, and they may be used without formal permission from that organization.) See, too, "Standards of Ethical Conduct..." which outlines the standards for special collection librarians. Many of these are applicable to reference librarians and are found in *The Library Handbook 2* (Chicago: American Library Association, 1995), pp. 453–456.

do not think about the question and adults automatically assume records are confidential. The American Library Association believes tradition and education support the librarian who honors confidentiality. The expectation of privacy is such that the majority of the library profession—law or no—observe the confidentiality rule. Courts support the library claim to confidentiality even though it is not a formalized law.

Freedom of Information and Censorship

Although the American Library Association (ALA) has clearly and properly taken a stand on the side of "intellectual freedom," censorship remains a persistent and pressing problem in all libraries at all levels of service. The ALA moves vigorously against the threats of the censor, and it is an ongoing issue discussed among librarians year in and year out. Two or three points are worth stressing.

The discussion of censorship must always include a look at the misguided individual who wishes all reference works (including dictionaries) with four-letter words were removed from circulation. Political groups often lobby for the removal of books with opposing views. A more insidious type of censorship is that of the publisher who withholds a reference work because it may inflame opinion or, more frequently, because it will not make enough money although valuable.

In or outside of the reference section the natural question is: "Should the library buy such titles?" A more refined point is that if the books are purchased, should they be limited to the reference section? This type of query, which deserves an answer, depends upon the individual library and the community. Librarians may concede that there are times when a "how-to-do-it" reference work, no matter how popular, should not be in the library. Is this a violation of the sacred creed of freedom to read? It is. The author's particular view is that there should be no censorship. Any book or any form of communication, which does not violate the law, should be available to the individual who makes the request.

A refutation of censorship might be that few criminals ever use a library, and the only real way that crime pays in a library is to write a book about it. And evidence indicates strongly that few criminals get their ideas from reading matter, whether it be pornography or how-to-do-it manuals.

Networks and Censors

While censorship of reference books, for the most part, has not been a serious problem, a more difficult situation presents itself with the international flow of data over computer networks and particularly the Internet. Even the most liberal of civil libertarians recognizes the difficulties involved with international networks. If nothing else, the reference librarian should be aware of the flash point discussions concerning the pros and cons of network censoring.

One legal method of evaluating material is to measure it against contemporary community standards of what is decent or obscene. The law is difficult to enforce in a nation with television, newspapers, magazines, and other forms of communication. It is impossible to enforce in a system, such as the Internet, which scans the globe. A basic community standard in New York, for example, may not be the same for New Delhi or for other points in the world. One may pass bills that ban indecent or criminal matter on the Internet, but the high cost of running down the elusive "publisher" will more than make the law unenforceable.

The plus side of the inability of any one person or country to censor material is that it opens the world to the clarion call of freedom. (Of course, the assumption is that the country involved has enough computers and laptops to spread the message.) On a minus side it equally opens up the world to hate and harassment on a scale not yet possible to envision.

An individual may press slander, libel, and harassment charges against another individual on the Internet. Who is to find the person or group of persons? Once found, say, in a far off part of the globe, who is to press charges?

The lesson for reference librarians is relatively simple. Leave this flow of information alone. Any effort on the part of the librarian to police or monitor what goes in and out of a library computer terminal is to ask for problems. One may post required legal rules, as done for copyright at the photocopying machine, but beyond perfunctory measures, the librarian should leave Internet freedom alone.

Hackers and Crackers

Another aspect of library ethics concerns the role of the hacker and cracker and information. The hacker tries to figure out how any code of data operates, and drops it at that. The cracker not only discovers how a database operates, but "cracks" into it, sometimes for nefarious purposes. The distinction may not always be clear, but hackers are the ladies and gentlemen of the information highway, while the crackers are the crooks and thieves.

There is danger in the ability of an unscrupulous for-profit cracker to find the key to germ warfare, secret weapons, and confidential government studies. In the 1990's, for example, a few Russian salespeople began peddling plutonium to the world. This is a less than appealing practice for those trying to check the atom bomb. At a more mundane level, crackers can intercept, read, and even change content of e-mail.

While neither the hacker nor the cracker is likely to take up headquarters in a library, the reference librarian should be aware of their existence. Steps should be taken to block anyone having unauthorized access to library files, whether they be public or private.

COLLECTION EVALUATION

The reference librarian from time to time must step back from the evaluation of individual sources and evaluate the collection as a whole. Thanks to rapid document delivery, networking, and interlibrary loan, the problem of collection evaluation has both eased and become increasingly complicated. It is easier as fewer titles are needed on the shelves. Electronic databases, which eventually will replace most printed works in the reference section of the library, have helped to ease the necessity for concerns about space and shelving. At the same time, the potential availability of so much (at a sometimes undetermined cost) has made collection development complicated. For example, is it better to purchase X periodical, or have it available online or on a CD-ROM, or simply order bits of it from a document delivery organization, or forget it entirely?

Similar puzzlers must be asked of the majority of reference sources, at least where networking (from the local area network to OCLC and Internet) is available. Collection evaluation is a study in itself, but reference source evaluation has three parts. First, the librarian decides what type of reference materials—books, periodicals, electronic databases, and so forth—to buy. Second, the librarian studies reviews and where possible the reference works themselves. The material is then accepted or rejected. Third, periodically the whole collection is examined to evaluate its overall quality and whether it is keeping up with the users' changing needs.

Librarians must continue to raise and answer the quality question because what may be adequate one year may be less than desirable the next. There are several points to consider in evaluating quality: (1) What is the optimum size of the collection for the particular library? (2) What type of materials should it contain, for example, should there be more emphasis on science than social science? (3) What are the cost considerations?

Additional factors to weigh include: (1) Who is going to use the collection, and will even the largest (or smallest) collection be suitable? (2) If a certain type of material is required this year, will the users' needs change so that a different type will be necessary the next year? (3) What resources are available from nearby libraries, and how much can service be improved through interlibrary loan document delivery, and use of databases? (4) If the budget must be cut, which type of material should be given more or less consideration?

Number and Type

Since answering reference questions may involve the resources of the whole library, and, for that matter, libraries and collections elsewhere, it is difficult to zero in on the precise type of materials to be evaluated. Normally, one concentrates on reference books per se. These are the titles that are dutifully marked as such, are listed in such annotated standard guides as *Guide to Reference Books*, and are categorized and reviewed by such services as *Library Journal* or *Choice*. Beyond that, the librarian will want to evaluate the serials collections (an obvious and integrated part of the indexes and abstracting services); the government documents and how they are treated; and, in more and more cases, the number and type of databases used directly or indirectly for reference service. One should consider the collection as a whole, as well as its parts.

Experience recommends shortcuts. Almost any survey of holdings finds that the reference collection (or, for that matter, any tested subject sections in that collection) which meets standards for both retrospective and current holdings accurately reflects the quality of the library as a whole. That is to say, if the reference collection, or a representative part of it, is good, the library is likely to be good. At times this test fails, as in a library where the rest of the staff is not of the caliber of the reference librarians, but these instances are unusual.

The next consideration concerns the number of reference works a basic collection should have, the number to be added each year, the number to be weeded, the number of dollars necessary for acquisitions, and so forth. Ideally, there is sufficient money to acquire everything that is needed, as well as materials on the periphery of need, but this is rarely the case. So some indication of numbers should be useful, some quantitative guide helpful.

Unfortunately—some would say fortunately—national or even regional standards or figures do not exist. Determining the optimum size of a collection within a library involves so many variables that an attempt to set one standard would be meaningless. There are negative answers to some questions that may be helpful: (1) Is there an ideal size for any given type of library? No. (2) Can one work out a ratio between size of the reference collection and of the rest of the collection? No. (3) Can one develop a useful figure by working out a ratio of the number of librarians and the number of potential users? No. (4) Can one determine the size of the collection by applying any statistical methods? No. (5) Is there a correlation between the size of the collection and the degree of successful reference performance? Yes and no, depending on who does the study.

Still, there are some rough guidelines for establishing the optimal minimum and maximum size of a good reference collection, including print and electronic formats. Generally, the best test of the right size is a simple one: Does this library have the amount of material to answer the reference questions that are usually asked? If the majority of questions are answered quickly and correctly by the available collection, then it is the optimum size. Simple observation and experience are the key to this evaluation exercise, and there are some practical hints on what to observe:

1. When a book or other source must be borrowed or when a librarian must call another library for information from a work not in the library, then purchase should be considered. When the source is needed more than twice in a single month, the work should be purchased - if, of course, funds are available.

2. When the users cannot find what is needed, then purchase of more titles should be considered. Here, of course, one must count upon interviews, questionnaires, and observations for answers to the frustration. A simple technique, which also helps establish contact between librarian and user, is to ask people periodically if they are managing to find what they want.

3. Both large and small libraries keep their collections updated and growing in size through purchases. When deciding what to buy, one may rely on reviews from *Choice* (about 700 reference titles considered each year), *Library Journal* (about 400 titles), and more specialized works. There is also the *American Reference Books Annual*, which annotates about 1,500 to 1,800 publications.

4. Keep track of unfilled requests. How many times and for what type of works did the library have to refer to another library? If, for example, X title is consistently used, but is not in the library, one suspects it would be a good idea to purchase the title. This is the case where a periodical statistical check can be most useful. What journals or articles, for example, had to be requested on interlibrary loans for X period of time to fulfill reference requests?

By now it should be apparent that determining the proper number of reference titles is more of an educated gamble than a statistically accurate measure. The variables help to explain the reluctance of individuals, committees, or even the American Library Association to assign numerical guidelines to size in the acquisition process.

Intrinsic Quality

Various rules and suggestions are given throughout this text about evaluation of reference titles in general and those categorized by form. When one evaluates a whole reference collection, this type of judgment is vital.

The mechanics of evaluating a collection in terms of quality include three tested procedures:

1. Isolate a representative list of *retrospective titles* (print and digital) and check to see if these are in the library. The list is considered statistically representative of a fair sampling for large libraries when chosen from a random sampling of titles in *Guides to Reference Books*, or for smaller libraries when chosen from titles in *Reference Sources for Small- and Medium-Sized Libraries*. In the former case, a list of about 450 to 500 titles would be available, whereas in the latter situation, the list would be no more than 100 titles. The library with a majority of these titles is likely to have a good collection.

2. A more accurate approach is to isolate two or three *subject areas,* particularly those areas of most interest to people who use the collection, and check availability of representative titles. In this case, a list of titles taken from the same sources cited above would include titles in the subject area. A similar technique is applicable when one turns to even more specialized bibliographies such as *Sources of Information in the Social Sciences.*

3. Isolate titles, again using lists, to check the *timeliness of the collection.* Here one might take a representative sampling from *American Reference Books Annual* for the past year, the list of reference titles that appears in *Library Journal,* or a list of titles in the six or seven library journals (or specialized subject journals) for the past six months.

Online and Other Digital Formats

As content and purpose is much the same, electronic database collections may be evaluated in a similar manner to print collections. The obvious difference is format and cost. In addition, the library should determine how many for fee databases should be available, which vendors should be represented, how much should be charged (if anything), how many librarians should be on duty to offer such services, whether there should be online training for laypersons, and so forth.

Note the emphasis is on "for-a-fee" databases. Obviously, the free sources are no concern in the traditional sense of evaluation. On the other hand the much used free databases should be examined closely for accuracy, current activity and numerous other points enumerated elsewhere in this text.

Budget

Few reference librarians are directly involved with the preparation of the library budget. However, two points must be made:

1. As many have observed, the budget is a statement of the ultimate goals, policies, and services of the reference section. It is a current view of where things stand, of just how much importance the library places on reference services. Furthermore, budget line items show the part of reference services (from personnel to online searching) deemed of most importance.

2. The reference librarian will be asked to recommend what is and what is not needed for the next fiscal year. Although not directly involved with the figures (i.e., with where the money comes from), the librarian at least is concerned with what it will mean not to get a particular request. Furthermore, librarians are the ones who must implement what is implied in the budget. Managing the budget is the concern of every reference librarian.

WEEDING

A constant ongoing aspect of reference source evaluation is the weeding process. Weeding is the removal of information sources from the reference collection. There are various ways of determining whether a particular work should be ranked as obsolescent or of little value to the reference librarian.

What follows concerns primarily printed titles. At this time there are few libraries with so many for fee digital sources that weeding electronic databases is a consideration.

1. Study the use of the title. This can be determined by a survey of how often the book is off the shelf. (Circulation records can be studied to see which books are checked out most frequently, but this is rarely the case in the reference section.)

2. Timeliness is often a factor, although not always. A source "ages" in the sciences and social sciences in only one to five years, although in the humanities sources can last up to twenty-five years or longer.

Weeding is a cost-efficient method of ensuring needed new space and keeping the collection efficient for use. Weeding is a delicate process. Conceivably, any book, pamphlet, CD-ROM, magazine, newspaper, or other written material can have reference value, particularly for the historian or anyone else concerned with social mores and records of the past. To discard such a work is akin to destroying the past. For example, one of the most difficult research problems is to locate materials in local newspapers of the nineteenth century.

Anyone who has sought contemporary opinion or statistical data or a biography of a little-known figure knows that there is no limit to the material that may be found in older reference works, certainly in books from both the general and the specific reference collections. Many of these older reference works, such as the early editions of the *Encyclopae-*

dia Britannica, are now classics, and are invaluable sources of material found nowhere else.

Understanding these warnings, there is still a need for judicious weeding. Libraries are always short of space, and this is particularly true in the reference section. Weeding clears the shelves of little-used, or sometimes never-used, materials. Actually, few works are discarded in larger libraries. They are sent off to storage. Smaller libraries cannot afford this luxury, and the material often is systematically removed.

Guidelines for Discarding

Each library must establish its own general and specific guidelines for discarding materials. As is true of acquisitions, each library has its own peculiar needs, its own type of users. It is important to weed materials to meet the needs of those users, not the standards established in a text or at another library. Yes, weeding is not much of a problem online, although the "favorites" or "bookmarks" can get quite out of control and should be periodically checked, as should the content of the library web page. CD-ROMs, though, can be weeded for much the same reasons as print.

Common sense is the primary guide to weeding. In 1999, for example, California launched a state-wide weeding program of school libraries. This was done in order to make space for a much delayed supply of new books. Well, what then to discard? It hardly takes a rule to weed a book published in 1950 with the prediction, "Someday man will land on the Moon." Or how about the "problem" of retaining or getting rid of a book called *I'm Glad I'm a Boy, I'm Glad I'm a Girl* with a passage which says "Boys are doctors. Girls are nurses. Boys are presidents. Girls are first ladies. Boys fix things. Girls need things fixed." Then there is the book in American history which "contained illustrations of American Indians in which they are colored brick red, and stories of happy slaves working hard and singing on the plantations."[5] Parenthetically—who says we have not made at least some social progress?

Beyond what good judgement tells one about weeding, there are some helpful hints:

Timeliness. Most of the reference titles that are used for ready reference have to be up to date. Older titles may be helpful historically, but are of little value for current material.

Reliability. Data and viewpoints change, and the changes must be reflected in the reference collection. Yesterday's reliable explanation of a given event or phenomenon may not apply today.

[5]"Library Books Long Outdated Will Be Gone," *The New York Times,* June 1, 1999, p. A19.

Use. Needs change from generation to generation, and yesterday's valued reference work may no longer be used by today's reference librarian, today's user.

Physical condition. Books wear out and must be either discarded or replaced with new editions.

Later editions. Most popular reference works go into several editions, and it is normally pointless to maintain earlier editions when the latest edition of a standard work can be obtained. Another linked consideration: duplication of materials. Perhaps a title was unique four or five years ago, but today there are more recent, even better titles in the field. In that case the older title may be discarded.

Language. Sometimes a foreign language work may be discarded because no one is using it. It may have been purchased at a time when the particular language was important to the library's users.

To make a wise selection of what should be discarded requires:

Thorough knowledge of the collection. The librarian should know how the work is used and by whom. Should a particular work be totally eliminated, should a new edition be purchased, or should a similar work be considered? These are all questions that vary from situation to situation and can be answered only by the librarian working closely with the collection and the public.

Knowledge of other resources. A librarian needs to understand the collections of regional and national libraries. Is at least one copy of what you propose to discard in a local or national collection for use at some later date? Obviously a much-used work, such as a ten-year-old copy of the *World Almanac,* need not be checked. But any material that is purely local, (particularly pamphlets and material without lasting value), anything more than fifty years old, and any items about which there is a question regarding use or value should first be cleared with the larger libraries in the region. Such an item may appear shabby and of little use, but may prove to be a unique copy.

Older works worth keeping. One must remember that age does not necessarily dictate whether a work is discarded. No worthwhile reference collection lacks, for example, a copy of the dated *Encyclopedia of the Social Sciences* or the mass of bibliographies and other guides that were published a number of years ago and are still basic works.

Encyclopedias. Maintain as many older editions as space allows, *but* try to obtain a new edition at least every five years, and preferably every year.

Almanacs, yearbooks, manuals. These are usually superseded by the next edition or the succeeding volume. Nevertheless, as the information in each is rarely duplicated exactly (new material is added, old material deleted), it is wise to keep old editions for at least five years, preferably ten years.

Dictionaries. In a sense, these are never dated and should never be discarded unless replaced by the same editions. An exception might be the abridged desk-type dictionaries. The unabridged works and those devoted to special areas are of constant value.

Biographical sources. Again, the more of these and the more retrospective the sources, the better. Only in a few select cases should any be discarded.

Directories. Like yearbooks, almanacs, and other such works, these are frequently updated, and the older ones (five to ten years) can generally be discarded safely.

Geographical sources. Inexpensive atlases may be safely discarded after five to ten years. More expansive, expensive works are invaluable. In fact, many gain in both research and monetary value over the years.

Government documents. Never discard these if they are part of a permanent collection. Discards should be considered where material is used only peripherally for pamphlet files. However, be particularly careful to check local and state materials before discarding.

In the subject areas, it is relatively safe to assume that except for botany and natural history, science books are generally dated within five years. The recurrent yearbooks, manuals, and encyclopedias may be discarded as new editions are obtained. In the humanities, discarding should rarely take place unless the material is quite obviously totally dated and of no historical or research value. In the social sciences, timely or topical materials may be considered for discard after one to five years.

Electronic Modifications

Most of the rules for adding or discarding reference materials are applicable to electronic databases. On the other hand, with more and more data going online and/or on a CD-ROM (or equivalent), much of the traditional picture will change. There will come a day when questions of additions and discards will be more concerned with what is available or not available in electronic formats.

The rules may change drastically for online books and journals. If virtually everything found in most libraries is available online in full text, why is there a question about additions or weeding? Answer, there is not. If the books and journals online are cumulative, as they are now, it will become more a matter of finding specific pieces of information—from a complete book to a bit of an article—than worrying about shelf space or the need to purchase a specific title. In other words, when the "universal library" is open to everyone, standard evaluative practices for addition and discard will have taken another turn.

With that, do not hold your breath waiting for the change. It is true current books, current journals will be, and are available online. But there is a massive amount of material which has yet to be digitalized, and for that libraries are needed in their old form of books and journals on shelves.

EVALUATION OF REFERENCE SERVICES

What constitutes ideal reference service? The answer is a high score in five areas: personnel performance, collection development, introduction of new technologies and reference services, evaluation of services and personnel, and administrative capacities. This section is concerned primarily with services and personnel.

Speaking from experience, reference librarians inevitably point out that happy librarians are those with good salaries and fair hours. Beyond the obvious: (1) There should be an intelligent division of labor so that, for example, x number of hours on the reference desk or instruction with CD-ROMs is balanced with X number of less strenuous hours. (2) Continuing education, particularly in the new technologies, is an absolute must. (3) Specialization should be recognized and rewarded. The librarian who becomes an expert on computers and electronic databases or in anthropology or in eighteenth-century criticism is a valuable asset at a reference desk. (4) There should be some scale to measure overwork, burnout and the hazards involved with the constant pressure of serving the public. The library should not wait until the librarian becomes ill or has to quit to recognize the stress factors in the job.[6]

Library Evaluation

There are numerous reasons for the evaluation of reference libraries. Some are literally required to meet demands of accrediting groups or administration directives. Some are traditional: The evaluation is built

---

[6]David, Tyckoson, "What's Right With Reference," *American Libraries*, May, 1999, pp. 57–163. A working reference librarian with a flair for analysis discusses both what is wrong and what is right with current reference services. He puts a strong emphasis on individual attention. Along the way are numerous hints about points to evaluate in reference work and about reference librarians. A considered opinion, which should be first on any reference librarian's reading list. Why? It is based on experience, common sense and a faith in the intellectual strength of the reference librarian.

into routine study of practices, the revision of the library policy manual, or management studies. Others are economical: Cuts or failure to increase budgets means scaling back services. Which services are to be cut, modified, and so on? Even without budgetary threats, the best system is one which is operated efficiently within standard budget requirements. This, in turn, factors in the purchase of new technologies, the place of the library in the economic changes in networks, and so forth.

The most common evaluation is relatively nonstructured and informal. Routine assessments of reference service are built into the annual activities of the staff. Unfortunately this has the drawback of putting too much emphasis on collected data and too little on qualitative measurements. It requires less effort, less staff time, and certainly less commitment, for example, to gather statistics on how many people use the Net than the degree of their satisfaction.

Evaluation results are usually measured against national standards for school, public, and academic libraries. (All of these are available from the American Library Association, and tend to be modified from time to time.) Then, too, in an age of networks and electronic communication, the library will be measured against other libraries of equal size, in similar communities, and with the same purpose and budget. Measurements vary from those that are more concerned with how many questions were answered (outcome measures) to measures which evaluate the ability to deliver this or that service in x or y amount of time. Still, no matter what standard or group of measurements is employed, the goal is to use evaluative systems suitable and practical for the particular library. To impose a scale, which may meet the needs of national managers but not those of the local reference librarians, is to impose chaos on any study. Before assessment tools are employed, there must be an understanding of what tools will or will not work in the particular library.

Generally the methodology employed and the tools used depend on the local library and what one is trying to discover about services. The purpose of the research study must be carefully decided and outlined. Failure to do so, if nothing else, may result in an endless add-on type of study that starts at no particular point and can never seem to reach a conclusion.

EVALUATION METHODS

Essentially any evaluative process can be analyzed in four or five steps. The first step is to determine the purpose of the evaluation, its goals, and precisely what one hopes to learn. Second, use a comparative ruler to measure the situation as it exists against a more ideal situation or against local or national standards. Third, decide which methods should be used to gather the necessary information and data. Fourth, determine how the methodology is to be carried out, that is, who is going to do what, at what cost, and under what time limits. After these preliminaries, one proceeds with the process, gathers the information, and makes any necessary modifications to the methodology.

Finally, the results have to be analyzed, and conclusions must be drawn from the results to assist in understanding and possibly changing the situation, which is under study.

The process of evaluation requires both subjective and objective methods, attitudes, and approaches. Emphasis should be, and tends to be, on objective methodology. There may be an almost mystical faith in the scientific method and in objective data, but the fact remains that it produces results. Scientific results convince governing bodies to provide more funds and persuade skeptics that improvements in service might be useful. At the same time, it is ridiculous to assume that a cumulation of statistical data on, say, how often people use the dictionary, will give anything more than just that—data—and will provide very little information about the quality of the collection. It is imperative that the objective studies have a fine focus and that they be balanced by subjective observations and analyses.

There are a number of desired or necessary qualities in evaluative instruments. Effective methodology should (1) demonstrate validity; (2) demonstrate reliability; (3) utilize the natural setting; (4) assess multiple factors in the reference process; and (5) include sufficient input, process, and outcome factors so that cause-and-effect relationships become apparent. In addition, the use of a standardized form to collect and report data should (6) utilize an adequate and unbiased sample; (7) provide for comparing data; (8) provide for timeliness of results; and (9) provide for interpretability.

Today most evaluations are conducted either by the library staff or by consultants. The staff usually performs evaluations, primarily because there are limited funds for outside help. On occasion, academic faculty, usually from a library school will study the library for a scholarly research effort. In such a situation, the library tends to be only one of a larger group that is studied and the specific evaluative techniques and findings may or may not be applicable to the particular library studied.

There is much more to the evaluation of reference services than data on successfully answered questions. The components of reference evaluation would go like this: One must look at (1) *answering success* based on obtrusive, expert judgment, librarian or patron report, or unobtrusive study; (2) *the cost* and tasks involved with reference services; (3) *the reference interview* and how reference questions are classified for the search; (4) the quality of the *reference collection,* including new technologies from CD-ROMs to Internet access; (5) the quality of the staff.

The most common approach for analyzing the reference process is the *obtrusive* method. Unfortunately, the descriptor is accurate enough: It means that everyone is well aware of the "obtrusive" presence of people, questionnaires, interviews, and the like used in the study.

Since this is the most-used approach, there are scores of examples in the literature. They include checking how long it takes an individual or a group of librarians to answer a set of questions and determining what methods are employed in selection of reference works or choice of databases in an online search. Other examples are found throughout this chapter.

The obtrusive method has the drawback of putting the subjects on their guard. With this method it is absolutely necessary to use easy-to-understand questionnaires and interview techniques, carefully explaining ambiguous statements. Most important, the librarians must be aware of the purpose and goals of the study, understanding that there is no hidden agenda, no secret threat.

If the objective methodology is carefully explained, the librarian will not be threatened by thinking the administration is trying to find a reason to dismiss them, to check their advancement, to increase the speed of answering questions, or of having a hidden motive behind the study. The real objective is to improve reference services, but how many librarians are able to believe this when they feel threatened? Of course, the good administrator should be able to calm such fears, but where there is a lack of faith in leadership, there will probably be problems with such evaluation techniques.

Unobtrusive Techniques

The *unobtrusive* approach is, as the name indicates, a method by which the subjects are not aware they are being evaluated. Usually, the unobtrusive test is divided into the factual query ("What is the height of the Empire State Building?") and the bibliographical question ("Who published *Death of a Salesman?*"). Surrogate information users, either directly or over the telephone, query the librarian who is unaware that an evaluation is under way. The method has become increasingly accepted. It is by far the most-used methodology for evaluating services today.

A simplified example of unobtrusive testing: 12 public libraries of various sizes and in various locations are visited by students with only one question. (The more usual unobtrusive test uses a battery of queries of various types.) The query in this instance is "What do you have on John Major?" All the libraries visited have the basic sources to afford a correct answer, for example, *Who's Who, The New York Times Index* and the *Readers' Guide* or *Magazine Index* in print or online. None of the reference librarians queried know the students' real purpose—that a test is under way. This is the first and most basic requirement for unobtrusive studies. The students have a list of points to observe and to comment on at convenient stages of the study or, if possible, at the conclusion. The students report back on several aspects of reference service given—the reception, the management of a reference interview, how the search was conducted, and, of course, the answer.

The methodology, although simplified, fulfills the need to test for: (1) the right, wrong, or incomplete answer; (2) the proper use of the reference interview, if used at all; (3) search strategies employed and reference works consulted; (4) the use of referral, where necessary, to another point in the library or to another library; and (5) the general attitude of the librarians. Some claim that an unobtrusive approach is not only better, but it does less internal harm because the staff simply does not know it has taken place.

Combining obtrusive and unobtrusive methods, experts have come up with new evaluation techniques and new jargon. The combination is known as *outcome studies,* that is, studies that evaluate the outcome of a reference transaction.

Surveys

Polls and surveys are as much a part of America as MTV, politics, and the automobile. Rarely a week goes by that a group of well-known masters of the query do not report on still another facet of American life. Librarians are familiar with the methodologies employed, and know the protests which are heard if the poll goes against X or Y group's ideas. (The questions are inconsistent with the answer. The questions point to only one acceptable answer. The survey failed to consider...and so it goes.) Criticism, right or wrong, is heard every time a survey is run.

What's the point of all of this for librarians? Surveys are a help, but not the complete answer. Surveys may be used in evaluative studies of service, but with some consideration as to their lack of reliability. Finally, unless a cursory study, the survey should be checked and edited by someone who is an expert in such matters. The reference librarian might turn to a reference source for the name(s) of such a person in the community.

Sampling

Sampling is a method of selecting a random or specific portion of the population and is used in opinion polls, market research, television popularity, and the like. The method is useful in analyzing aspects of reference service, such as the kinds of reference questions posed by users.

Records should be maintained on questions asked of the service: How many were there? How were they answered? Who asked them? But if done too frequently, the amount of paperwork will take time away from providing service. A better approach is to sample every few months. Some libraries pick two or three days a month every three or four months, and on those days record complete information on the reference queries made. This type of sampling, without interfering with the regular conduct of the reference service, indicates basic trends and, if done in a complete fashion, will show user satisfaction or lack of satisfaction.

The sampling technique is employed, too, for questioning users. The usual procedures are to select blocks of time in a day, week, month, or even year and sample user reaction by means of a questionnaire.

Interviews

The personal interview is often a key part of a survey. Here the person making the evaluation sits down with the librarian and in a structured way tries to determine, through the discussion or interview, the character of reference services, and in some cases, the abilities of the librarian. Both evaluations, of course, might be considered in an interview.

Individual interviews will show how the librarian with a low batting average for questions analyzes the query. In contrast, how does the librarian with an excellent record do the same? Do librarians think of various approaches, sources, and interview techniques, or are they stuck in the proverbial question-and-answer rut? Is success due to education, natural verbal ability, intelligence, energy, knowledge, intuition—or what? We now have only a vague notion of the success profile. Individual interviews and analysis of the data could yield solid answers.

A more common type of interview is one in which the reference services user is asked about the success or failure of those services. The responses are often less than trustworthy because the users believe they will be supporting the librarian by giving what they think are "correct" answers or they think the answers really do not matter.

As an evaluation tool, an interview usually takes place between the reference librarian and the interviewer and between the interviewer and individual users of reference services. Others, of course, can be questioned, from the head librarian to the nonuser. There are great advantages to interviews as an evaluating technique, particularly when the interviewer has training and is able clearly to differentiate fact from fiction, opinion, and bias. The drawbacks result when the respondent and the interviewer are at odds, when the respondent is inhibited by oral questions, when the interviewer intimidates the respondent, and when the respondent is trying to make a good impression. Still, when handled skillfully, an interview will often reveal information that can be obtained in no other way.

The available guides to evaluation describe a rather traditional interview methodology:

1. Ask a sampling of students about their ease in obtaining sources.

2. Talk with a sampling of students and faculty to gain insight into their satisfaction with services.

Interviews do work and do produce information, but there are so many variables, and they are so time-consuming, that the technique is rarely used.

Observation

"I could tell by the way he left the reference desk that he was not happy with the answer." "The reference interview seemed to go well." "There never is anyone at the reference desk." "No signs, no indication of where to find the reference people."

All of the above are based on observation. The first two are subjective observations of reference librarians in action. The last two are observations of fact. Of the four statements, the last two are the more valuable because they are observable conditions. The statements illustrate the rewards and the possible witch-hunt aspects of simple observation of people's actions and structured conditions.

Given the problem of observation, an ultimate requirement is that it be systematically channeled by measures which will ensure accuracy and eliminate, as much as possible, the human factor. This is done in most library studies, particularly where an unobtrusive study is made of reference services.

Quantitative Studies

In quantitative studies the librarian is dealing with statistical data or with known quantities that may be changed and measured by variations on a system, practice, goal, and so forth. For example, one may measure the number of referenda questions asked, and vary results and evaluation by using one reference librarian instead of two and changing the hours of the questions, the place of the questions, the amount of time, and so on. No matter what is done, it can be measured quantitatively.

The usual employment of quantitative data is in measuring circulation, hours, number of questions asked, number of users, and so forth. Here the raw numbers can be juggled and studied, but at least the numbers are accurate. This is particularly true today as most libraries employ computers to keep track of everything from circulation to reserve items to number of cards issued.

Given the raw data of quantitative studies, the librarian may use it for almost anything from annual reports to justification for hiring more staff. Internally, too, the figures are useful as explained by the counted reference questions in the previous example. Information on figures concerning queries assist in collection development.

Quantitative measurement is preferable for most managers and many librarians because it does deal with data and not the problematic area of quality. It is, for example, much easier to count reference questions or the number of people who use CD-ROMs daily than to ascertain the quality of the answers and the quality of the layperson searches.

Qualitative Studies[7]

Where the librarian measures the "quality" of this or that, the human factor must be taken into consideration. The advantage of such a measure is that it covers various elements of the real world. The problem is that there often is a lack of detachment, of objectivity, which can thwart the best-constructed qualitative evaluation.

Usually the unobtrusive qualitative study is favored to evaluate personnel. And this is discussed in the next section.

EVALUATING LIBRARIANS

Almost without exception a set of procedures exists for evaluating and guiding reference librarians, as for all employees of the library. Certain elements are found in personnel policy statements. There usually is some indication of the daily activities of the reference librarian from number of hours at the reference desk to duties in the collection development.

The primary benefit of a written personnel policy statement can be summarized in one word—fairness. Policies may or may not work, depending on who wrote them and who interprets them, as well as on the given sense of understanding or misunderstanding between the parties involved.

Recognizing the vagaries of human nature, the usual policy statement is general. It rarely spells out what to do when one librarian takes exception to the rules governing Monday evening hours. At the same

[7]Herbert White, "Public Library Reference Service—Expectations and Reality," *Library Journal*, June 15, 1999, pp. 56–58. A plea to let reference librarians, rather than administrators and outside evaluators, decide how to improve service. "Reference librarians certainly know better than anyone else what they could be doing and are not being allowed to do."

time given policy sections can be quite specific, for example, the salary scale and antidiscrimination clauses.

The literature of reference service runs over with surveys, which attempt to draw an accurate personal profile of the happy, successful reference librarian. Much of the statistical fallout is predictable: (1) Daily contact with all types of people requires an interest in conversation, and enthusiasm for helping. (2) The librarian is confident without being aggressive. (3) The librarian is imaginative, creative, and able to make quick turnarounds when either the question or the response has been misinterpreted. (4) The librarian has a memory for details and is able to follow clues with the skill of a Sherlock Holmes.

Evaluation Forms

Normally the library has evaluation forms that are filled out by the librarian's immediate supervisor. A self-evaluation is less often used, but can be useful. Performance ratings tend to get particular attention during the early months and years of a reference librarian's employment, but they probably should be used in later years too. "Probably" because it depends on the type of library, the administrator, and the librarian, among other things. If at all possible, there should be mutual agreement among all parties involved on the types of evaluation employed for testing the experienced librarian.

Peer Evaluation

There are different approaches to discovering whether or not a reference librarian has one or all of the required magic qualities. Peer evaluation is a useful technique to improving reference services, but as the process implies it has rewards as well as dangers. The results are based on the day-to-day activities of the reference librarian. Evaluation is by peers and peer groups who, literally, watch the librarian in action. Criticism may be mild ("Not advisable to turn a pencil in your hand during the interview") to highly critical ("Never seems to listen to the person with the question.") to praise ("Demonstrates an unusual ability to get on with patrons."). The rewards are improved service and, under most circumstances, a happier reference librarian.

The obvious pitfall is that the system smacks of the "self improvement" approach whereby peers point out, often with politically correct attitudes, what is wrong with the person being evaluated. Another problem with this approach, as with any in which the qualifications of the individual are tested, is that the focus is often on shortcomings. And this carries over from the individual to studies of the library as a whole.

Competency Measures

The competencies of the reference librarian may be measured in numerous ways, although the most telling test is simply how well questions are answered. Other equally major tests:

1. Is the librarian keeping up with new technology, for example, with CD-ROM, online searching, Internet, and so forth?
2. What knowledge does the librarian have of reference and related sources?
3. How well does the librarian negotiate the reference interview, the search, and the analysis of the results?
4. Does the librarian have a positive attitude about people and the reference process? Kindness, tenacity, patience, and determination are only a few of the required personal and intellectual traits.

Performance Measurement

Using statistical data to measure satisfaction of the user with the reference service, the time it takes to answer a question, the number of questions answered, and cost per query in performance analysis tends to be favored more by managers than by working librarians. To be judged against a preset scale seems more appropriate for the performance of a worker on a production line than for a professional. Today it rarely works or has the cooperation of staff.

Such measurement not only lacks support, but also is costly and time-consuming. And trying to determine the worth of a reference section by how many questions are answered in a given time is too crude a method to produce any effective evaluation.

Reference librarians will agree that some measure of performance is needed. The difficulty is ascertaining the measures to employ. The simplistic, numerical approach is not enough because it may give a totally misleading picture of service.

In a discussion of how managers may evaluate research-and-development results in industry, a team of management consultants offers advice that applies to evaluating reference services and librarians as well: (1) Focus should be on measuring outcomes, not personal behavior. Every reference librarian has a personal approach to service. This should be honored as long as the behavior does not interfere with the natural flow of daily activities. (2) Make the measurement system simple. The best systems are based on the collection of data on six to eight key indexes. (3) Make the measurement as objective as possible. Industry techniques may differ from those appropriate to libraries and librarians, but the foregoing three golden rules are applicable to any method of measurement.

Stress at the Reference Desk

Working with, talking with, and helping people are by definition stressful situations. Even under the best of circumstances reference work requires a lot of concentration and energy, and a reference librarian may be forgiven for the occasional thought that being alone on an island might not be a bad idea. And when the library is noisy and the person asking a question is less than cooperative, then true stress sets in.

What causes stress for the reference librarian? Or another way of putting it, is there anything that does *not* cause stress at the reference desk? It depends on the situation, the personality of the librarian, and a dozen other variables. Still, one may generalize. Although meeting interesting people is one of the positive aspects of the job, rude patrons are a major stress. While the variety of reference work is enjoyable, the workload can be hectic. And there is never enough time. Problem solving and learning are major benefits, and yet anyone who has worked at a reference desk has experienced a nagging sense of inadequacy. Often, a question refuses to be isolated so that it has a specific meaning, and once it is clarified, the resources available do not give a current, correct answer. In other words the challenge and the stimulation are always there, but so is the stress.

Reference Burnout

Experienced reference librarians have written about stress and reference "burnout." Increasing demands on the librarian result in this all-too-familiar fatigue syndrome.

There are as many ways to meet the burnout problem as there are librarians and libraries. A few common approaches: (1) Every seven or so years the librarian is given a sabbatical or time off to relax in some other aspect of the profession. (2) More assistance is given at the reference desk by paraprofessionals who can field the 60 to 70 percent of questions that are no more than directional and occupy an inordinate amount of the reference librarian's time. (3) The actual number of hours at the reference desk is limited, and often rotated. Some find the average of 15 to 20 hours too much, and they should be given the opportunity to do other tasks. (4) Continuing education that includes everything from online searching to philosophy helps. (5) Finally, the supervisor should be open to the librarian's suggestions on how to avoid burnout. Anything that is reasonable should be considered.

SUGGESTED READING

Bernie, Sloan, "Electronic Reference Services: Some Suggested Guidelines," *Reference & User Services Quarterly,* vol. 38, no. 1, 1999, pp. 77–81. Practical guidelines for service which cover: administration, services, clientele, personnel, infrastructure, finance and evaluation.

Dow, Ronald, "Using Assessment Criteria to Determine Library Quality," *The Journal of Academic Librarianship,* no. 4, 1998, pp. 277–281. How does a reference librarian measure the quality of service? This is part of a study of how to go about assessing the impact of the library on its users. Various approaches are discussed, some traditional, some rather new. At any rate, the author urges the librarian to move away from counting books and resources to evaluating how they are not used by patrons.

Hayward, Tim and Judith Preston, "Chaos Theory, Economics and Information: The Implications for Strategic Decision-Making," *Journal of Information Science,* vol. 25, no. 3, 1999, pp. 173–182. And now for something entirely different. Well, not quite, because the chaos theory has been around a bit. What is out of the ordinary is the application of it to management and how to think of the future. An interesting approach for supervisors in or out of reference services.

Hermans, John, "Catch the Knowledge Management Wave," *Library Journal,* September 1, 1999, pp. 161–163. This is an annotated bibliography of the best books—as well as websites and listservs—covering what the author describes as knowledge management. While the books are directed to companies, much of the information is of value to library and information systems managers.

Holt, Glen et al., "Placing a Value on Public Library Services," *Public Libraries,* no. 2, 1999, pp. 98–108. How does the librarian place a dollar value on service? The answer is necessary to explain budget needs. And the answer is varied from the proper use of cost benefit analysis to time methods. The methods were employed in one situation, probably applicable to others. The result: for every $1 spent the user received $4 in services. In the same issue see a related article: Roger Kemp, "A City Manager Looks at Trends Affecting Public Libraries," pp. 116–119.

Lochstet, Gwenn and Donna Lehman, "A Correlation Method for Collecting Reference Statistics," *College & Research Libraries,* January, 1999, pp. 45–53. Two university librarians demonstrate an improved way of compiling reference services and reference services statistics. It is a "less time-consuming procedure" and is more accurate.

Logan, Rochelle, "Ready, Set, Plan: Community Analysis Help Online." *Public Libraries,* July/August 2000, pp. 220–223. The author discusses the Public Library Association's planning process for library managers and how it is augmented by a website which produces online documents for the planner. Other resources are suggested in the quest to understand the community.

Lynch, Mary Jo, "Compared to What, Or Where to Find the Stats," *American Libraries,* September, 1999, pp. 48–50. The director of the American Libraries Association Office for Research and Statistics reveals how to find statistics, which can be understood, concerning libraries and their operations. She shows how those same members can be used to make a case for additional funding.

Nitecki, Danuta and Peter Hernon, "Measuring Service Quality at Yale University's Libraries," *The Journal of Academic Librarianship*, vol. 26, no. 4, 2000, pp. 259–273. The authors show how a new process of measurement was used at Yale and how it can be employed in other libraries. The primary question: how valuable are library services in meeting the information needs of its users? Their methodology shows how to find an answer about service quality and user satisfaction.

Nolan, Christopher, *Managing the Reference Collection*. Chicago: American Library Association, 1999. An excellent short (231 pp.) guide to everything from how to develop a reference policy for collection development to evaluating and weeding practices. Suggestions are as practical as they are based on actual experience. Should be "must" reading for anyone involved in reference management of collections.

Rieh, Soo Young, "Changing Reference Service Environment: A Review of Perspective From Managers, Librarians and Users," *The Journal of Academic Librarianship*, May, 1999, pp. 178–186. A lively discussion of issues and trends in reference services and how they are evaluated, not only by managers but by the public at large. Along the way to evaluate reference services. Sometimes the conflicting approaches of the public and the ideal are not considered. They will be after anyone reads this fine article.

Smith, Mark, *Internet Policy Handbook for Libraries*. New York: Neal Schuman, 1999. What policy statements should the library have which govern the Net? Thanks to a survey and study of libraries, the author comes up with a practical answer—an answer which will fit into the plans of most libraries. While aimed for schools (K-12) and public libraries, much of what is found here is applicable to academic and special libraries.

Watson-Boone, Rebecca, "Academic Librarians as Practitioner-Researchers," *The Journal of Academic Librarianship*, March, 2000, pp. 85–93. In her analysis of articles published in *JAL*, the author not only summarizes types of in house research, but outlines in some detail which each entails, e.g., "practice-based research methods" is broken down into: action research, case study research, evaluation research, experimental research, etc. For each there are examples.

Welch, Jeanie, "Laser Lights or Dim Bulbs? Evaluating Reference Librarians' use of Electronic Sources," *Reference Services Review*, no. 1, 1999, pp. 73–77. A practical discussion of means and methods of evaluating reference librarians at work in the electronic age. "Guidelines for assessment of reference librarians' effectiveness in providing service to patrons using electronic sources," are offered.

Whitlach, Jo Bell. *Evaluating Reference Services*. Chicago: American Library Association, 2000. A leader in the reference field, the author offers a pragmatic view of how to evaluate reference services. Reference sources, service to patrons, collection of data, funding and many more points are covered in this basic guide to the subject.

INDEX